ON
JEWELLERY

Liesbeth den Besten

ON *JEWELLERY*

A COMPENDIUM
of international
contemporary art jewellery

ARNOLDSCHE Art Publishers

To Jim, my love and support for so many years,
and to Vincent, Charlotte and Jasper, my most precious jewels.

Contents

Introduction

This book has been a long time in the making. It started as a simple idea to compile differ-ent lectures into book form, complete it with images and to publish it. However while starting to rewrite these lectures, new ones emerged, and inevitably the urge came to write about other aspects of jewellery that I hadn't lectured on before. My aim was not to write an academic book on jewellery, but rather a readable one that reflects on current tenden-cies within contemporary jewellery. Therefore the book is dependent on examples, many of which have been reproduced, while others have just been described. I think it is import-ant to mention the fact that I have seen the majority of these examples in reality. After all, images can be misleading, particularly with jewellery, where you cannot see the measure-ments, or feel and hear the materiality – characteristics which are so important in relation with the body and wearing. Philippe van Cauteren, the artistic director of S.M.A.K. in Ghent, Belgium, in an open letter (dated April 2010) to sculptor Henk Delabie expressed his ideas about the mendacity of the image of an artwork in publications. He thinks that it '… can hardly be called a document. It is flimsy, a two-dimensional archaeological "dis-covery" of something that does not exist the way we perceive it.' With good reason, he talks about a 'second-hand way' of getting to know art works.[1] Unfortunately that is all I can offer the reader in this book: an indirect introduction to pieces of jewellery or works of art through images and my interpretation of them.

A person who is engaged in contemporary jewellery, like me, has to explain an awful lot. For instance, that you are not a maker ('no, I did not make this brooch, I bought it in a gallery'), or that one can indeed be professionally involved with jewellery as an art histor-ian, or that there exists another type of jewellery rather than the regular stuff most people wear. You have to explain that there are jewellers across the world, graduated from art academies, who create this other kind of jewellery. And how their work differs from com-mercial or precious jewellery because it is an artistic expression, and that its value is not determined on the material it is made of. You then explain that the history of this kind of jewellery is rather recent, but that there are specialised galleries, private collectors and museum collections. That fairs are organised, competitions are held and books are pub-lished, but that it is still a rather unknown field. There is nothing wrong with explaining but sometimes you become weary of it. Why is the subject so out of reach? Why is it seen as something trivial? Why do museums and universities still hold on to age-old hierarchical distinctions between the fine and applied arts?

My own history with jewellery started in 1980. As a young history of art student at the University of Amsterdam, I had developed a chief interest in modern and contemporary architecture. However, in December 1980 there was an article in my daily newspaper under the heading 'The New Jewellery Art Wants to Give Shape to an Idea'.[2] It was about Paul Derrcz, who had just won the first Françoise van den Bosch Prize, and his Galerie Ra in Amsterdam. This was the first article about jewellery in a newspaper that I had ever seen or read. Up until that very day, jewellery had never attracted my attention, apart from when I went through a phase of wearing several silver rings on both hands, as youngsters used to do in those days. The matter discussed in the article intrigued me, even though I hadn't the slightest idea about what this kind of jewellery would be like. But the article was cut out (I still have it in my archive) and put away. I didn't think about jewellery anymore until one of our teachers at university, the highly acclaimed De Stijl specialist Professor Hans Jaffé, assigned his seminar students the task of researching the relationship between fine and applied arts – not from the books but by 'fieldwork'. So he ordered us to visit galleries and to look with our own eyes. Galerie Ra and its artists turned out to be a fascinating starting point for my investigation, and a few years later, in 1985, I wrote my thesis: 'Jewellery Design and Fine Art: Connections Between Jewellery Design and Geometrical Abstract and Conceptual Art in the Netherlands, 1967 to 1980.' In the 100-page-long study I interpreted the developments in Dutch jewellery in the second half of the 1960s and the beginning of the 1970s as a process of emancipation and democratisation, similar to tendencies in the other arts, applied arts and society. I found that there were direct connections between jewellers and fine artists around 1970. And I concluded that both approaches – the geometrical abstract and the conceptual – were the arteries that nourished Dutch jewellery design. In 1985/86, I had the opportunity to create an exhibition on the subject of my thesis in the Van Reekum Museum in Apeldoorn. The exhibition *Sieraden: vorm en idee* [Jewellery: Form and Idea] also involved contemporary jewellery from other countries. This marked the beginning of my life-long fascination with jewellery.

It is clear to me that this book could do with the subtitle 'from a Dutch perspective', as I am fully aware that my personal and cultural background has influenced my take on things. The fact that I was born and grew up in a particular part of the world and in a particular time in history is my luck and my limitation. I grew up in a period of affluence in the capital of one of the richest countries in the Western world, where things were mine for the taking; I did not need to search for art or contemporary jewellery, for a museum or a jewellery gallery, they were just there. It took me quite some time before I learned that there was also interesting new jewellery made outside of Europe in the United States, Australia and New Zealand. While I did not actually witness the first important manifestations of new jewellery in Holland at the end of the 1960s, having been just a child at that time, I was nevertheless raised in the same atmosphere of cultural and social awareness that gave way to this movement.

Although I have tried to be international in scope with respect to this book, people from the United States, Latin America, Australia, New Zealand and Asia may have trouble with my Eurocentric approach; people from Eastern and southern Europe may chide me for my Western European orientation; while people from Germany, Austria or Italy may reproach me for being directed too much towards the Netherlands. And they are all within their right to do so.

In 1985, Peter Dormer and Ralph Turner coined the notion 'the New Jewelry'.[3] Terms can be complicated and, especially if they are used too strictly, tend to be rather more limiting than explanatory. In some literature it may seem as if the New Jewelry was a movement with clear aims, which in fact it was not. All the same, I think it is a nice concept and I like to use it at times, because it reflects so well a certain mentality prevalent around 1968: the deep-rooted conviction that everything was changeable and should change, and a trust in the future that seems rather naive from today's perspective. The New Jewelry is not so much a style as it is a loose, international and vital tendency that breathed new life into jewellery. This happened in different places around the world – almost simultaneously – but under different conditions and with different results.[4] In fact, the differences between

European and American jewellery were tremendous during this period. In 1994, the American writer Susan Grant Lewin put it like this: 'European jewelry is by and large more occupied with problem solving and conceptual issues. It reveals a narrower focus and is more exclusive than the generally inclusive approach to materials and subjects found in American work. In the United States one can find more personal narratives and emotional expression than in the cooler, more restrained European work.'[5] This appreciation holds true until the 1990s, when, from that point on, jewellery gradually became global; a fusion of styles and tendencies that could not be resolved from local sources alone.

In Europe and America around 1970, the aspect of economic growth and of growing travelling opportunities and artistic and intellectual exchange contributed to a mutually understood energy in the crafts. The urgent need for renewal and breaking with tradition was felt on both sides of the ocean but the message wasn't shared. Peter Dormer and Ralph Turner summarised the New Jewelry like this: 'What emerges is the growth not so much of an international style, as of international variety, in which ideas and themes rather than national cultures provide the common threads.'[6] They categorised the new trends in three groups: 1) controlled expressionism, 2) exaggerated expressionism, and 3) design-based '... where "simple good taste" tends to rule'.[7] These clever categories had the advantage that they also could include American jewellery, but it excluded a conceptual tendency in jewellery that was becoming more and more significant around that time. However, it is to Dormer and Turner's merit that in 1985 they had already defined the leading characteristic of the contemporary jewellery, namely that it was international (which eventually resulted in the global jewellery known today), diverse and not restricted to a certain style. Although the prefix 'new' may look rather time determined and comparative, it is a good notion – one that was also applied in other fields of the arts, such as new ceramics, new textiles, new glass and new theatre. The sensation of 'newness' in the 1970s can still be recognised many years later.

The new jewellery was created by a young generation of makers mostly born just before, during or just after World War II. They grew up in a period of reconstruction, and for the first time in history the number of students in this sector, many of them female, grew spectacularly.[8] Almost everywhere around the globe, this new generation of jewellers was looking for alternatives to precious materials and conventional ornamentation. They turned to (new) industrial and synthetic materials, such as Perspex, stainless steel and aluminium, often combining them with precious materials and discovering the sculptural possibilities of jewellery along the way. The body and wearability were central to the work of many jewellery artists in the 1970s. Reproducibility and attempts to reach a broader (preferably younger) public were also issues in those days, and concepts such as avant-garde jewellery, objects to wear, sculpture to wear and wearables began popping up in newspaper and magazine reviews of exhibitions.

These tendencies were not only noticeable in different European countries but also on both sides of the ocean, although an intensive exchange of ideas had not yet taken place. However, there were early contacts, for instance between England and the Netherlands, thanks to Ralph Turner (who was the director of Electrum Gallery in London) and Jerven Ober (former director of the Van Reekum Galerij in Apeldoorn).[9] In Germany, Fritz Falk, the then director of the Schmuckmuseum in Pforzheim, organised five exhibitions on international jewellery under the title *Tendenzen* [Tendencies], which began in 1968. They exhibited experimental jewellery from Western and Eastern Europe, Australia, Japan and the United States. Thanks to the Kunst + Werkschule, Pforzheim had already begun to attract young international jewellery students from as far afield as the United States and

Japan. In 1974, the Austrian Peter Skubic organised an international steel symposium, *Schmuck aus Stahl* [Jewellery in Steel], inviting artists from six different countries – among them Gijs Bakker (NL), Anton Cepka (SK), Otto Künzli (CH/DE), Emmy van Leersum (NL) and Fritz Maierhofer (AT) – to experiment with this industrial material in order to find new artistic applications. Around 1970, American artists such as Stanley Lechtzin (jewellery artist) and Helen Drutt (collector and protagonist of contemporary jewellery since 1966, teacher and gallery owner since 1973) started to travel to Europe while European artists such as Claus Bury, David Watkins, Wendy Ramshaw, Gijs Bakker and Emmy van Leersum began travelling in the US. In the 1970s, Helen Drutt's gallery and house became a meeting place for artists of many different nationalities. But the restrained, abstract European work and the sculptural, narrative American jewellery were worlds apart. Gijs Bakker once told me he could not understand how Helen Drutt appreciated North American and European jewellery simultaneously. Clearly there was a mutual recognition between artists from different countries and continents – not so much in styles and themes but rather in the vigour to change existing ideas about jewellery and to try and make jewellery that was a sign of its time. The New Jewelry had problems with its identity from the outset. The difficulty was not only in the positioning of the maker, away from old-fashioned crafts notions such as the goldsmith (Ger. *Goldschmied*, or Nl. *edelsmid*, literally meaning one who forges precious metals) but also in the identification of the field or practice, in order to distinguish it from fine, precious, fashion, costume or commercial jewellery (to name just a few). Different names gained popularity and are still used interchangeably: contemporary jewellery, studio jewellery and art jewellery (mainly used in the US), research jewellery (mainly used in Italy), jewellery design and last but not least author jewellery or jewellery d'auteur (Ger. *Autorenschmuck*, or Nl. *auteurssieraad*). But all of these names have their own difficulties:

1. Contemporary jewellery indicates that it is made now and that it is 'of our time', whereas it actually covers a period of time that spans at least forty-five years and that has seen big shifts; therefore it is not very precise.

2. Studio jewellery, so well defined by Amanda Game and Elizabeth Goring as 'jewellery produced by individuals, working in their own studios, usually alone, at most with one or two assistants, who deliberately control every aspect of producing a piece of jewellery from original idea to finished work',[10] only refers to the 'where' and 'how' of jewellery production and is therefore too limited.

3. Art jewellery indicates that either art and jewellery are similar or that jewellery is an art form; however, this view is not shared outside the world of jewellery. To be more precise, museums, universities and academies do not view jewellery as an integral part of the visual arts. Like ceramics, glass, furniture and textiles, it is separated off into the category of the applied arts, which has a lower ranking. There are only few modern art museums in the world that challenge these age-old hierarchies. The concept of art jewellery is used without hesitation, though, in the US. In Susan Grant Lewin's view '… its most salient feature is its involvement with the ideas of art: vision, intellect, and concept. In fact, it is more about art than about jewelry.'[11] Cindi Straus in *Ornament as Art*, the book showcasing Helen Drutt's collection of jewellery, thinks jewellery *is* art; it is 'another art form'.[12] Oppi Untracht, the author of the important handbook for jewellery makers is of the same opinion when he writes of the '… acceptance of jewelry making as a valid medium for creative expression on a par with other visual activities. This viewpoint declares that the jewel is an art form capable of achieving the status of what is termed "a work of art". For those whose definition

of a work of art includes the implication that the object created must have no practical function, the ability of jewelry to make this transition is simplified because jewels are, in essence, non-functional objects.'[13] We can dispute whether functionality or non-functionality is the issue. In my view, the issue is rather that because of its long history and the connotations derived from this, jewellery has obtained a reputation of being supplemental, superficial and female – in Western society these are all negative associations, especially when combined. Those who use jewellery as a medium for artistic expression have to fight many prejudices. Although there is much written about art jewellery today, the term is not accepted outside the realm of jewellery – at best, jewellery is accepted as 'an artistic discipline'. In short, we can say that although we can adopt the name, it still doesn't provide an entrance ticket. The concept art jewellery is often used in a political way, as the manifestation of an attempt to bring jewellery to a supposedly higher level. In my dissenting view, this fight for legitimising jewellery as art is not significant as such, and it is also confusing: art jewellery is *not* more about art than about jewellery, as Susan Grant Lewin argues; art jewellery is exactly about jewellery *not* about art. Jewellery is the source and – mostly, but not necessarily – the outcome. But I do endorse the viewpoint that contemporary jewellery should be presented in a broader context than the jewellery scene alone because it has meaning as an artistic expression.

4. Research jewellery (It. *gioello di ricerca*) can be explained as a way to describe the artistic process. In the words of Italian art historian Maria Cristina Bergesio, research jewellery reaches: '… from research into forms and materials, […] onwards to more conceptual, philosophical reflections'.[14] Although the idea of research is significant within the context of artistic research, the notion suffers from obscurity because it is mainly used in Italy.

5. Jewellery design (Nl. *sieraadontwerpen* or *sieraadvormgeving)* was mainly used between the 1960s and the 1980s. The Dutch words *sieraadontwerper* and *sieraadvormgever*, both meaning jewellery designer, were introduced at the end of the 1960s to distinguish between the designer and the craftsman/maker; that is, between the concept and the handwork. Its meaning was to emphasise the fact that a piece of jewellery was the result of a process of design instead of just the making, of rational thought instead of emotion or intuition.[15] It referred to the discussion of the concept versus the handwork (which was supposedly done by intuition), of which Gijs Bakker is still one of the main protagonists today. Although rather useful for quite some time, the notions of jewellery design and jewellery designer are no longer valid to describe the field as it has developed today, although one can still come across them in current literature. The need to dissociate from the craftsman or artisan is not so much of an issue today. Theorists have convincingly disputed the supposed distinction between the mind and the hand, and today we now feel that we are able to 'think through our hands'.[16]

6. Author jewellery or jewellery d'auteur is derived from the notion of the auteur film, which was introduced in the 1950s in France by theorists such as François Truffaut and André Bazin. Cinéma d'auteur refers to films that bear the artistic stamp and creative vision of the director or auteur.[17] This notion indicates that film is an art form, equal to literature, fine art, theatre, and the like. Etymologically the word auteur (Lat. *auctor*) means designer, creator and spokesman and is derived from the verb *augere* meaning to increase, grow or enlarge. An auctor is a finder, maker, creator and also a spokesman and an innovator. The addition of the word author is therefore meaning-

ful, because it denotes a creative process. When I introduced the term *auteurssieraad*, I did so with reference to etymology and film history, to indicate that this kind of jewellery is made by an individual maker and bears the stamp of his or her artistry and vision.[18] As is prevalent in film theory, the notion of auteur supposes content and a certain continuing artistic 'standard of reference' that might even progress from one collection of jewellery to the other.[19] In other words, it assumes that there is something that might be called artistic growth. Although this concept seems appropriate, it is not generally adopted, perhaps because of its rather luxurious, elegant flavour. Because of this, it also has a sense of isolation and pride, which makes the notion of author jewellery the zenith of disapproval in discussions about the position of contemporary jewellery. Another problem lies in the fact that it refers just to the tangible object, while contemporary jewellery is also known for its conceptual work.

You cannot force linguistic usage; the acceptance of a word depends on many factors. In this book I do not stick to one notion; I use different ones alternately because I think this reflects quite well the status quo of art jewellery – contemporary jewellery, author jewellery – at this very moment.[20]

What do we understand as jewellery? A question that seems easy to answer, we envision necklaces, chains, bracelets, rings and brooches, or to put it in more popular terms, baubles, bangles and beads. But this is too limited; badges, medals, crowns, tiaras, chains of office and other official regalia, in fact every item that is worn on the body and is additional to it, excepted hats and scarves, should be listed under the concept of jewellery. Traditionally, that is to say in the Western world, jewellery originates from goldsmiths and is therefore observed as an applied art form. Jewellery is categorised within the realm of objects that beautify, decorate, signify and have a practical function. But jewellery has no utility; it is practically useless, apart from the historical fibulae (pins) that were used as fasteners for cloaks in ancient times and the cufflinks that are the only remaining piece of typical male jewellery today. A piece of jewellery is not an implement, a utensil or an appliance, which all have a straightforward and unambiguous purpose.

The function of jewellery is manifold and rather complex compared to that of other examples of applied arts, crafts or design, such as cups, cars, curtains or cutlery. Decorating, embellishing and signalising can, in essence, be seen as the main functions of jewellery. Jewellery is supplementary to humans; without man, jewellery only partially serves its function. To be more precise: the function of jewellery can be defined as the meaning it adds to the person wearing it and therefore to people in general who recognise its meaning and who can use this for their own benefit or purpose. More than any other functional object, jewellery is related to people. Yet it is exactly this that remains so difficult to grasp and that causes jewellery to be overlooked as *merely* additional and *just* decorative; in other words, as superfluous.

Because the function of jewellery is not obvious, it is important to make a categorisation. This categorisation can also help to understand where contemporary jewellery finds its place. Function, when talking about jewellery, should be understood as meaning. The function of jewellery is its meaning in the public and the private realm:

1.   Social and religious: Distinguishing is an important function of jewellery both in history and the present day, ranging from classical signs such as insignia and chains of office to wedding rings, medals, religious charms and (political) badges. Conveying

status has always been an important social function of jewellery. The lavish application of precious materials on the body reveals the wealth and importance of the wearer (who today is usually female).

2. Economical: Capital investment is in some cultures and social classes a serious function for jewellery. In the public realm, precious jewels convey status, but jewellery that is purchased for economical reasons is not necessarily worn; it can also remain locked in a safe forever.

3. Ornamental: Jewellery enhances, embellishes or beautifies the wearer; this function is appreciated in every culture and in every historic period.

4. Sentimental or memorial: Memory is primarily an important private function of jewellery. Jewellery carries reminders of people, events and happenings in life, which are significant for the wearer yet invisible for the viewer. Examples of public memorial jewellery are the red poppies worn in the weeks preceding Armistice Day (11 November) in the Anglo-Saxon world.

5. Magical: Jewellery is worn for health and safety, such as amulets or special minerals with the idea of healing or defence.

6. Symbolical: Next to the finery, the capital investment, the decoration, the memory and the magic, there is yet another function, one that takes the limelight and puts the others into the shade – that a piece of jewellery is a sign on the body. The signalising function of jewellery is strengthened by its inherent uselessness and by the fact that it is worn on the body, whereby it makes its entrance into the world. Jewellery, whether fine, costly, traditional or avant-garde, can be read as a symbol, precisely because it is brought into the public domain. A tiara or crown is a symbol of royalty; a piece of jewellery purchased in a gallery is a symbol of exquisite taste and knowledge. Jewellery is a sign that can be read: an expression of one's social situation and identity.

The first function of jewellery – the social and religious meaning – often takes on a ritualistic, performative and overt character known to all of us. A piece of jewellery can be publicly and solemnly presented, taken up and put on someone else's body in a ritual of adorning (medals) or belonging (wedding rings), where only then its function starts to become visible and its meaning is established. Within this context I will present some examples of the public function of jewellery as symbols of honour, love, power and dignity, remembrance and status in 'the spectacle of the everyday', in order to underline how many codes and messages are to be read in jewellery.

The medal, worn on the left side of the breast (on top of the heart), is a piece of jewellery that symbolises honour and recognition. In 2009, for the first time in fifty years, the Willemsorde, the highest Dutch military award, was granted to a Captain Kroon. It was pinned on his uniform by Queen Beatrix during an official ceremony, which was then concluded with the receiving of the accolade, a pat on his shoulder. Just one year later, Kroon was accused of drug dealing and illegally possessing firearms. From that point, the Willemsorde played a significant role not just in the legal proceedings but also in the public debate. Kroon and his lawyer, the accuser and the press, mentioned the medal many times as sign of honour. The accused appeared in court in full regalia, which added to the drama of a hero balancing on the edge between good and evil.[21]

Love and jewellery are closely related, with the wedding ring representing a symbol of love and also one of faith. The moment of exchange during a wedding ceremony has a highly symbolical meaning. It may therefore have been disappointing to the two billion

people witnessing the British royal wedding of 2011 that Kate Middleton could not give her
prince a wedding ring because he had decided not to wear one. Hers was made from an exclusive gold mined in Wales, perfectly suited to mark her transition from a middle-class woman to a duchess and the wife of a future king.[22]

Power and dignity are symbolised in jewellery that is mainly worn on the breast and the head. In some countries, such as the Netherlands, Germany and the United Kingdom, mayors have a chain of office. In other countries, such as France, Belgium and Italy, mayors have a sash as their official distinguishing sign. This distinguishing jewellery, meant for public exposure, does undoubtedly have a different meaning and invoke different rituals in different countries. However, I can only explain the Dutch situation, which I have researched in the past.[23] One of the things that struck me during my investigation was the fact that the chain of office represents a very delicate symbolic tradition that resists the idea of innovation. Of course the chain stands for power, distinction and dignity, but it also stands for tradition and history, and is therefore almost untouchable: a mayor cannot move too far away from the myth. The mayor should wear the chain of office during certain, precisely described situations, for instance when he/she leads the council meeting or when officially meeting civilians. Most civilians appreciate the chain of office as a treasured symbol of the mayor's dignity. A visit without the chain is robbed of its importance, devaluated as it were. The use of this symbol can be manipulated though. Newspaper images of the mayor of Amsterdam for instance, made in the 1960s and 1970s, show that he only used his most humble chain (councils often have more than one chain, mostly due to the redrawing of municipality boundaries) during this period of upheaval. Apparently it did not seem appropriate to wear a more prominent sign of power in those days. Today, the mayor of Amsterdam again wears the beautiful sculptural chain, created by crafts artist and designer Harm Ellens in 1923. While the installation of a new mayor is concluded with the solemn hanging of the chain around the neck, the reverse – the taking off and laying down of the chain – is also an act full of symbolism. If a mayor takes the chain off during the council meeting, he/she withdraws from office. Dramatically photographed, these symbolic and telling moments find their way to the newspapers. From all of these narratives, we can conclude that the chain of office is a 'conversation piece' par excellence, whose effect radiates on to others.

A piece of jewellery is one of those small and intimate artefacts completely suited to remind one of a person or an important moment in life. Remembrance can also be shared in public. As mentioned earlier, the red poppy badge has become the most familiar symbol of remembrance in Commonwealth countries. The symbol of the red poppy originates from the famous poem 'In Flanders Fields' by Major McCrae, written in May 1915, after the first slaughters on the Ypres battlefields. The poem, describing the flowering battlefields, received widespread publicity and inspired some women in the allied countries to wear the red poppy as a symbol of remembrance. By 1920 the symbol had been adopted as the official badge of remembrance in the UK and the US. It is worn on 11 November on Armistice Day and in the preceding weeks when it is sold to raise money for charitable work. Television presenters, at the BBC for instance, are usually the first to start wearing one at the end of October. The red poppy is a rare example of a wearable symbol that unites people all around the world. There is a lively trade in these red paper badges, and it has brought about a large industry of gadgets decorated with this flower. This illustrates one of the few examples of the adaptation of a piece of jewellery on other items.

Buttons or badges (the words are used interchangeably) are excellent means for communication and alliance. As Philip Attwood forcefully explains, the word badge is used in the United Kingdom while the word button is used in the United States: 'The two terms […] say something about the history and functions of these objects – and also perhaps of the two countries themselves.'[24] The button is a twentieth-century invention described by Attwood as 'a protective disc of clear plastic and a paper disc bearing a message positioned between a circular disc of metal and a metal collar, with a sprung steel pin inserted in the back'.[25] Medieval badges, openly signs of alliance to a Lord, find their contemporary counterpart in signs of membership, such as those of the Rotary organisation. In our modern times buttons are used to express a political message. As a cheap and an easy conveyer of slogans, they were very popular during the 1970s and the 1980s, while today they are used a lot in all kind of creative projects and playful actions. Madeleine K. Albright, Secretary of State under the Clinton administration, made use of this connotation of badges and buttons by wearing brooches from her extensive collection of costume and fine jewellery that hold a special message in a certain political context – the collection was put together with this aim. In an exhibition and book, *Read My Pins: Stories From a Diplomat's Jewel Box*, she tells how she used jewellery diplomacy as a subtle way to tell her political opponents and the media how she felt about certain issues.[26] The practice began when she was ambassador to the United Nations and Saddam Hussein called her a serpent. When she next met with Iraqi officials, she wore a snake brooch. She observes this play as a typical gender issue: 'I love being a woman and I was not one of these women who rose through professional life by wearing men's clothes or looking masculine. I loved wearing bright colors and being who I am. So the pins kind of evolved, and then they became signals to other foreign ministers. It was kind of fun because they actually noticed what I was wearing'.[27]

Exceptional, precious jewellery provides status; one can even say that some exceptional jewels have status. The most famous diamonds in the world bear fancy names, such as Koh-i-Noor, Cullinan, Blue Princess, Heart of Eternity, Pasha of Egypt, Eureka and Star of South Africa. There are only a few that are named after a famous owner, such as the Hope Diamond. It is unclear who decides on the name, especially because the history of such exceptional diamonds is often one of fast changing ownership. The Hope Diamond belonged to the French crown jewels in the eighteenth century. After the French Revolution, this blue diamond disappeared for some time until it was purchased in England in 1812 by Philip Henry Hope and as a result received its name. Subsequently, the stone frequently changed owners until 1958, when jeweller Harry Winston donated it to the Smithsonian Natural History Museum in Washington, D.C.

Film stars Elizabeth Taylor and Richard Burton are among the few twentieth-century socialites who have a diamond named after them, partly because of the enormous amount of money (over one million dollars) Burton paid for it, partly because of the turbulent love life of Burton and Taylor that was frequently publicly displayed. The diamond was set in a necklace and was worn by Elizabeth Taylor on several occasions, every time again underlining her position as a Very Important Person.[28]

The military order, the royal wedding ring, the chain of office, the poppy, the button, Madeleine Albright's diplomatic brooches and Elizabeth Taylor's trinkets stand far apart from the subject of this book, contemporary art jewellery. However these narratives and connotations play a role in the creation and perception of contemporary jewellery. By focusing so extensively on these pieces that are almost regarded as public property, I hope to reveal some of the mechanisms that start working when we look at author jewellery. Although we may not do this consciously, we know how to read jewellery because jewellery plays a role in our personal lives and in society. Jewellery conveys meanings and incites readings. It is a given, which one way or another determines the appreciation of contemporary art jewellery.

During the last forty to fifty years, jewellery has evolved into an artistic and reflexive practice. As in the visual arts, the applied arts and design, boundaries are blurred, and artists (makers, creators, designers) borrow freely. Contemporary jewellery not only involves the baubles, bangles and beads, but also photography, installation, performance, video and so on. In my view, this new freedom in jewellery should not be confused with the freedom in the visual arts. In visual arts, one can say anything, convey even the most horrified and objectionable messages; one can give way to all emotions, from disgust, horror and aversion to immorality, perversity and provocation. Some theorists and artists observe having the freedom to be amoral as an important task of art in today's society. In the applied arts, this is almost unthinkable, although the borders are being breached here as well. A series of jewellery by Munich based Stefan Heuser, made from human fatty tissue from a liposuction clinic, is a recent example of jewellery breaching the boundaries of disgust, horror, distaste and immorality. However, since it is still a piece of jewellery its message is emasculated. As a wearable, beautifully made, decorative and conventional object (a pendant that looks like amber, fig. 1) its message – when worn – is not divulged to the incidental viewer.[29] In this case the medium (a piece of prototypal jewellery) adds something to the message (a jewel made of human fat) only when you know the full story; the message is not readable from the object alone. Stefan Heuser's work is exemplary for today's reflexive approach to jewellery: jewellery observed and researched as a phenomenon, envisioned as a work of art, created as a piece of jewellery and perceived as a controversial piece that needs a spirited wearer but finds its utmost power of expression when combined with the full knowledge of the concept, material and history.

> 1

> fig. 1

1   The letter was published at the opening of Henk Delabie's exhibition at Galerie S&H De Buck in Ghent, in Nov. 2010.

2   Saskia de Bodt, 1980. 'Onderscheiding voor ontwerper Paul Derrez. De nieuwe sieraadkunst wil vormgeven aan een idee', in *NRC Handelsblad*, 18 Dec.

3   Peter Dormer and Ralph Turner, 1985. *The New Jewelry: Trends + Traditions*. London: Thames & Hudson. In this book I use the phrase 'the New Jewelry' as a reference to Dormer and Turner.

4   The Studio Jewelry movement in the US can be traced back to the Wearable Art movement of the early 1940s. The style of working was biomorphic, Surrealist and Modernist. In the 1960s, Pop and Funk became new sources for non-precious jewellery. Towards the end of the 1960s, American jewellery became sculptural and narrative, quite distinct from the restrained and geometrical approach in Europe at the time. New Zealand's equivalent to New Jewelry is the Bone, Stone, Shell movement. Actually it was not a movement but the title of an exhibition held in 1988, which brought together the work of a generation of makers, born in the 1940s and early 1950s, who worked with natural and found materials, rope and thread, as a kind of bricoleurs. Their work embodied a new awareness of New Zealand's bicultural character.

5   Susan Grant Lewin, 1994. *One of a Kind. American Art Jewelry Today*. New York: Abrams, p. 26.

6   Peter Dormer and Ralph Turner (see note 3), back cover.

7   Ibid. p. 23.

8   As far as I know, the number of jewellery students and schools has never been researched in depth, neither in the different countries nor internationally. It is clear, however, that for instance, in the Netherlands the number of students

started growing towards the end of the 1960s. Later the number of jewellery departments at academies, polytechnics and universities also increased, while private schools such as Alchimia in Florence, and summer schools such as Opere (by Ruudt Peters) also emerged. In the twenty-first century the number of jewellery students is still growing.

9   Ralph Turner invited Emmy van Leersum and Gijs Bakker for a show in the Electrum Gallery in 1972, but before this date they had already been invited to show their work in the Ewan Philips Gallery in London in 1967. In 1974, the Electrum Gallery invited the Dutch BOE groep for the exhibition *Revolt in Jewellery*. The Van Reekum Galerij in the Netherlands organised different exhibitions with British jewellers, such as *British Jewellers on Tour in Holland* (1978) and *The Recurring Theme: Susanna Heron* (1982). During this period, the museum also purchased jewellery by British jewellers for its collection.

10 Amanda Game and Elizabeth Gore, 1998. *Jewellery Moves: Ornament for the 21ˢᵗ Century*. Edinburgh: NMS Publishing, p. 5.

11 Grant Lewin (see note 5), p. 13.

12 Cindi Strauss, 2007. *Ornament as Art: Avant-Garde Jewelry from the Helen Williams Drutt Collection*. Stuttgart: Arnoldsche in association with The Museum of Fine Arts Houston, p. 13.

13 Oppi Untracht, 1985. *Jewelry: Concepts and Technology*. New York: Doubleday, p. xxi.

14 Maria Cristina Bergesio, 2006. 'No Body Decoration!', in Maria Cristina Bergesio (ed.), 2006. *No Body Decoration: Research Jewellery as a Redefinition of the Human Body*. Lucca: Pacini Fazzi, p. 40.

15 The notion was easily adopted and spread very fast. There are numerous Dutch newspapers and magazine articles from around 1970 where the notion is introduced and explained.

16 See: Glenn Adamson, 2007. *Thinking Through Craft*. Oxford/New York: Berg. His book opens with the sentence: 'Thinking through … craft? Isn't craft something mastered in the hands, not in the mind? Something consisting of physical actions, rather than abstract ideas?' About the same time, Israeli jewellery maker Esther Knobel published a book about her work under the title *The Mind in the Hand*. Jerusalem: Carmel, 2008.

17 Film is of course a much more complex process of creation, involving many parties, such as the producer, scriptwriter, cameraman and actors.

18 See my prologue in *Sieradiën … een noodzakelijke zotheid*. Rotterdam, 2005. In March 2005, I wrote an introduction for an exhibition catalogue: 'Author jewellery an unknown story…', in *Silver – med mera*, Åsensbruk: Dalslands Museum & Konsthall.

19 Adapted from André Bazin.

20 In the subtitle of this book the notion 'art jewellery' is prominent. One has to choose and in this case it seemed appropriate to adhere to the term most used internationally.

21 Captain Kroon was cleared of the charges in Apr. 2011.

22 The use of Welsh gold in British royal wedding bands is a long-standing tradition.

23 In the period between 1997 and 2001, I was an advisor to an official working group of Dutch mayors, under the auspices of the Nederlands Genootschap van Burgemeesters [Society of Mayors of the Netherlands]. It was our aim to investigate the possibility of new/contemporary designs for mayoral chains of office by commissioning jewellers and designers. Over the years designers were linked to communities, and designs, sketches and models were made and discussed. The eleven models, the result of this project, were exhibited in 2001 in the Stedelijk Museum in Amsterdam. Of these eleven, two were realised: one by Philip Sajet and one by Ted Noten. While in the following years three other chains were realised by Philip Sajet, Annelies Planteijdt and Arnout Visser. During the project, I researched the history and symbolism of chains of office. The research and the results of the project were brought together in a publication, which was offered to every mayor in the country: Liesbeth den Besten, 2001. *De nieuwe keten van de burgemeester, een verslag van de werkgroep ambtsketens*. Amstelveen.

24 Philip Attwood, 2004. *Badges*. London: British Museum Press, p. 5.

25 Ibid.

26 Madeleine Albright, 2009. *Read My Pins: Stories From a Diplomat's Jewel Box*. New York: HarperCollins. The exhibition *Read My Pins: Madeleine Albright* was held at the MAD, New York, from 30.9.2009 to 31.1.2010.

27 Eleanor Clift, 2009. 'The Ambassador's Jewels', in *Newsweek*, 28 Sept.

28 Elizabeth Taylor owned an extensive jewellery collection, about which she also published a book: Elizabeth Taylor, Ruth A. Peltason and John Bigelow Taylor, 2002. *My Love Affair with Jewelry*. New York: Simon & Schuster. Taylor's motto on the book is: 'Here, in my own words and as I remember them, are my cherished stories about a lifetime of fun and love and laughter… I've never thought of my jewelry as trophies. I'm here to take care of it and to love it, for we are only temporary custodians of beauty.'

29 The jewellery of Stefan Heuser was shown in March 2008 in Galerie Wittenbrink FUENFHOEFE in Munich; in 2009 the artist presented jewellery made from mother's milk, and in 2011 he presented jewellery created from sleeping pills, viagra and other medicines.

I. The Meaning of Jewellery

In this chapter, I will discuss the meaning of jewellery in general, including art jewellery. It is not about content, but about what meanings society/mankind attribute to jewellery. Jewellery functions on different levels – social, cultural and individual. Every historical period, every social group and class and every culture has different views on jewellery, its meaning and suitability for rituals and daily use. By taking jewellery in general as the subject of this chapter, instead of this very small sub-category called art jewellery, I try to reconstruct a small history of the meaning of jewellery. In doing this, we will encounter remnants of older meanings that still form part of our view on jewellery today.

A text by Roland Barthes sheds light on jewellery from quite an unusual angle and offers new insights into jewellery. Therefore in this chapter I will go into his essay rather extensively, elaborating on some aspects mentioned in the text, commenting on it and supplementing it with – in my view – missing points. In the second part of this chapter, I will try to adopt some ideas found in Barthes's essay by analysing some examples of contemporary author jewellery.

The French theorist Roland Barthes is seen as one of the early pioneers of the theory of fashion. From 1957 onwards he regularly published articles and essays about fashion in academic journals and in the women's magazine *Marie Claire*. Barthes saw fashion as a complex system of signs used to communicate and exchange information. His book *Système de la Mode* (1967) epitomises his thinking about fashion.[1] He spent many years working on this book in which he analyses the rules of the underlying system of fashion. The book is a rather indigestible study of fashion – though not of fashion as such, but of the description of women's fashion ('written fashion' as Barthes puts it) in French fashion magazines. The book, simultaneously known as a magisterial effort and as the most boring book ever written about fashion, is in his own words 'a book of method'.

Few people know that Barthes also wrote an essay about jewellery; the essay entitled 'From Gemstones to Jewellery' is rather contrary to a methodological undertaking. Instead, the literary text is full of imagination and rich in ideas. The essay, first published in the leading Parisian art magazine *Jardin des Arts* in 1961, reflects some essential ideas about jewellery. Barthes writes about the magic of the gemstone and of gold, and the role of the detail in fashion. It is interesting that the author begins exploring jewellery's origins with the gemstone, which in his view is 'inhuman' and as such 'inert', because it comes from deep under the ground 'where humanity's mythic imagination stored its dead, its damned and its treasures in the same place'.[2] In Barthes's description of the gemstone (hard, pitiless, infernal object), it may seem as if he places jewellery right in the centre of a moral dilemma. But in his time notions such as 'blood diamonds' or 'conflict diamonds' were not an issue (if they had been, Barthes probably would have written about it). It is only fairly recently that the mining of gemstones (and gold) is observed as a problem that encompasses ethicality, slavery, war, pollution of the environment and poisoning of miners and people living in the immediate surrounding areas of the mines. Barthes refers to something else, namely to the very character of stone. For Barthes, stone is inhuman because it is an inanimate substance and therefore regards 'the stubbornness of the thing to be nothing but itself; it is the infinitely unchanging. It follows then, that stone is pitiless; whereas fire is cruel, and water crafty, stone is the despair of that which has never lived and will never do so, of that which obstinately resists all forms of life.'[3] It is curious to see with how much force he succeeds in describing this 'inanimate object' using anthropomorphist characterisations. The purity of the diamond is compared with sterility and infertility: '... the diamond is like the sterile son emerging from the deepest point of the earth, non-productive, incapable of rotting down, hence incapable of becoming the source of new life.'[4]

It may seem disappointing to approach jewellery from the side of the gemstone. However, knowing that the English word 'jewel' actually means gemstone, that early jewellery consisted of gemstones sewn on to the clothing (of men and women), and that for most people jewellery is indeed represented by a metal setting with one or more glistening stones, it is legitimate. The origin of Western jewellery lies in the setting of stones. These (mostly) gold settings were replaceable and recyclable, and what remained was the invulnerable stone, which was qualified by its weight (carat), colour and purity.

About the glister of the diamond, which gives it a magical power, Barthes observes: 'For centuries, Christian humanity felt deeply [...] the opposition between the world and solitude; thanks to its fire-like sparkle and its coldness, the diamond was this world, this abhorrent and fascinating order of ambition, flattery and disappointment, condemned by so many of our moralists...'. Here, Barthes refers to an aspect of jewellery that is often neglected in our discussions today; the fact that jewellery by its very nature represents worldliness: 'This cold fire, this sharp, shining object which is nevertheless silent, what a symbol for the world of vanities, of seductions devoid of content, of pleasures devoid of sincerity!'[5]

In the film *Gentlemen Prefer Blondes* (1953) Marilyn Monroe sang in much paler words the glory of the diamond, in a rather cynical song 'Diamonds Are a Girl's Best Friend'. In the film, she appears dressed in a pink evening dress, bejewelled with diamonds, a choker and two bracelets and surrounded by an army of men. In this classic song, the worldliness of diamonds is underlined by putting diamonds on a par with currency:

> *The French are glad to die for love.*
> *They delight in fighting duels.*
> *But I prefer a man who lives*
> *And gives expensive jewels.*
>
> *A kiss on the hand*
> *May be quite continental,*
> *But diamonds are a girl's best friend.*
>
> *A kiss may be grand*
> *But it won't pay the rental*
> *On your humble flat,*
> *Or help you at the automat.*
>
> *Men grow cold*
> *As girls grow old,*
> *And we all lose our charms in the end.*

But square-cut or pear-shaped,
These rocks don't lose their shape.
Diamonds are a girl's best friend.

Tiffany's!
Cartier!
Black Starr!
Frost Gorham!
Talk to me Harry Winston.
Tell me all about it!

There may come a time
When a lass needs a lawyer,
But diamonds are a girl's best friend.

There may come a time
When a hard-boiled employer
Thinks you're awful nice,
But get that ice or else no dice.

He's your guy
When stocks are high,
But beware when they start to descend.

It's then that those louses
Go back to their spouses.
Diamonds are a girl's best friend.

I've heard of affairs
That are strictly platonic,
But diamonds are a girl's best friend.

And I think affairs
That you must keep liaisonic
Are better bets
If little pets get big baguettes.

Time rolls on,
And youth is gone,
And you can't straighten up when you bend.

But stiff back
Or stiff knees,
You stand straight at Tiffany's.

Diamonds! Diamonds!
I don't mean rhinestones!
But diamonds are a girl's best friend.[6]

I will not embark upon a complete textual analysis, but this song can teach us something about jewellery. The message of the song somehow reflects our deepest prejudices about jewellery (and girls):

1.   That jewellery is vain.
2.   That jewellery is for dumb blondes.
3.   That jewellery is money.
4.   That jewellery is about showing off.
5.   That jewellery is an investment.
6.   That girls are corruptible.

These ideas are so deep-rooted that they even affected Roland Barthes, as we will soon see. Of course we can object and say that this applies not to contemporary art jewellery, the kind of jewellery this book is about. We can argue that art jewellery is definitely not about intrinsic values, but about meaning – which is absolutely true. But it should be clear that art jewellery has to fight against prejudices that are fed by ideas about jewellery that have a very long history, much older than the history of contemporary jewellery. It may be one of the reasons why contemporary art jewellery is often not recognised as an artistic expression.

Now back to Barthes and his essay about jewellery. Barthes values gold and diamonds in a different way. The diamond, he thinks, has a symbolic quality because it glistens. He calls it '… a paradoxical substance, both lit up and stone cold: it is nothing but fire and yet nothing but ice. This cold fire, this sharp, shining object which is nevertheless silent, what a symbol for the whole world of vanities, of seductions devoid of content, of pleasures devoid of sincerity!'[7] Gold in his view is an intellectual substance, because it is convertible and because it can 'appropriate everything'. Gold is, according to Barthes, superlative and 'absolute richness'. But as an intellectual substance it also has power: '… as a sign, what power it has! … the sign par excellence, the sign of all signs.'[8]

Barthes does not talk about the medieval and Renaissance view on gemstones, which was completely different from our modern view. And therefore he does not mention the pieces of coloured glass and enamel that were, in medieval times, as valuable as gems because they provided colour, as gems did. Colour was an important phenomenon in those days, specially intended for objects of a divine or noble character. Only the rich and well to do could afford to wear colourful garments. Red pigments, for instance (made from rare snails and worms), were extremely hard to get and therefore expensive. Cathedrals and religious sculptures were polychromous, and even the church windows were made of stained glass, providing beautiful colourful effects when the sun shone through them into the holy space. There are accounts of medieval visitors of cathedrals who expressed their amazement and respect for the superterrestrial beauty of this spectacle. Colour, light and sparkle suggested a direct connection with the divine revelation.

In those days, gold and gemstones (particularly sapphires, rubies and pearls) were observed as divine materials because of their colours and rarity. Gems were not faceted, but polished instead. Medieval and early Renaissance jewellery combined the devotional, religious and the worldly. Clare Phillips, curator at the Victoria & Albert Museum in London, writes: 'Stones were chosen not just for colour but also for their supposed healing and spiritual protective powers, which were extensively written about and widely accepted. According to the treatise on lapidary written by Marbodus, a Bishop of Rennes in the eleventh century, the sapphire's virtues included not only protection against physical injury, fraud, fear and envy but also the promotion of peace and reconciliation, healing for ulcers, eyes and headaches and the safeguarding of chastity'.[9] Although the medieval virtues attributed to stones were quite far reaching, a modest echo is still recognisable today in the so-called 'health stones'. Today's gemstone therapy even claims to be a new science of healing.

In the second half of the thirteenth century, increased levels of affluence started to be considered a problem. Therefore in 1363, King Edward III of England enacted a law that forbade families of low standing, such as artisans and peasants, to wear gold or silver jewellery. This ban seems like an echo of much older laws from the Byzantine world, laid down in the Codex that Justinianus compiled in the year 529, which tried to regulate the use of gold and gemstones. Clare Phillips writes that due to the stipulations in the Codex 'the finest materials were only available to jewellers' workshops within the palace in Constantinople, where a hereditary caste of skilled craftsmen produced jewellery for the emperor, his family and the court'. And furthermore that 'every man and woman had the right to wear a gold ring', but that the use of pearls, emeralds and sapphires was restricted to the emperor.[10] Laws like these were designed in order to save jewellery's status for the traditional centre of power where it belonged, namely the court and the church. Of course, this was a lost case, and soon everyone who could afford to invested his money in gold and stones as a safe investment and as a way to show off.

Barthes mentions that in the Middle Ages and during the Renaissance period, gemstones were worn by men and women alike – which is an important fact to consider. In a famous painting by Hans Holbein, King Henry III is featured with his whole massive body entirely bejewelled. It was only in modern times that jewellery became exclusively associated with women and gradually gained a negative connotation – women having a marginalised social position but also the power of being the living showcase of their husbands' wealth and power. Barthes calls this the 'mythology of woman'. He writes: '… as always with human society, a simple pattern is quickly invested with unexpected meanings, symbols and effects. Thus the primitive showing-off of wealth has been invaded by a whole mythology of woman: this mythology remains infernal, because woman would give everything to own gemstones, and man would give everything to own that very woman who wears the gemstones that she has sold herself for.'[11] At this point Barthes's ideas about women and gemstones are not far remote from the message that 'Diamonds Are a Girl's Best Friend' provides. Barthes goes on to describe this radiant jewellery as 'a singular, dazzling, magical object, conceived as a way of ornamenting and thus making woman look her best.'[12] And here Barthes especially refers to French literature from the period of the Second Empire (the second half of the nineteenth century), such as *Nana* by Emile Zola, which is dense with ideas about the power of gemstones and its 'capacity to induce human Evil',[13] – also one of the themes of Art Nouveau jewellery with its representation of the tempting and pernicious femme fatale in colourful glass, stones, horn and gold.

Roland Barthes concludes his article with the assumption that today (that is, the 1960s) not only has 'the mythology' of woman changed (the femme fatale is on the decline), but that of the gemstone, too. He thinks the gemstone is hardly worn any more: 'They are', he writes 'of historical value only, sterilized, embalmed and kept away from the female body, condemned to sit in a safe.'[14] Jewellery has become secularised and democratised, just like society has. 'In short', he says 'there has been a widespread liberation of jewellery; its definition is widening, it is now an object that is free, if one can say this, from prejudice: multiform, multisubstance, to be used in a variety of ways, it is now no longer subservient to the law of the highest price nor to that of being used in only one way, such as for a party or sacred occasion: jewellery has become democratic.'[15] This is an interesting fragment; it is as if Barthes has written down a proclamation of New Jewelry. The keywords and ideas – liberation, a widening of definition, free from prejudices, different formal possibilities, multiple materials, different applications, liberated from the intrinsic material value, democratic – are all valid with respect to New Jewelry as well. However, it would be another twenty-four years before Peter Dormer and Ralph Turner described the contours of the new ideas and the new freedom in contemporary jewellery and coined the concept of New Jewelry.

The liberalisation of jewellery, as observed by Barthes in the 1950s (his essay being published in 1961), brought about the creative use of every conceivable material for jewellery, even cheap, fragile and non-sustainable materials like paper, wood and plastic, as Barthes describes. Jewellery was no longer there to show off a price, and as Barthes writes: 'when jewellery imitates some precious substance, gold or pearls, it is shameless; the copy, now a characteristic of capitalist civilization, is no longer a hypocritical way of being rich on the cheap – it is quite open about itself, makes no attempt to deceive, only retaining the aesthetic qualities of the material it is imitating.'[16]

So in 1961, in a pre-New Jewelry period, Barthes refers to a new kind of liberated jewellery that is secularised and free of conventions. It is tempting to see him as a visionary, but it is not very clear to which kind of jewellery he is actually referring. Notwithstanding Barthes's explicit execution of the death sentence on precious jewellery ('condemned to sit in a safe'), expensive and extraordinary gemstones were, and still are today, worn in certain circles; it is the rationale of the existence of such great jewellery houses such as Cartier, Van Cleef & Arpels and Boucheron. Not mentioning any of these houses in particular, he calls this kind of jewellery 'jewellery of bad taste': '... what defines bad taste in a piece of jewellery is curiously that which was once the very sign of its prestige and of its magical qualities: namely its highest price; not only is jewellery that is too rich or too heavy now discredited but conversely, for expensive jewellery to have good taste, its richness must be discreet, sober, visible certainly but only to those in the know.'[17]

The other kind of jewellery Barthes is referring to – the liberated jewellery – is less obvious. What kind of jewellery is he actually talking about? Knowing that Barthes was famous for his theory on the system of fashion, which was based on an analysis of fashion magazines, he must have been well acquainted with the work of the famous French paruriers, who specialised in designing catwalk jewellery and commercial, relatively cheap bijouterie for the shops.[18] The heyday of so-called costume jewellery was the period between 1920 and 1990, with a peak in the years 1950 to 1970, exactly the period when Barthes studied French fashion and wrote his essay about jewellery.

Costume jewellery is a phenomenon that has been extremely strong throughout most of the twentieth century in France due to the French fashion culture and industry. In the 1920s, fashion designer Gabrielle (Coco) Chanel, who was known for her dictatorial style and provocative attitude, declared that fake is more beautiful than real. In an interview she stated: 'Nothing looks more like a fake jewel than a beautiful jewel. Why get mesmerized by a beautiful stone? One might as well wear a cheque around one's neck'.[19] Her revolutionary attitude laid the foundation for the unprecedented success of costume jewellery in the twentieth century.

Paris was a centre for costume jewellery with many workshops: a creative (home) industry that employed thousands of workers. In her book about costume jewellery, Florence Müller recalls the post-war period in costume jewellery as follows: 'Every imitation stone was celebrated in the quotations of the nineteenth century or the Second

Empire. Haute couture costume jewelry was now accepted, and its artistic value was held up in contrast to the absence of creativity in fine jewelry [i.e. by the big jewellers' houses, LdB]. The Maharani of Baroda bought jewels from Roger Jean-Pierre [one of the best-known paruriers in this period, who worked for Schiaparelli, Balenciaga, Dior, Grès, and Balmain, LdB] in order to have them reproduced in fine jewels by Indian jewelry-makers, who are devoid of any imagination'.[20] It is this kind of jewellery to which Barthes refers in his essay. Anyone who cares to spend some time studying this subject will be astonished by the high quality and experimental joy of French costume jewellery. These Parisian paruriers in their liberal attitude towards materials and imagination can be observed as fore-fathers, or at least one kind of forefather, of the contemporary art jewellers of today. The quality, imagination and adventurousness of the jewellery of paruriers such as Lina Baretti (for Schiaparelli), Cissy Zoltowska, and that of Elsa Triolet who, in the 1930s, made excellent jewellery for Schiaparelli using unusual materials such as dried cotton coated with artificial mother-of-pearl, porcelain, palm wood and leather, is unique and may explain Barthes's enthusiasm about what he called 'the liberated jewellery'. This kind of jewellery must have been known to Barthes, because it was published in every fashion magazine, but what he is actually referring to in his essay is another type of jewellery – that is the casual, ready-to-wear, cheap variation of the adventurous catwalk pieces.

For Barthes, the story of jewellery stops there at this very moment when jewellery, as he puts it, becomes part of the clothing, becomes a detail. In Barthes's view, the jewel is an accessory, a thing that supports, not a thing in itself, not a 'singular, magical object'. Therefore Barthes calls a piece of jewellery a next-to-nothing, because it is cheap and available in boutiques instead of expensive jewellers' shops. However, we shouldn't mis-understand him; according to Barthes this next-to-nothing has a significant power pre-cisely because it is detached from the clothing. It is exactly this that gives fashion or a style meaning. He states: 'What is new, if you like, is that the piece of jewellery is no longer on its own; it is one term in a set of links that goes from the body to clothing, to the accessory and includes the circumstances for which the whole outfit is being worn; it is part of an ensemble, and this ensemble is no longer necessarily ceremonial: taste can be everywhere, at work, in the country, in the morning, in winter, and the piece of jewellery follows suit.'[21] In Barthes's view, this detail is very important because it is 'able to modify, harmonize, animate the structure of a set of clothes' and even 'underlines the desire for order, for composition, for intelligence' in getting dressed.[22] Thus, the tiniest detail has meaning and is able to affect the personality, not because it is precious but because of its next-to-noth-ingness. Here, Barthes makes a clear division between the 'singular, dazzling, magical jewel', which is an ornament, 'thus making woman look her best' and the 'depreciated' (because it is secularised, democratised and feminised) detail with its ultimate power of signification.

Although Barthes's essay is about one specific segment of jewellery – that of the libertarian costume jewellery and its democratised offspring – his thoughts give some interesting clues to jewellery that need to be investigated deeper:

1.   The idea of jewellery as giving meaning.
2.   The idea of jewellery as a democratised copy.
3.   The idea of jewellery as a singular, magical object.

Jewellery can hardly be worn naively, apart from some casual jewellery that is put on in a daily habit, just like putting on one's shoes, and the social or inherited jewellery (wedding ring, the ring of a loved one passed away) that has become part of one's personality and that is never put away. Most other jewellery will demand some understanding, involvement and commitment, not to say intelligence in choosing it and wearing it in a satisfying way. This has to do with the fact that jewellery is a surplus, an extra; it is not part of the clothing and it has no other function than completing the clothing and attracting attention from others.

Jewellery is often conceived as a sign, as an object that gives meaning. People are used to reading jewellery, whether it is a conventional gold heart, a medallion or a name on a chain, a wedding ring, a pearl necklace, a piercing, a glittering fake bijou, a medal, an ethnological or antique piece of jewellery or a unique handmade piece of art jewellery. Having said that, I should add that it is also the wearer that makes the meaning of a piece, attributing stories, memories and their personality to it, charging a piece of jewellery with meaning.

Historically, clothing and jewellery were subject to many codes. You could tell by the clothing which village or region someone came from; the jewellery revealed the social position of the wearer. These codes were not written down but were generally accepted and known to everyone. In the Netherlands, one of these codes was about pearls, a natural material that was restricted to certain social strata. Wearing a string of pearls was the female Dutch bourgeois adaptation of a court style that had never fully developed in the Republic of the Seven United Netherlands (founded 1588) and in the post-republican royal nineteenth-century society. The wives of the governors and the rich citizens in the towns wore pearls; it was their sign of respectability and social belonging. In the countryside, men and women had their own special ways of showing off: gold was widely accepted as jewellery, as well as diamonds, garnet and red coral. Poorer families used silver, wood, textiles and even pewter to express their sense of belonging to a community or a religion.

It is said that the flourishing of the traditional costume until the first decades of the twentieth century was a conscious reaction towards the growing influence of fashion and city life. Every little village had its own colours, fabrics and forms of dresses, shoulders, sleeves, skirts, caps and trousers. Villages that were only ten minutes apart could have completely different outfits. Although called 'costume', this clothing was not completely uniform: every woman could change details (fabrics, colours, embroidery, lace, accessories) to her individual taste. There was a certain amount of uniformity in the jewellery, though. The female cap bells and forehead jewellery, amongst other items, and the male buttons and trouser plates were all part of a certain system of signification, differing in each village and even between different religious communities in a village. Jewellery was also a sign of matrimony, which enabled young men to make up their mind easily: to court or stay away. Jewellery was as readable as an identity card.

But what about today's author jewellery? It has a reputation of not wanting to be part of fashion and clothing, a position which is in line with the fundamental approach of the author (auteur, creator) who is solely responsible for his or her work. In fact, any relationship with fashion is denied and a piece of author jewellery is never intended to become a next-to-nothing. Yet, a piece of jewellery also exists and lives through the wearers and viewers and can become a sign that bears a more general meaning when being used (i.e. worn). In most countries, contemporary jewellery was also immediately recognised as a sign, with the abstract forms containing another meaning beyond the presumed neutral one. People experienced from the outset that such a work of jewellery, when placed on the body, acted as a sign. In the Netherlands around 1970, these ornaments by artists such as Emmy van Leersum (fig. 2), Gijs Bakker and Nicolaas van Beek became signs of good taste and, for some years, favourites among the cultural avant-garde elite in Amsterdam because they gave meaning to the wearer, placing him or her in the centre of intellectual and aesthetic connoisseurship. The jewellery designers, on the other hand, did not consciously work with these ideas and connotations. Of course they registered how their pieces worked as signs on the body, but the semantic aspect of jewellery was not what occupied them. They were interested in the formal aspect of the design of jewellery and believed in a piece of jewellery as a neutral abstract object.

> 2

In Scandinavia, Tone Vigeland must have been very well aware of the different meanings of jewellery. Her jewellery plays with the idea of the private and the public, of the soft and the aggressive, and furthermore it presents a Nordic austerity and solidness. While her steel and silver necklaces and bracelets may look like heavy armours, on the body they get a different meaning – at least for the wearer (fig. 3). When worn, they appear not to be stiff and heavy at all but flexible, soft, light and fluid, like textile. There is a decisive difference in how the viewer observes these pieces and how the wearer experiences it. They create a safe distance, the monumental necklaces providing the wearer with a powerful and invulnerable outlook. Through the ages and in many cultures, the neck and chest are special places on the body, as is the head, where power, dignity and status are celebrated. Vigeland uses this semantics, while at the same time protecting the wearer with an almost elastic and light structure that feels like a comfortable second skin because, as Vigeland says: '… it must concern itself with the body. It should enhance the wearer. It must feel nice, even sensual …'[23] It is a beautiful rendering of jewellery's dichotomy. Jewellery can involve conflicting characteristics: being frightening or imposing and shielding, private and public, at the same time individual and part of a culture and an idiom. In her essay about Norwegian jewellery, Jorunn Veiteberg points to the fact that 'Foreign commentators […] tend to emphasize the Norwegian character of Vigeland's jewellery. This is a reference to the "barbaric" or aggressive expression that the use of iron nails gave her jewellery around 1980.'[24] Apparently Veiteberg does not feel quite at ease with these national references. Yet the words 'furrowed' and 'weathered' that Veiteberg, in the same essay, lifted from the national Norwegian anthem to characterise the conditions and lifestyle of the country, seem equally suitable to Vigeland's jewellery. They give her objects meaning when worn on the body, supporting the style and consciousness of the wearer.

> 3

In New Zealand, the New Jewelry took on a completely different shape compared to Europe, America and Australia. Bone, Stone, Shell was the southern Pacific take on contemporary jewellery that developed some ten years later than in the rest of the world and was inspired by local materials and cultural issues.[25] This jewellery, predominantly made in the 1980s, was simple and made from natural materials. Wearing a piece composed of paua (shell), flakes of stone, mother of pearl, bone and fibre expressed a newly discovered identity; being New Zealand, a mixture of European blood and South Pacific culture. Or as New Zealand critic Damian Skinner put it: 'The story of New Zealand contemporary jewelry is, like the settlement of New Zealand itself, a tale of successive waves of peoples and cultures washing onto the shores of this far flung group of islands. The resources on which New Zealand contemporary jewelry draws include Pacific and Māori adornment, and European modernism.'[26] In the work of Warwick Freeman, one of the protagonists of contemporary New Zealand jewellery, this often results in jewellery with a striking

> 4

emblematic character. Although he uses symbols that have a different meaning outside the borders of his own country, he has been exhibiting and selling his work successfully in Europe since 1989. The meaning of his jewellery is, however, stronger in New Zealand than elsewhere. *Fern, Fish, Feather, Rose* (1987, fig. 4) for instance, deals with a sentiment unknown to Americans or Europeans. As Skinner explains, the rose in New Zealand is 'an introduced species. Brought to New Zealand by British settlers, the rose wages a war of affection with native plants in public and private gardens all around the country.'[27] The group of brooches *Fern, Fish, Feather, Rose* deals with this New Zealand ambivalence. The fern, fish and feather are recognisable and beloved references to New Zealand's flora and fauna. Freeman added the rose on purpose and registered people's reactions: 'People said: I don't like the rose, take the rose out. Where's our agreed us gone? And I'd say: well, no, the rose is the key, that is the us, part of the us. These were small conversations but I was surprised how many people were offended by the rose.'[28] The series turns out thus to be a work about national identity. This is an often-recurring theme in the emblematic work of Warwick Freeman (fig. 5). Other New Zealanders, such as Alan Preston, Areta Wilkinson, Jason Hall, Niki Hastings-McFall and others also have a preference for indigenous materials, symbols and identity issues.

> 5

References to conditions of place and culture, or to descent and background, have proved to be pivotal in the appreciation and understanding of contemporary jewellery. Therefore this jewellery can be interpreted as a support. It supports one's style, not completely according to Barthes's idea of completing and affecting a set of clothes (the fashionable way) but as an expression of the personality of the wearer, giving it meaning.

THE IDEA OF JEWELLERY AS A DEMOCRATISED COPY

Danish jewellery artist Mette Saabye uses the badge to question the singular status of jewellery. Most art jewellery is one-off, and even if it is made in a series of three or five or even seven, it maintains the character of the one-off because it is made by hand, repeating the design several times. Mette Saabye's *One of … in a million* is a series of badges featuring motifs from her one-off brooches, such as *The Puppy Fido* and *The Puppy Putin* brooch. With *One of … in a million*, Saabye has created 1,000 brooches that show reproductions of her one-off brooches. The artist copies her own work, making objects with desirable images of singular and one-off objects made by herself. They suggest they are something special but they can't possibly measure up to the real thing because they miss all the tactile and visual sensations of real jewellery. Mette Saabye's gold badge, however, is different in character (fig. 6). With this, she offers the client a genuine original, big, fat gold brooch – a badge wrapped in gold leaf – questioning value and singularity in a very cool and appealing way. It is a badge about fake and real, about real gold and its value, a piece of jewellery that democratises the status and aura of gold.

> 6

Another artist who uses the badge is Noon (Passama Sanpatchayapong). She considers its round surface a playground for experiments with form, colour and technique. Using this approach, she created decorative accessories – the *Extra Button* series – in a limited edition and at affordable prices, customising the design for each occasion (fig. 7). In 2010 and 2011, she made different editions on this theme: a shiny voluminous series of twelve different forms (made by rapid prototyping used in making wax forms, then electroforming and plating), a flat series in fifteen forms (made by laser cutting), and brightly coloured copper forms. The shiny series shows different rounded forms in three finishes – 14 ct gold, rose gold and black rhodium. The appearance of Noon's buttons is rather

> 7

extreme, especially that of the shiny and brightly coloured ones with their large rounded voluminous forms. The flat buttons present a bare, undecorated surface in 'non-colours' (white, grey, black), bearing a resemblance to utilitarian plastic components (from machines and the like) and also to jewellery forms such as the medallion. Noon uses the idea of the badge as a kind of philosophical and material playground. The badge is only visible on the rear side, where you can see how the idea of the badge – a flat round surface with two small holes to hold the pin – is used as a foundation for many different forms. They are engraved with her brand and *edition 2010–2011*. Because she uses industrial and semi-industrial reproduction techniques, she is able to multiply her designs and customise them for different exhibitions, shops and events. The name *Extra Button* refers to the fact that they present something extra to the original. As such, they present a transformation of the mass-produced item into an individualised accessory.

The work of Dutch jeweller Philip Sajet is characterised by his great skill and his preference for gold and coloured stones. He is a real goldsmith, but one who despises people's lust for diamonds and other status symbols. In his jewellery he mocks this desire. For around ten years, Sajet has worked with copies of legendary diamonds such as the blue Hope diamond (figs. 8, 9). He obtains these stones from a company in the German town > 8, 9 of Idar-Oberstein. The company claims to make exact copies, made from rock crystal, yellow quartz, smoky quartz or onyx, of the original diamonds. Sajet's fabulous rings are good examples of Barthes's notion of jewellery as a democratised copy 'retaining the aesthetic qualities of the material it is imitating' and realising the dream of being the owner of a jewel with mythical references. There can be no misunderstanding about their fakery, yet they are genuine pieces of jewellery, made by a skilled artist, at affordable prices – at least seen in the light of real diamonds, which are only available for the happy few because their prices rise up into the millions.

> fig. 4   > fig. 9

Atelier Ted Noten (ATN) has recently started copying work of Ted Noten himself. It began by making sculptures by assembling together different ready-made objects. *Nightbird*, for instance, consists of a tyre, crowned with a gold pig wearing a pearl chain. These one-off sculptures were then manipulated by computer and rapid prototyped to become pieces of jewellery in gold, titanium or resin. *Nightbird* became the model for a series of jewellery: a one-off gold ring, titanium rings in a series of twenty-five (fig. 10), a bracelet in white > 10 resin (3-D printed in a limited edition) and the pink resin *Miss Piggy* rings (3-D printed in unlimited editions). ATN sees this work as a natural evolvement, from the handmade haute couture one-off assemblage and gold ring to the industrially produced prêt-à-porter *Miss Piggy* rings. As Ted Noten stated, his final goal is to offer every woman on earth a cheap and genuine Ted Noten copy. An idea that ATN also worked with is vending machines, such as the Amsterdam red-light district vending machine (2008–09), where people could buy a red-sprayed metal ring for € 2.50. It sold 3,000 copies in one year.

Danish jeweller Kim Buck preceded Noten with his vending machine in the Århus Art Building in 2003, where he sold inflatable 'gold bracelets' of metal foil, together with a piece of paper warning the user: 'Gold can damage your morals'. The bracelet is a copy of a gold bracelet, or should we say a pastiche: nobody would ever think the thing is made of real gold (fig. 11). Buck is the champion of the genuine use of copies. In many of his pieces, imprints of brooches, earrings, necklaces, hearts and the like are made in square gold, silver or resin plates which are beaded on to necklaces or worn as brooches.

> 11

In 2003, Buck made a range of jewellery for the centenary of the famous Georg Jensen Company of silversmithing, using Jensen's brooch *Number 100* as an imprint on his designs for a ring, brooch, pendant and cufflinks. It is interesting to see how Kim Buck manages to use a historic classic from the Jensen collection – which itself is already an industrial copy – as a copy in his own industrial design called *Floral Shade* (fig. 12). We might call this the final victory of industrial copying processes. This particular range of jewellery by Kim Buck was only for sale in Asia, whereas Jensen has shops all around the world. But by doing this, Jensen could maintain a kind of exclusivity for the *Floral Shade* collection, which actually contradicts the mechanical manufacture at a company like Jensen. This clever play with original and copy, exclusivity and edition, as a result of the collaboration between an industry and a goldsmith–designer, especially designed for the Asian market, is a rare example of intelligent design and good marketing within contemporary jewellery.

> 12

THE IDEA OF JEWELLERY AS A SINGULAR, MAGICAL OBJECT

When Barthes mentioned jewellery as a singular, magical object in his essay, he referred to an aspect of jewellery that is often neglected in our discussions today: the fact that jewellery by its very nature is appealing, enticing and imposing. Jewellery enhances the body; it is a very special addition, one that is different from clothing. Jewellery, precisely because of its additional, redundant nature, is a sign. Most power-jewellery is worn on the head or on the chest – rulers, whether royal, elected or self-acclaimed, wear their symbols of power there: the crown, the chain of honour and the medal. As symbols of power these objects are indisputable; their message is fixed, their appeal is magical. Examples of other jewellery, such as fine jewellery by the great jewellery houses, elaborate on this signifying quality. The lavish use of gemstones, diamonds, pearls and gold in spectacular necklaces lend an aura to the wearer. And on a reciprocal basis, the wearer, if she is truly famous or royal, or wealthy and a socialite, lends an aura to the jewel. There are books written on this subject and just by reading the picture captions, a world of signifying power is revealed. I have picked out some of those and listed them here[29]:

> fig. 12   > fig. 15

'Queen Margherita in court dress wearing her magnificent royal necklace together with the Stuart emerald brooch.'

'Twentieth Century-Fox production chief Darryl F. Zanuck sits between Joan Bennet (left) and Merle Oberon, who is wearing her Cartier emerald bead necklace, at a nightclub in the 1930s.'

'Daisy Fellows photographed by Cecil Beaton in 1937. Among the wonderful jewels she is wearing is the "Tutti Frutti" necklace by Cartier, Paris, as it was originally created for her in 1936. She is also wearing two diamond bracelets by Cartier.'

'The Duke and Duchess of Windsor in December 1955, dancing at the Lido, the Champs-Elysée cabaret in Paris. The Duchess is wearing her Van Cleef & Arpels invisibly set ruby and diamond foliate ear clips, her sapphire, ruby and diamond hinged bangle designed as a peacock's feather by Cartier, Paris, 1946, her ruby bead, emerald and diamond necklace of Indian inspiration by Cartier, and her pearl necklace (which the Duke inherited from Queen Mary)… '

Without knowing how these jewels exactly look, we get the picture. The last description is of special interest because it reveals that it was apparently accepted in certain circles to wear even two conflicting necklaces at the same time (an antique, regal string of pearls and a fashionably designed piece in an Indian style) and to combine those with mismatched ear clips and a bracelet (not to mention the rings she was possibly wearing as well but which are not visible in the photo). In the wearing of jewellery, no socialite was as avid and as exuberant as the Duchess. Her presence gave the singular, magical objects extra value. Fine jewellery is as much about material value, the glitter and shine as it is about ownership; both determine its magic.

In author jewellery, we hardly find examples like these; author jewellery prefers to stay away from formal and societal traditions. And if the language of shining power play is used, then we should be aware that it could be a game with a malicious message, as in the *REAL* jewellery series by Gijs Bakker, where fake and real stones blend in a unity of illusion (fig. 13). However, in contemporary jewellery there is another power play that until now has not > 13 been clearly identified as such. I am referring here to the aura of uniqueness in individual one-offs having nothing to do with shining materials, but everything with the authorship of the creator. Swiss artist Bernard Schobinger, for instance, began using consumer-society goods and leftovers at the end of the 1970s in a remarkably forward and aggressive way. Tops of plastic tubes were chained with gold wire, a bent nail combined with a diamond hung from an earring, plastic combs were linked with cobaltite wire; he also created remarkable aesthetical compositions with dangerous used saws and broken bottlenecks. The aggression and directness of Schobinger's anti-jewellery made during this period was recognised in the art world as well, where his work was exhibited on different occasions. Even today Bernhard Schobinger is one of the very few jewellery artists who has resigned from the jewellery scene, preferring instead to show his work in a fine art context.

Younger generations in jewellery also succeed in creating pieces that are empowering and imposing because they are cheeky and fanciful products of their time. When worn they attract the eye and are signs of the open-mindedness and taste of the wearer and of their financial status. Thus, a hilarious necklace assembled from the oddments of today's consumer culture by Lisa Walker can become a singular magical object (fig. 14), just like > 14 the plaster and pigment ornaments of Mia Maljojoki (fig. 15) or a brooch by Felieke van > 15 der Leest depicting a plastic zebra in a crocheted suit (fig. 16). However, most such pieces > 16 of author jewellery do not immediately appeal to people outside the inner circle. Their appearance is too unfamiliar or too pale, and their extraordinary size, unconventional materials and expression are more repulsive than attractive. What people miss most is having a standard. The price of gold and gemstones is set and under constant pressure, which contributes to their magic appeal, yet with cheap and trashy materials we enter the realm of the everyday where magic fails.

The shine and magic of jewellery is foremost in its costly materials; even one single diamond set in a piece of jewellery makes it radiate, and the simplest golden ring is still a ring of gold. There is an obvious connection between shine, magic, fame and money. That shine and magic coincide with economics is emphasised in the opening page of Atelier Ted Noten's website. It shows how the price of the *Eveningbutterfly*, a massive 18 ct gold (*Nightbird* series) ring, changes per day, fluctuating with the freak changes of the market. In his own mocking way, Noten succeeds in diverting our attention from jewellery to economics. Although traditionally in many different cultures, gold was seen as a divine material, in the Western culture gold was and is foremost appreciated because of its economic value. This property of gold, therefore, determines our appreciation of jewellery. For some artists, it became the subject of ongoing research, resulting in pieces that question the singularity and magic of precious materials. Otto Künzli is one of them. Key pieces are the *Gold Makes you Blind* bracelet (1980), *The Swiss Gold – The Deutschmark* performance (1983), *Cozticteocuitlatl 1995–1998 B.M.* and the gold pendants *Traces of Movements* (2007). Künzli has made his fascination functional in multifaceted jewellery by leading our thoughts to the sinister side of gold. By doing this, he is able to uncover conventions and assumptions and place the role of jewellery in our society in a clear light.

> 17

The title of a collection of 121 silver and gold pendants, *Cozticteocuitlatl 1995–1998 B.M.* (fig. 17), comes from the Aztec's notion for 'the yellow faeces of the gods'. With this work Künzli opens up many layers of thought about gold. The reference to a lost culture that practiced human sacrifice for the gods, whose 'excrement' was so much desired by people from another continent that it caused the gradual decline of this culture, is only the overture for further reflections on the subject of desire and greed. The pendants with their uncanny shapes, from hearts to bombs, question the price we are willing to pay for our desires. The addition *B.M.* in the title means 'Before Mouse', a reference to Künzli's fascination with 'the new world' and America's own history and myths. In the 1990s, Mickey Mouse became a recurring motif in his work.

The story of the Aztecs, who lived in the region now known as Mexico, illustrates the clash between the non-Western and the Western approach to gold and to value. Gold was found in many places and was observed as a godly material. It was not used as a currency; instead the Aztecs bartered using cacao beans. In 1519, when the Spaniards under the lead of Hernán Cortés arrived in present-day Mexico, they were searching for a legendary rich civilisation. It took Cortés two years to destroy the Aztec capital and society. Innumerous amounts of gold and jewels were shipped to Spain. The legends of El Dorado were soon known all over Europe. El Dorado, the man completely covered with gold dust, was a legendary figure somewhere in the mountains of South America, who regularly took a bath in a crystal clear mountain lake. Eventually the legendary El Dorado became an utopian dream, a place of unknown affluence where the streets were paved with gold. Many sixteenth- and seventeenth-century Spanish, Dutch and Portuguese expeditions were targeted at finding El Dorado. In 1532, the Spaniards found an Incan civilisation in present-day Peru where gold was widely available. The story goes that the value of the booty send to Spain was so big that it caused inflation in Europe.[30]

In Indonesia gold also had a mythical and magical appeal. Dayak myths observe gold as the source of the world. There are versions of this myth which see the creation of the world in relation to the creation of specific forms of splendid jewellery and enigmatic creatures, half human half jewel. In this creational myth, gold and jewels are as sacred and magical as the gods. This belief, this worship of gold, gemstones and jewels, is to a certain extent comparable with the European medieval outlook on those materials. With the arrival of the Renaissance and humanist science and philosophy, the Middle Ages were looked upon as barbarian and primitive. A process of secularisation did the rest: magic faded while trade and commerce rose. Gold and gemstones lost their godly, magical aura and became economic commodities.

In our deritualised and disenchanted society, people are devoid of shared symbols, myths and beliefs, but they do share receptiveness for everything impressive, unique and expensive. The aesthetic impact of a non-precious piece of contemporary author jewellery can also be profound outside the inner circle of jewellery aficionados – at least when certain conditions are met, such as excellent craftsmanship and the transformation of a non-valuable material into something outstanding. Therefore the wooden necklaces by Norwegian Liv Blåvarp stand out as 'singular objects' (fig. 18). Her voluminous collars enclose > 18 the neck in a dramatic way. These collars cannot be avoided and lend lustre and power to the wearer even though they don't shine and glisten themselves. The power referred to here is not a political, administrative or noble power but the power of those who 'have taste', those 'in the know', those who dare to present themselves like this and those who can afford to – setting the wearer apart from those who cannot afford nor dare to wear these pieces.

Manifold examples like these can be found in contemporary jewellery. Mirjam Hiller's astounding sculptural brooches, sawn out of powder-coated steel plate in bright colours, impress in their hybrid and exquisite expressiveness (fig. 20). They are as singular as the > 20 stout sculpted plastic bangles by Peter Chang or the paper necklaces by Janna Syvänoja, both made from recycled material. In fact author jewellery is often a bold statement carried on the body, even leaving room for social comment, like, for example, the 'objects of desire', jewellery sculptures about animals in our society by Sari Liimatta. Plastic toy animals, cut open, set with patterns of needles or beads, may seem repulsive for some – a polar bear nearly drowning (fig. 19), a circus tiger, a bejewelled horse decorated with paper price > 19 tags, but with this jewellery, Liimatta succeeds in balancing the critical line between the inconvenient message and a stunning and magnificent style. These are real objects of desire for people with brains and guts, objects which have an aesthetic impact on those who wear and those who observe them.

The meaning of jewellery, even author jewellery, is – more than we normally think or would like to admit – dependent on underlying traditions, attributions and systems of value that have a long history; this forms jewellery's own language.

The examples of author jewellery discussed in this chapter bear signs of art because they are driven by an urge for autonomy and originality. However, they are limited by size, weight and fastening because they connect to the body. It is exactly this connection with the body, the wearer and the wearing which gives them meaning. The autonomy claimed by author jewellery is only partly true, as such namely within the confines of the phenomenon of jewellery.

When talking about fashion jewellery, Roland Barthes talks about 'great energy'. According to him jewellery 'holds the ultimate power of signification'. This power of signification is the central issue of contemporary author jewellery: it is not merely decorative, and it can hardly be completely conceptual, but its meaning is in the remarkable statement on the body – an effect that is enhanced by the personality of the wearer. The singular aesthetic pieces of jewellery as discussed above are super accessories, having meaning and beauty that go hand in hand.

1   First published in English in 1983. *The Fashion System.* New York: Hill and Wang.
2   Roland Barthes, 2006. 'From Gemstones to Jewellery', in Roland Barthes, 2006. *The Language of Fashion.* Oxford/New York: Berg, p. 59.
3   Ibid.
4   Ibid. p. 60.
5   Ibid.
6   These are the complete lyrics from the song as derived from Marilyn Monroe's page at Reel Classics: *www.reelclassics.com/Actresses/Marilyn/diamonds-lyrics.htm.*
7   Barthes (see note 2), p. 60.
8   Ibid.
9   Clare Phillips, 2008. *Jewels & Jewellery.* London: V&A Publishing, p. 28.
10 Clare Phillips, 1996. *Jewelry: From Antiquity to the Present*, London: Thames & Hudson, pp. 33–4.
11 Barthes (see note 2), p. 61.
12 Ibid. p. 63.
13 Ibid. p. 61.
14 Ibid.
15 Ibid. p. 62.
16 Ibid.
17 Ibid. pp. 62–3.
18 For more information upon this subject see Florence Müller, 2006. *Costume Jewelry for Haute Couture.* London: Thames & Hudson.
19 Ibid. p. 25.
20 Ibid. p. 33.
21 Barthes (see note 2), p. 63.
22 Ibid.
23 Cecilie Malm Brundtland, 2003. *Tone Vigeland: Jewellery + Sculpture. Movements in Silver.* Stuttgart: Arnoldsche, p. 30.
24 Jorunn Veiteberg, 1995. 'Norwegian Jewellery 1900–1995', in Jan Lohmann and Lise Funder, 1995. *Nordic Jewellery.* Copenhagen: Nyt Nordisk Forl., p. 134.
25 The name is derived from the exhibition *Bone Stone Shell: New Jewellery New Zealand*, Crafts Council of New Zealand Wellington, 1988, which travelled around Australia.
26 Damian Skinner, 2010. *Pocket Guide to New Zealand Jewelry.* San Francisco: Velvet da Vinci, p. 37.
27 Ibid. p. 29.
28 Damian Skinner, 2004. *Given: Jewellery by Warwick Freeman.* Auckland: Starform, p. 44.
29 These descriptions are borrowed from two books: Penny Proddow and Marion Fasel, 2001. *Bejeweled: Great Designers, Celebrity Style.* New York: Abrams, and Stefano Papi and Alexandra Rhodes, 1999. *Famous Jewelry Collectors.* London: Thames & Hudson.
30 In the 1970s, world-explorer Victor Wolfgang von Hagen wrote a book about this subject: *The Gold of El Dorado: The Quest for the Golden Man.* London: Paladin Books, 1978.

II. A Short History of Jewellery and Photography

Contemporary jewellery cannot be dissociated from developments in the fine arts. The arts in the 1960s and 1970s are characterised by a multitude of attitudes and isms which have a few things in common; the tendency towards immaterialisation and conceptualisation, and the need to break up traditional media and find and investigate new ones, such as photography, film, video, book, performance and happening. Photography, an important means in the avant-garde arts, also entered contemporary jewellery and has become generally accepted today. Those jewellery makers who held a reflective position towards their métier were the first to discover photography as an artistic tool. For them photography was the appropriate agency to create a context for their jewellery. They used photography in a documentary and expressive way as a means for research and comment; however it is not concerned about photography as a medium but rather about the artist's perception and reflection on jewellery.

Besides the expressive use of photography as a means in jewellery there is also the functional use of photography intended for publication in newspapers, magazines and exhibition catalogues. Photography was discovered as a promotional tool that could show jewellery from a different perspective. This chapter starts with functional photography and continues with photography as a means of research. It ends with discussing how contemporary jewellery artists use photography as a visual and expressive means.

FUNCTIONAL PHOTOGRAPHY

In the Netherlands, between 1967 and 1970, the rather large pieces were shown on models – beautiful young girls, their eyes heavily made up. These pictures related to the fashion photography of the time. The images showed the models full size, photographed from below, looking up and sometimes in a dramatic pose or with special effects around the head. These models looked powerful and self-confident rather than modest, elegant and pleasing. The message of this photography was evident: it was positive, full of energy and power, future-focused and confident, expressing that this jewellery was meant for the young and new generation.

Yet most jewellery photography at that time was object-based. Because the focus in jewellery design changed gradually to the abstract object, photography also gradually changed. If we compare the photography in Karl Schollmayer's book *Neuer Schmuck: Ornamentum humanum* (1974) with other jewellery photography of the same period in the Netherlands and the United Kingdom, we will notice a difference that is due to the character of the objects. Schollmayer's selection, involving mainly German and some mid-European and Scandinavian artists, shows a predominantly painterly, expressionistic tendency. The jewels are photographed against a rather 'scenic' background of structured

> 21

surfaces, such as fabric, a mirrored surface, marble, rice or seeds. The abstract Dutch and British jewellery of the same period (not in Schollmayer's book) is photographed in an abstract, clean way, without any distractions such as dramatic lighting effects or backgrounds. The photography of these objects seemingly floating in an endless space is aimed at underlining their *objecthood*, their uncompromising entity as an art object, as shown in an image of a neckpiece by David Watkins (fig. 21). This kind of photography remains dominant today, though there is a growing concern in re-establishing the relationship between the object and the subject, or between jewellery and the body.

We may wonder what the reason for this object-focused approach is. Besides the obvious practical and customary reasons, there must be a deeper reason, perhaps having something to do with a fear of vulgarisation. In advertisements for commercial jewellery, the relationship between jewellery and models is quite common, but any association with this world was consciously avoided by the avant-gardists. When jewellery, such as author jewellery, is photographed as an object, it gains a different meaning. Isolated and removed from its normal context, the artistic integrity of the piece is not obscured by any circumstantial intrusion. But conversely it also becomes completely unclear what we are looking at because the connection with the human body is missing and measurements and attachments are obscure. This dilemma became a growing point of concern. With the gradual change of focus from a piece of jewellery as an art object to an everyday object, room was made for another approach to jewellery in photography, which was meant foremost for publications. The involvement of art photography was crucial in this process.

ART PHOTOGRAPHY

By the 1980s jewellers had already begun to investigate the relationship between jewellery and man in photography commissions. These commissions, ordered by jewellery artists and created in close collaboration with the professional photographer, were meant to redress jewellery's relation with the human body. But there was also an aspect of 'upgrading' at work.

A fine and early example is found in Marion Herbst's overview publication including humorous black-and-white images by professional photographer Paul de Nooijer, released on the occasion of the Françoise van den Bosch Award 1982 prize-giving ceremony. At this time, photography had been discovered as a new art form; on several occasions art photographers were invited to make photographic works about jewellery. In these photos, which although commissioned were highly autonomous, pieces of jewellery were treated as props in artistic configurations. At the end of the 1980s, a commission given to six art photographers by the Françoise van den Bosch Foundation was a case in point, resulting in a special publication about Françoise van den Bosch.[1] Dutch jewellery artist Ruudt Peters made it his policy for quite some time to commission art photographers. He invited them to create their impressions of his jewellery for a range of publications.[2] Earlier in this period, in 1983, when the awareness about the loss of contact with the human body was growing, Ruudt Peters made a series of white steel and plaster collars, which were photographed on beautiful young men, young Adonises, who did not just resemble classical statues but also flirted with the camera at the same time. Peters's *Dedicated To* series from 1989, a collection of metal bowls, although photographed without models, dealt with the relationship between people through the use of objects.

The Swiss jewellery artist Bernhard Schobinger holds a very interesting position in this respect. His wife, the well-known art photographer Annelies Štrba, has been photographing his jewellery worn by their two daughters since the 1980s. Her early style has a characteristic, casual and misty, unfocused appeal (fig. 22). In their first collaborative project published in 1988, Schobinger marked Štrba's rather gloomy black-and-white images with handwritten, vertically positioned captions.[3] The union between the vulnerable girl and the powerful, at times aggressive jewels interpreted by Štrba is a highlight of contemporary jewellery photography. Her photography is neither documentary nor objective but adds something to the item photographed.

Photos of jewellery could also attain an artistic appeal by using well-known and important personalities as models. This happened all over Europe. In 1987, Ruudt Peters asked photographer Michel Szulc-Krzyzanowski to make a series of portraits of five Dutch protagonists of contemporary jewellery, wearing his *Symbol* bracelets (fig. 23). In the same year, Otto Künzli asked architects to pose for his *A Roof Over One's Head* series (1986/87), while Orfebres FAD (the Catalan association of goldsmiths) mobilised the cultural in-crowd of Barcelona for a photo shoot with contemporary jewellery. The images appeared in the catalogue accompanying the exhibition *Joieria Europea Contemporània* [Contemporary European Jewellery], at that time a rather unknown phenomenon in Catalonia, although the jewellery department at Escola Massana under the lead of Ramón Puig Cuyàs had a good reputation. The introduction text to the catalogue addresses the aspect of wearing jewellery: 'Jewellery is an art whose ultimate purpose is its integration with the human body. Often the piece of jewellery does not come into its own or project itself until the moment it is worn. At other times it is ambivalent in nature, with its own autonomy as object outside its natural context.'[4] Reflecting these ideas, the expensive colour catalogue presented a photographic section with full-page staged portraits of well-known personalities wearing these unknown, strange jewels. The theatrical, light-hearted photography in the catalogue was received as a refreshing approach in the countries at the centre of the New Jewelry.[5] In the same period, the *Ornamenta* exhibition in the Schmuckmuseum Pforzheim in 1989 invited well-known people from sports, fashion and industry to present their favourite object, while well-known jewellers were asked to design a special piece for this prominent person. The only thing missing were photographs of the VIPs wearing the jewellery.[6]

PHOTOGRAPHY AS A MEANS FOR ARTISTIC RESEARCH

In the 1970s, as a result of a conceptualised way of working and under the influence of simultaneous developments in the fine arts, photography became a new means for the jewellery artist as well. Gijs Bakker used photography to materialise, or 'freeze', his immaterial shadow jewellery, which was the result of lacing up a woman's waist, ankle or arm with the aid of a gold wire in 1973. The next year he made two head profile ornaments, one for Fritz Maierhofer and the other for Emmy van Leersum, which are often published worn by the models themselves. Bakker did not include the pictures of the shadow jewellery on the model in his oeuvre catalogue (2005, fig. 24). It is an interesting case, demonstrating a relative uneasiness with photography in jewellery. The denial of the photos raises questions about which is the true shadow jewellery. Is it the temporary imprint on the body (action), the record of this imprint (photo), the gold wire put in a signed jewellery box (tradable and exposable art object, fig. 25), or the combination of the images and the object? The images are in fact the only remaining evidence of an action, and the title of the work *Shadow Jewelry* refers to this result, not to the used object that can be observed as a simulacrum. Furthermore, the object, a simple bracelet of gold wire, was in fact not the same thing as the wire that was used to make the imprints in the human body.[7] The gold wire, presented in archetypal green velvet jewellery wrapping, is Gijs Bakker's wink to his métier. In the case of the profile ornaments, photography has a less important function in the full appreciation of the work because the objects actually show what their title says, whereas in the case of the gold wire there is no direct connection between the thing and the title. This is also the case for a second shadow jewellery piece, made one year after the first, which shows a leather band with a stainless-steel disc on top of it. Only when it is worn – on the upper arm under the clothing – does its function become clear. In the appreciation of this work photography is indispensable.[8]

Another meaningful use of photography is found in the work of British jeweller Susanna Heron. While working in America for a year between March 1978 and March 1979, Susanna Heron embarked on a completely new mission in body adornment. Heron studied jewellery design at the Central School of Art in London from 1968 to 1971 and was mainly interested in jewellery as an extension of the body. In 1969, inspired by Oscar Schlemmer's film *Stick Dance*, she made a spiral costume of green ribbon and a wire frame. The theme recurred in 1978/79 in New York when she started experimenting with photography. First there were photographic prints of a cardboard spiral, curving from and around her head downwards over the shoulder, like the *Curve* made of acrylic and spray paint, and ultimately she worked with light projections. They were created in cooperation with her partner, photographer David Ward. The result was an interesting series of black-and-white photo-

> 26

graphs documented in a catalogue (fig. 26).[9] David Ward recorded: 'It is rather difficult to describe how two people can work together on something like a photograph – the photographer seems to be in the position of complete control. We projected slides onto Susanna. She had a big mirror and composed the light on herself while I composed the photographs. I don't think either of us could have anticipated the resulting images but we both like them. The theatrical or dramatic quality was intentional – they might almost be stills from a performance.'[10] Susanna Heron stopped making jewellery soon afterwards in 1982 and turned to fine arts, making sculpture, photography, prints, drawings and large scale public art works.

'Light jewellery' inspired other artists as well. In 1986, Johanna Dahm coordinated a summer school about the subject in Salzburg, and in 1987, she worked with students at the Fachhochschule Düsseldorf on the same subject. In an article, she reported on these workshops in text and illustrations, discussing the problem of light projection and the controversies that arose between the models and the directors. Although this temporary and immaterial work is almost 'nothing', as Dahm writes, '... we were still dealing with a concrete search for expression.'[11] The workshop reflected very well the spirit of the time.

In the 1970s, Dutch artist Robert Smit started using the then brand-new technique of Polaroid SX-70 instant colour photography.[12] Smit trained as a goldsmith at the Staatliche Kunst + Werkschule in Pforzheim, but he might be called a double talent as he has been working successfully both in the realm of jewellery and the fine arts while in more recent years integrating both of these attitudes in his work. In 1976, he used the Polaroid technique to make a contribution to the exhibition *Jewellery in Europe*, organised by Ralph Turner, as a final goodbye to jewellery. In the beginning of the 1970s, the climate in the Dutch jewellery scene was radical; there was no place for Smit's rather expressionist and painterly way of working with gold, the material he loved above all. Besides, his work had become increasingly large and sculptural. Smit sold his goldsmith's equipment in 1972 and started drawing. In his view, drawing is the basis of every artistic expression and should be explored as an action. According to him there will always be a difference between the imagination and the concrete result, and every tangible and visible result is relative. This fundamental approach led him to investigate the medium of drawing by using instant photography. He made some series of Polaroids of different movements of his hand while drawing; the line was drawn afterwards. These photos are suggestions of possible drawings. In another series of Polaroids entitled *To my pencil* from 1975 his hand is playing with a pencil.[13] In 1976 when Ralph Turner invited Smit to join the exhibition *Jewellery in Europe*, the artist had already withdrawn from jewellery and was involved instead in drawing and investigating the conceptual and artistic process. Yet he decided to join the exhibition and submitted a series of more than hundred Polaroids of a man seen from behind, dressed in a white suit and holding two packets of Peter Stuyvesant cigarettes in his hands in changing positions. This *Everyday Adornment* (1975, fig. 27) is commented by Robert Smit in the catalogue: 'Now it is time to enjoy looking at The Filter Flavour Craftsmanship Show (synchronous movements of my favourite hand-adornment […].'[14] These 'favourite hand adornments' can be explained from his new artistic interest, yet they also present a perfect anti-jewellery statement at the same time.

> 27

There was a quite radical attitude in the air at that time and the *Jewellery in Europe* show presented a platform for this. However, the reviews were not particularly positive; an anonymous correspondent in *ArtScribe* laid his finger on the problem when he wrote: 'I do not know the full significance of the fact that jewellers are now bent on filling applications for membership of the artistic avant-garde. This would depend upon whether their applications succeed, and upon how much credence you give to the remnants of the avant-garde idea anyway.' According to this reviewer much of the exhibited work '[…] consists of drawings, photographs, written notes and diagrams, jottings and other bits of visual marginalia [which] cannot be worn anywhere.'[15] During this period many artists used photography incidentally. In 1977, Hans Ebbing made *Full Evening's Jewel*, a Perspex brooch filled with ink dripping slowly from the brooch onto the clothing, thus creating a gradually increasing stain. The process was recorded in a series of photographs and was part of a Dutch exhibition about Body Art.[16] Jan Tempelman made temporary jewellery with gold leaf on the body, which were documented in photographs and drawings. *Bracelet 80: A Photoreport of Jan Tempelman* (1980) was a numbered artist's book in fanfold format using SX70 Polaroid photography. The subject of this photo-document is the transformation of a gold wedding ring into a bracelet, accompanied by a series of photos of a woman's mouth that by the end is laughing.

This way of working keeps up with simultaneous avant-garde art movements in its choice of medium and its rebellious and non-object, non-jewellery character. Anti-jewellery thinking was especially prominent in the Netherlands. There might be a relationship with

> fig. 26   > fig. 27

the Dutch cultural governmental policy in those days, which was very prolific and supportive of those jewellery designers who worked in experimental ways. During the 1970s, the Nederlandse Kunst Stichting [Dutch Arts Foundation] and the Bureau Beeldende Kunst Buitenland [Visual Arts Office for Abroad] – both sub-divisions of the Ministry for Cultural Affairs – organised a range of travelling exhibitions involving the new jewellery. There were exhibitions organised on serial jewellery and on Body Art; others dealt with visual art, fashion and jewellery on an equal footing. In a stimulating cultural climate like this, artists will automatically put their neck on the line.

It cannot be coincidental that in Vienna, the centre of the Wiener Aktionismus [Vienna Actionism], the Yugoslavian born jeweller Peter Skubic made a piece of jewellery that is even more radical than any of the Dutch anti-jewellery projects. The surgical implantation of a small steel disc in his arm is a rare example of Body Art in jewellery. Skubic reported this 'happening': 'On November 4th 1975 I underwent an operation and had a small steel implant inserted under the skin of my lower arm – JEWELLERY UNDER THE SKIN. On May 27th 1982 the implant was surgically removed, to be kept and secured in the casket-shaped bezel of a ring.'[17] Photographs were used to document the operation while radiographic photographs proved the existence of this invisible jewellery in his arm. The idea of the invisibility of jewellery is essential in this project and the reason why the steel implant, after its removal from the body, was set in a special ring to be locked away forever. Ten years later, in 1985, he elaborated on this idea in his series of twelve abstract black-and-white photos entitled *The Inside of a Ring*, which did not show actual rings but instead gave hints to experiencing jewellery. This project shows the final dematerialised stage of invisible jewellery: jewellery that only exists in your imagination.

Photography plays a minor role in the work of another Viennese artist, Manfred Nisslmüller. Since 1976 Nisslmüller has been making conceptual work about the meaning of jewellery, mainly in the form of texts but also in the form of images, objects and jewels. His series *Anonymer und Nichtanonymer Schmuck* [Anonymous and Non-Anonymous Jewellery] from 1977, which uses photography, drawings and images from magazines presented in A4 format, questions jewellery. In Nisslmüller's philosophical approach, jewellery 'can happen', it is up to the viewer to discover, like the military equipment in one of the photos that is like a jewel for the ruler on the platform.[18]

Three young German jewellers Gerd Rothmann, Otto Künzli and Gabriele Dziuba showed series of photographs of jewellery on the body in the exhibition *Goldschmiede dieser Zeit* [Jewellers of Today], organised by the Kestner Gesellschaft in Hanover in 1979. Here we see another way of using instant photography (in this case mostly photo booth snapshots) that can be characterised as documentary. Again, the medium was very helpful in communicating the artists' concept. Otto Künzli used photography to investigate the effect of geometrical jewellery on the body. The pictures only show part of the male body, from waist to shoulders. A series of four-shot sheets of photo booth photos from 1976 show a male torso stretching a string and geometric shapes between his hands and holding this in different positions against the body: vertically, horizontally and diagonally (fig. 28). This analysis of the relationship between lines and forms, and the human body resulted in gold and silver objects, which also entered his photographic investigations. Other series of machine pictures show small bullet brooches composed in geometrical patterns on the body. Furthermore, they show the body from the side with a ball or a cylinder brooch pinned on the breast, or with a ball held under a wire that is laced up around the upper arm. In an interview, Künzli says: 'In 1976, I tried to get rid of everything that was still left of the formalism from my education in Zurich. I was looking for new relations between

> 28

the body and the jewel. Because I didn't want to go on working just formally but wanted to find a good way to deal with the matter, I started reducing all elements to what they were actually. A rod became a rod again, an object that you had first to take in your hand to see what you could do with it. In doing this, I searched for the most elementary things. With rubber bands, drawing pins and tape, I looked for a relation to the body. I experimented with these materials in photo booths, and these images helped me along.'[19] Instant photography helped Künzli to develop his ideas about jewellery.

Arbeit für die Hand [Work for the Hand], from 1979 to 1980 (fig. 29), is a series of > 29 large-format photographs that may be observed as one of the results of Künzli's previous instant photo researches. It consists of a black acrylic cassette filled with some mysterious elements, such as three sharp, flat steel triangles, three small steel rods and three larger ones, and five elastic rings. There are twenty-four photographs showing the different ways of wearing these objects: between or around the fingers, adorning the hand and at the same time fixing it in certain positions. The photographs are indispensable for understanding this work. In 1982, they were part of the exhibition *Körperkultur* [Body Culture], organised by Otto Künzli and Gerd Rothmann, about the relation between jewellery and the body. Documentary photography was an important medium in this project, offering unforgettable images such as Otto Künzli's brooch for two people, his ring for two people, the X-ray of the *Kugel für die Achselhöhle* [Bullet for the Armpit] and Gerd Rothmann's casts of arms and ears.

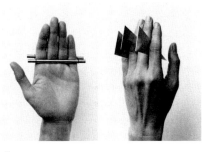

> fig. 29

Although these projects have been developed under the influence of Body Art they are fundamentally about jewellery and about the function of jewellery. To this end, photography served on two levels; that of the artist and that of the audience. Photography enabled artists to investigate their ideas while also giving them the possibility to communicate these to the audience. Investigation and documentation run parallel.

In the 1980s, colour photography became a powerful medium for Otto Künzli. He mostly operated the camera himself. The colour photos of his *Wallpaper* collection from 1983 did not just serve documentary purposes; they also had a promotional function. Künzli invited several friends to be models, who had to bridge the gap between these – at that time considered to be – enormous brooches and the body (fig. 30).[20] The collection > 30 answered the Postmodernist need for ornamentation with large geometrical and mathematical polystyrene forms covered with wallpaper. The client could choose from different types of paper and different colour variations. The audience perceived it as a true liberation as it provided fun on many levels. Otto Künzli's *Beauty Gallery* from 1984, however, was different because atypical objects (frames) were used as jewellery that only existed in the photo series. *Beauty Gallery* is a photographic project that refers to traditional portrait galleries. It features a series of beautiful women, in full colour, all wearing a picture frame like an uneasy necklace or a laurel wreath around the upper part of the body. These frames, meant to beautify a painting, have a remarkable impact on the body as they are at the same time honouring and enclosing the model.

Künzli's works *Breakthrough* made from wall paint and mirror glass in 1987, *Eye* made from gilded copper in 1988, *Eyes*, a series of ten Cibachromes from 1989/90 and *Ring* made from gold and mirror glass in 1988 form a series of works based on the principle of reflection. Photographs and mirror lenses form a substantial part of these works. *Eyes* only exists in the sequence of photos, made by Künzli himself with the aid of spectacles with mirror lenses and the reflection of different people's eyes in these glasses. *Ring* only comes to life in the photograph *Ring worn*, or – of course – when the wearer sees their own eye gazing

> 31

back from the shiny bottom of the gold ring (fig. 31). These works are the output of the artist's creative research into ideas about voyeurism (the walls having eyes), the gaze and introspection.

The heydays of photography as research were over around 1990. Since then we have seen a growing need for this medium to create the right context for jewellery. The awareness that man adds something to jewellery resulted in the celebration of the human body as the best stage to show a piece of jewellery. Staged photography became popular. This does not mean that jewellers needed a complete scenery (though this sometimes happens), but they became very keen on finding the right models to show the work.

Robert Smit has always photographed his work himself. In 1985, after a long period of absence, he returned to jewellery with the collection *Ornamentum Humanum*. The photographs made for the occasion show a rather average man – the opposite of the glamorous photo model – wearing the remarkable and bold expressionistic gold pieces on his simple T-shirt. The in-crowd knew that this supposedly average man was Rob van Koningsbruggen,

> 32

a well-known painter and good friend of Robert Smit (fig. 32). The photos, which may as well be observed as portraits of Van Koningsbruggen, reveal something about the world behind the work. They were a provocative statement about Smit's work, referring to its completely different background, and dismissing the new Dutch jewellery of that time: 'This so-called modern jewellery – fruit of a collectively shared shortage of imagination – is without any meaning … the physical prove [sic] of an artificial beauty that shows no interest at all in establishing a serious, meaningful commitment to the wearer'.[21]

In 1996, Hilde De Decker published a book that looked like a children's picture book, printed on thick inflexible cardboard. *Eva's Kussen* [Eva's Cushion] was a mutual enterprise between De Decker, a photographer and a graphic designer. The glamorous cover shows the face of a beautiful model and is designed as a women's magazine cover with the appropriate layout and an extra text exclaiming in French 'Sois belle Eva!' [Be beautiful Eve!]. During this period at the start of her career, the work of De Decker had an obvious political character, dealing with traditional conceptions about the role of the woman as mother, wife and mistress. In the book her jewellery served as elements in the images of a pamph-

> 33

leteer (fig. 33). There were no captions, so the story of the jewellery remained unclear. The book with full-page staged photographs, complete with some emblematic imagery taken from other sources, might be observed as an example of book-art in jewellery. The artist directed it, and worked on it in collaboration with other professionals, as an extension in a different medium of the themes she explored in her jewellery and objects.

For many jewellers staged photography is a good way to provide a context for their jewellery. Swedish designer Pia Aleborg, who is also active in the fields of costume and set design, used stage-photography on different occasions to contextualise her jewellery.

Apartfrom (2005) is depicted in photographs taken on the spot, as it were (fig. 34). The jewellery, made from such domestic mess as electric wire, socks lying about, a top, chains and frills, is shown by some quite average models in an average domestic environment. The photos were published as a brochure. French artist Benjamin Lignel also uses this medium, creating posters, leaflets and paper mailings and collaborating with different professional photographers. *La Disparition* (2010), is a photo-publication documenting a series of badges with gradually dispersing clouds.

In 2011 Octavia Cook and Lisa Walker, both from New Zealand, were the models for their own jewellery. Cook, in line with her work, makes very elegant and glossy images that provide her exhibitions with just the right bourgeois atmosphere. While Walker, on the contrary but in line with her jewel assemblages, shoots casual snapshots that can even be labelled as 'bad photography'. In the hands of these artists, photography becomes an important vehicle that enhances the meaning and expression of their jewellery. Publications are an obvious destination for images, but photographs are more often also being treated as an integral part of exhibitions, as recent shows presenting the work of Nanna Melland, David Bielander, Octavia Cook (fig. 35) and Lisa Walker have proved.[22] As such they can have an important function in the perception of jewellery, transforming an abstract form into a wearable one.

PHOTOGRAPHY AS A COMPOSITIONAL ELEMENT

In the 1960s, photography had also already been used for its imagery as a material or element in jewellery. There may have been an influence from British and American Pop art in the way both Reinhold Reiling and Gijs Bakker used figurative photographic elements in their work. Reinhold Reiling, who studied and taught in Pforzheim, a German centre of the jewellery industry, used photo-etching between 1967 and 1969. Casual family pictures were etched in a coarse-grain raster technique on a gold surface. During the same period in the United States, J. Fred Woell and Robert Ebendorf made jewellery by using photographs, comics and logos in a narrative way. The incorporation of another medium – a medium of reproduction in jewellery – had an obvious aim. In 1960s America, photography was used alongside ready-made second-hand materials as being representative of 'the American way of life' and as a way to mock American society.

Gijs Bakker's use of photography in jewellery also has a communicative aim. For example, the early *Bibs* from 1976, showing different naked male and female breasts printed on linen bibs, can be observed as anti-gala necklaces (fig. 36). Choosing the right imagery is vital, while any printed matter stands at Bakker's disposition: specially-made photos, as well as cut out images from magazines, newspapers, posters and postcards among other things. The bejewelled décolletage of seven different queens, four different naked male and female breasts, the crossed arms of the artist seen from above, a giant rose with dewdrops, sports heroes cut from newspaper articles, the sequence of a penis in different stages of erection joined as a pearl chain, images of luxurious cars – anything can become a piece of jewellery.

Unlike the Americans, Bakker did not apply photography as a mere compositional element. Instead he transformed an image into an ornament by isolating a substantial part of it, shaping it in the form of a necklace or brooch and sealing it in PVC. Later, after 1985, mounted details in gold, pearls or precious stones became the very indicators of his message. Appropriate to his own ideas about design and craft already formulated in the 1960s and 1970s, Gijs Bakker has a rational way of putting different elements together, using solutions that have an industrial origin and appearance (sealing in PVC, covering with Perspex). Bakker creates jewellery as a designer, being responsible for the concept and the design and relying on the skills of craftspeople to realise his designs.

The combination of newspaper pictures of famous sportsmen (the new society stars) with gold and gems was clever and funny. In the *Sports Figures* brooches from 1985 to 1989, precious materials replaced certain elements in the picture: tennis player Lendl is in action behind a gold rod while soccer players Kerkhof and Kleton kick a cultivated pearl. This play with banality versus luxury is brought to an extreme in the *Bouquet Brooches* from 1989 where diamonds, sapphires and tourmalines are mounted on cheap frumpy postcards of a bunch of flowers. Today these jewels might seem pretty harmless. But in the 1980s, these pieces by Bakker were quite shocking because the taboo on the use of gold and precious stones was still very strong. The combination of cheap photography and precious materials proved to be the right vehicle to present his ironical comments on jewellery and society.

> 37 The *Waterman* brooch from 1990 (fig. 37) consists of a black-and-white photo of a naked man seen from the back, emptying a bucket of water over his head. Bakker replaced the water drops for seventy-seven diamonds. It was a statement again of a jewellery maker who likes to ridicule people's need for shine by using an abundance of it. He picked up the theme again ten years later in 2001 in the car brooches *I Don't Wear Jewels, I Drive Them*, which now used enormous stones. The title of the jewellery refers to an Alfa Romeo advertisement. According to his biographer Ida van Zijl 'the "insolence" of setting huge precious stones into photographs of luxury cars produced jewellery with an unabashed costliness rivalling that of Cartier.'[23]

Today, more jewellers are using photographic imagery for its pictorial and iconographical properties. The German jewellery artist Bettina Speckner, one generation younger than Gijs Bakker, is as much dependent on photography as the Dutch jewellery designer is. While both use the same combination of materials, a photo on top of which precious stones are mounted, the outcome is completely different. Speckner entered the jewellery scene in 1992, yet her poetic and pictorial approach is like a denial of Bakker's provocative stance.

Irrational, romantic and surrealistic are qualifications that can be attributed to Speckner's photo brooches and necklaces, which are created from combinations of pearls, shells, coral and precious stones. Speckner works with fragments of photographs made by her, landscapes, nature, plants, everyday still lifes and some cityscapes.[24] She also uses antique portrait photographs such as ferrotypes as a material for her jewellery.[25] Every image is like a canvas to be worked on. Speckner applies photo-etching and photo-enamelling techniques to consolidate pictures on zinc or silver. Both techniques have their problems. The photo-etching can be done in Munich but is poisonous and complicated. The photo-enamelling is an old and nearly extinct technique used for photos on graves and is executed in the workshop of one of the last Portuguese craftsmen familiar with the > 38 techniques (fig. 38).

The first images Bettina Speckner used were taken from her mother's photo album. Her mother made these pictures as a sixteen-year-old girl when travelling to the United States in the 1950s. Speckner says: 'Actually there was nothing to be seen on these pictures, but it was the intention which touched me.'[26] This experience of the invisible, of knowing that you cannot see what should have been in the picture, the actual reason for making the photograph, gave her new insights in the workings of photography and imagery. She started making her own photos, though she never makes a picture with the intention to use it in jewellery: 'It is somehow two completely different things. Only much later I see the "jewellery quality" of a photo. The last years I became more proud of my own photographs. That is why I made my [...] book, showing also some of my photos. Some of those are more than 15 years old.'[27] While photographing she tries to come near to the sensation of the captured moment. In her studio her workbench is filled with images, ready to be picked up and used.

The photos in her jewellery are often hazy and a bit grubby, landscapes are empty, left alone or just inhabited by a few cows. Sometimes we see electricity poles and cables, a house, a harbour, some chairs – remnants of human activity. The historic human figures have the same silent, frozen, character; they pose and gaze in the eye of the camera. Speckner's intense treatment gives them an abstract quality, yet she tells her own story on top of them. Sometimes an added stone seems like an echo of an element in the image or an unevenness in the old material. In a brooch from 2003, showing a group portrait of

> fig. 39

three men, two sitting and one standing, with hats, the formality of the composition is magnified by seven split raw diamonds arranged in a symmetrical grid (fig. 39). In some > 39 jewels, stones and other elements are scattered around, seemingly at random, disturbing the image in an uncanny way. Images have power over us, their content is compelling, and Speckner, aware of this, directs our eyes. Her intention is pictorial, though not narrative. Imagery, pearls, precious stones and ornaments are like words in the hands of a poet: they create a rhythm and incite new meanings. The borderline between embellishing and extending, distorting and hurting and between 'the everyday and the far away' is very narrow in this work.

Bettina Speckner can be observed as a pioneer in the use of photography as an artistic medium in jewellery. Today more and more jewellers apply photography in jewellery, all in their own individual way. Most of them make incidental use of it. Some jewellers who work or have worked with photography are Truike Verdegaal, Kirsten Haydon, Machteld van Joolingen, Iris Nieuwenburg, Jantje Fleischhut, Suska Mackert, Carolina Vallejo, Ramón Puig Cuyàs and Hiroki Masuzaki. The attachment of photography to metal is a new problem for jewellers. Jantje Fleischhut and Iris Nieuwenburg developed special varnishes to consolidate their images. Iris Nieuwenburg works on the basis of existing imagery – in her case, reproductions from images of historical interiors; Kirsten Haydon works with her own photos made during a residency in Antarctica.

The eye is an intriguing subject for brooches. References to the evil eye seem obvious, but I cannot abandon associations with the female gaze (the majority of brooches are worn by women, after all). Truike Verdegaal used portrait photos in some of her *Mirakel* jewellery from 2003, making special use of the gaze of the portrayed person, enhanced by a thick, milky white mineral called ulixite. When the brooch or necklace is worn, the staring portrait will not immediately catch your eye because of the thickness of the mineral under which the portrait is mounted. When confronted face-to-face with the gaze of the portrait, however, things change. A brooch that breaches the privacy zone, a brooch staring back, can be an overpowering experience. In early antique sentimental lockets, eyes instead of a full portrait were sometimes depicted as a remembrance to a loved one. These eyes inspired Suska Mackert to make a large series of contemporary eye-medallions using cut-out newspaper photos glued onto a plastic badge (fig. 40). In this way, by using her extended newspaper archives, she created a simple but highly appealing contemporary 'customised' series that allowed people to dream and associate freely. In his *Utopos* jewellery from 2007 to 2009, Ramón Puig Cuyàs also used fragments of portrait images (reproductions), in which the eye and the hands get special significance. The brooches deal with cosmos and humanity. The graphical constructions built on top of the photos respond to the imagery while at the same time referring to human installations and depictions of the universe (fig. 41).

> 40

> 41

In the early days of the New Jewelry, avant-garde jewellers inspired by developments in the fine arts began using the newly discovered instant photography as a means for artistic research. Furthermore, photography was discovered as a way to communicate ideas about jewellery, both in art photography projects inspired by jewellery and in staged photography of jewellery on models. In this way jewellers tried to establish a connection between their rather abstract jewellery objects and the wearer. At first they made use of famous models, VIPs and fellow artists. Later, ordinary people or the artists themselves were discovered as the ideal model for art jewellery. Nowadays, photography is used as imagery in jewellery more and more. At first it served mainly 'political' motives, commenting on jewellery and society. Gradually it evolved into an ornamental and pictorial medium, often the basis on which a composition is superimposed. Staged photography is used to enhance the meaning of the jewellery. The jewellery artist is not just the director but sometimes also the model and even the photographer of the image. Art jewellery is part of our present-day 'culture of images' and happily knows how to benefit from it.[28]

1   The book was initiated and edited by the chairman of the foundation Jerven Ober, who was also the director of the Van Reekum Galerij in Apeldoorn where he presented the first proofs of the 'new photography' in the Netherlands: photography as a form of art. It is an interesting coincidence that photography and jewellery started a process of liberation and innovation around the same time. Today, art photography has gained status in the art market, in museums and among collectors.

2   Ruudt Peters, *Interno* (photographs: Foekje Detmar, 1991), *Passio* (photographs: Tono Stano, 1992), *Ouroboros* (photographs: Winnifred Limburg, 1995), *Lapis* (photographs: William Ropp, 1997) and *Vinkhoek* (photographs: Johannes Schwarz, 1998). See also Chapter III.

3   Bernhard Schobinger (ed.), 1988. *Devon, Karbon, Perm: 62 Ausgewählte Objekte 1984–87, fotografiert von Annelies Štrba,* Richterswil. In later publications photographs by Annelies Štrba were also integrated.

4   Maria Teresa Carné, et al., 1987. *Joieria Europea Contemporània*. Barcelona: Fundació Caixa de Pensions, p. 16.

5   In 1993, the Dutch *Tekens & Ketens* [Chains & Signs] exhibition looked like a rehearsal for the Barcelona catalogue featuring Amsterdam VIPs and others photographed by Michaël Ferron.

6   Wilhelm Mattar, 1989. 'Prominente zeigen ihr Lieblingsstück, Künstler schmücken Prominente', in Michael Erlhoff, Fritz Falk, et al., 1989. *Ornamenta I: Internationale Schmuckkunst*. Munich: Prestel, pp. 284–97.

7   In retrospect, Gijs Bakker thinks that this is an omission: 'They really miss, they belong to the gold thread, they are in the collection of Benno Premsela together with the gold thread in the box.' Gijs Bakker, conversation with the author, Amsterdam, 19 Nov. 2007.

8   Ida van Zijl, 2005. *Gijs Bakker and Jewelry*. Stuttgart: Arnoldsche, no. 119, p. 249 (illustrated as an object, without model).

9   Susanna Heron, 1980. *Bodywork.* London: Crafts Council Gallery.

10 Ibid. p. 26.

11 Johanna Hess-Dahm, 1987. 'Almost Nothing', in *Art Aurea*, no. 3, p. 43.

12 The technique was developed by Dr Edwin Land and brought on the market in 1972. It was an improved version of his first Polaroid instant camera, which was available in 1948. The SX-70 became very popular among artists because of its spontaneous, direct nature. It was used by quite some artists as a means of research.

13 These Polaroids by Robert Smit are printed and described in the exhibition catalogue Els Barents, et al., 1981. *Instant Fotografie.* Amsterdam: Stedelijk Museum, pp. 54–8.

14 Ralph Turner, 1975. *Jewellery in Europe: An Exhibition of Progressive Work.* Edinburgh: Scottish Arts Council, p. 48.

15 *ArtScribe*, no. 3, summer 1976, pp. 14–5.

16 Travelling exhibition *Met het oog op het lichaam*, NKS, the Netherlands, 1978.

17 Peter Skubic, 2001. 'Jewellery under the Skin', in Helen W. Drutt English, Petra Zimmermann, Florian Hufnagl, et al., 2001. *Peter Skubic: Between. Schmuck/Jewellery.* Stuttgart: Arnoldsche, p. 133.

18 See exhibition catalogue *Schmuck – Tischgerät aus Österreich 1904/08–1973/77.* Vienna: Galerie am Graben (unpaginated).

19 John de Greef, 1984. 'Otto Künzli, behang', in *Bijvoorbeeld*, 16, no. 3, p. 2 (translation by LdB). This article was illustrated with portraits of Dutch jewellers and other people from the scene wearing a Künzli *Wallpaper* brooch.

20 Wearability was an important issue in the 1970s and 1980s. Different artists in different countries were working with this theme, including Pierre Degen (UK), Susanna Heron (UK), Jan Wehrens (NL/D), LAM de Wolf (NL), Joke Brakman/Claudie Berbee (NL) and Marjorie Schick (US). See also Chapter VI.

21 Discussion between Robert Smit and Gijs Bakker, 1986. 'Godert van Colmjon in gesprek met Gijs Bakker en Robert Smit: Een onpersoonlijk lijf tegenover de borst van Rob van Koningsbruggen', in *Museumtijdschrift*, nos. 3 & 4, p. 170 (translation by LdB).

22 Nanna Melland, *It's all about Love*, Centro Disene, Cine y Television, Mexico City (MEX), April 2010; David Bielander, *A Theatre of Appearances*, Galerie Biró, Munich (DE), March 2011; Octavia Cook, *Shangri-La*, Anna Miles Gallery, Auckland (NZ), April 2011; Lisa Walker, *Wearable*, COBRA Museum, Amstelveen (NL), Oct.–Dec. 2011.

23 Van Zijl (see note 8), p. 44.

24 Bettina Speckner also makes jewellery without photography. In the catalogue published for the Förderpreis der Stadt München in 1999, there are plenty of examples of jewellery made of gold or silver and precious stones or beads alone. However, photography holds a prominent place in her work.

25 A ferrotype (also called tintype or melainotype) is a photographic process invented and patented in the United States in 1856 by Prof. Hamilton Smith of Kenyon College, Ohio. It is a wet-plate process. In America it became the most common photographic process until the introduction of the modern gelatine-based processes and the invention of the reloadable amateur camera by Kodak at the end of the nineteenth century. The technique was relatively simple and fast to make, therefore relatively cheap and very durable. The image is actually a negative but due to the black background it appears as a positive. Ferrotypes are therefore unique images. According to Bettina Speckner, ferrotypes were only made in the United States.

26 Email from Bettina Speckner, 14 Dec. 2007.

27 Email from Bettina Speckner, 14 Dec. 2007. The book she is referring to is: Bettina Speckner, 2007. *The Everyday and the Far Away.* Munich: Galerie Spektrum.

28 Photography is again used for research or as a method of documentary for temporary body-related jewellery, these kinds of on-the-fringe and body jewellery projects are further discussed in Chapter V and VI.

III. Beyond the Showcase

In June 2004, students from the jewellery class of Otto Künzli at the Academy of Fine Arts in Munich devised a remarkable way of showing their jewellery: the glass house of Galerie Marzee in the Netherlands was to become their stage. The students invited the audience to enter one by one as VIPs. Each VIP received a piece of jewellery and a small card with information considering the piece: artist, year, title, material and price. Guests walked on a red carpet and talked to complete strangers about 'their' piece of jewellery, photos of each other were taken, waiters with trays filled with glasses of champagne circled around; everybody was a star. There were no showcases. The visitors were the display. The presentation reminded me of what must have been one of the first jewellery happenings in the world, an event that has been recorded in many writings and that has a legendary status.

> 42

It was on 31 January 1970 when Gijs Bakker and his partner Emmy van Leersum showed their so-called *Clothing Suggestions* on models (fig. 42). These *Clothing Suggestions* were tight-fitting, white elastic suits with special bulbous elements at the knees, elbows, hips, breasts or shoulders, and the fabric was hardened with polyester. Some of these elements were extremely pronounced, like a cube around the penis, spheres on the hips

> 43

or an open frame around the breasts (fig. 43). These futuristic suits expressed the view of Bakker and Van Leersum on modern jewellery. Jewellery should follow or intervene with the natural shape of the body, and these formal accents were used to express these ideas. They wanted to present their ideas about clothing as being related to the body and as confrontational as possible therefore they invited a group of friends, all committed to art, to wear the suits on this special occasion.

On a Saturday afternoon, the models, dressed in the suits, entered the Art & Project gallery, a new visual art gallery in Amsterdam. The gallery space was empty except for the people wearing the *Clothing Suggestions* and the invited audience. The public had nothing but themselves. Gijs Bakker remembers, '… it was an unplanned happening. Our friends [wearing the *Clothing Suggestions*] and the visiting public all came in at the same time. It was a shocking confrontation.'[1] Many newspapers and magazines covered it; one reviewer mentioned that the show 'raised astonishment, enthusiasm, outrage and even anger'.[2]

There are thirty-four years between the Amsterdam happening and the Munich VIP reception, and although there is a world of difference between them there are also some similarities. What bind these happenings are the tactics of surprise and the idea of asking people to serve as a display for the work. In doing this, Bakker and Van Leersum entered into a confrontation with the common conventional jewellery and art world. But they also subtly pointed at the fact that an ornament worn on the body is much more controversial than a painting on the wall and that it needs commitment of the wearer. That is the reason why they asked friends, among them some well-known fine artists, designers and gallery owners, to wear their suits.

The Munich students also worked with the idea of commitment, asking the public to participate by wearing a piece of jewellery that was chosen at random. In contrast to this, the commitment with the event in 1970 was real and deliberate because the models could choose beforehand which suit they wanted to wear. It was really felt as an act of engagement because the suits were controversial and in some cases – such as the one with the open showcase around the women's breasts – also rather daring. There was no room for neutrality or pretending. In both cases the audience was taken by surprise. Instead of watching a regular gallery presentation, the audience had to get involved in what was going on, they had to do something for it, had to change their passive observer's attitude. Both events are proof of the artists' wish to engage the audience somehow. Today our perspective has shifted; there is no need to make confrontational work the way it was done in 1970, but the need to confirm the relation between jewellery and wearer and to present jewellery outside the fixed rules of a gallery or museum show seems more urgent than ever before. This chapter discusses new ways of presenting jewellery.

INSTALLATIONS

Many jewellers observe the showcase, the usual place for jewellery in shops, galleries and museums, as a kind of a trap, a place that isolates jewellery from the world and people and turns them into rather unidentified, in a way commodified, objects. The museum showcase stresses the preciousness and uniqueness of a piece of jewellery. When an object or a piece of jewellery enters a museum collection its appreciation is changed. Its significance has increased but so has its isolation. The glass vitrine hinders the creation of meaning: the object now has an art status. In a gallery, a showcase stimulates buying instead of reflection, and the object is treated like a commodity, an object of desire. Another problem with jewellery galleries can be their restricted and fixed possibilities. A gallery only has a certain amount of showcases, walls and space, meaning the artist must adapt their exhibition to fit within these confines.

The presumed problem of distance, alienation and limitation gave way to new views on presentation, avoiding the showcase, sometimes also avoiding the gallery, by creating specific environments in order to create the right context for the work. This movement away from the showcase had already started in the 1970s but became increasingly popular in the 1990s. Installations, events and the use of special locations became important instruments for jewellery artists in presenting their work.

In jewellery, the notion of installation is generally used to describe exhibitions that are conceived as contextualised environments. The notion derived from the fine arts where it actually has a different meaning, and is used to describe all sorts of hybrid artforms related to public space, such as environments, site specific works and happenings. Therefore the origin of the word should be expatiated before applying it to jewellery. The history of installation art goes back to the 1950s with the introduction of happenings, events and environments. They developed as a way to break up classical and formal conceptions of art, which were considered too restricted. In fact, it could be observed as an anti-painting movement. Happenings, events and environments combine different media, including video, audio, computer and projection. The American artist and critic Allan Kaprow is seen as the person who introduced the notions 'happening' and 'event'. In 1958, he published a seminal article in *Art News* magazine entitled 'The Legacy of Jackson Pollock' as homage to the artist who had passed away in 1956. In his article Kaprow valued Pollock's non-conformist and liberated mind. About what Pollock has taught us he is clear: 'Pollock, as I see him, left us at the point where we must become preoccupied with and even dazzled by the space and objects of our everyday life, either our bodies, clothes, rooms or, if need be, the vastness of Forty-Second Street.'[3] And he goes on to describe how any material, sense or sensation are 'materials for the new art'. These are prophetic words. Kaprow's first groundbreaking happening, known as *18 Happenings in 6 Parts*, performed at the Reuben Gallery in New York (1959) was a highly conducted spatial, audio-visual and multidisciplinary composition in three gallery rooms, in which the public were to move according to a prescribed track and time score.

Installation art has developed from these early sources of event, happening and environment since the beginning of the 1960s. As with the early happenings and events, later installations still make an appeal to the public. The works ask for involvement and reflection, content is not easily read. There is an interaction between objects and the space around them, and the public is invited to experience the relationship between these different elements. Thus an installation is a work of art involving all the different components together with space, in an attempt to establish a new connection with the public. Installations are site-specific, made for a special place, room, building or situation, and therefore have a temporal character.

In jewellery, notions such as event and installation are loan words, words that have lost their actual meaning in favour of a rather one-dimensional one. In most cases, the installation or event in jewellery is not meant to substitute jewellery but to present it. In that sense, it is far remote from installation art, which is not about presenting or replacing: an installation is an artwork. Yet, there is a connection in the fact that both try to enhance the viewing and try to establish another profounder relationship with the viewer by making an appeal to the viewer's knowledge, sensibility and imagination. However, whereas installation art and events are self-contained and self-fulfilling, jewellery installations and events are in general instrumental and didactic. Yet there are exceptions to this 'rule'. The main protagonist in this field is Otto Künzli.

In 1980, Otto Künzli was invited to exhibit at a gallery in Basel, Switzerland. While preparing his show, the gallerist repeatedly stressed the fact that it was not a jewellery gallery but a serious fine art gallery. The artist was expected to make a fine-art show. Therefore he suggested leaving the room empty and personally marking each visitor with a red dot, the commonly known symbol in the art world which indicates that a work is sold. But apparently this was not what the gallery wanted, and so the show was cancelled. For Künzli it meant the start of his so-called drawing-pin brooches – first only available in red and later available in all colours – that have since been sold by the tens of thousands. From 1992 onwards, Künzli succeeded in fulfilling his previously refused wish on a much larger scale, not by marking the public but by marking non-commercial art galleries and museums where he showed his work with a red dot on the facade. This red object is a round industrially enamelled metal disc with a diameter of 20 cm. In this way, Künzli managed to turn the red dot into a personal brand that in some cases remained on the facade as a memento of the artist's presence at the venue. Künzli even gave instructions as to where the red dot should be placed: 'So far there are two possibilities for placing the Red Dot. One is somewhere at the edge of the architecture, as in Oslo and in Munich, or associated to the "logo" of the museum as in Glasgow. The latter only makes sense if the logo is placed in a prominent place and large enough.'[4] When invited to join the group exhibition *Closer*, by making a work of art or jewellery that would reflect on a work of art from the collection of the National Museum of Ancient Art in Lisbon, Künzli decided to only mark the museum with his red dot: 'Today I do not insist anymore on having a solo exhibition in the particular museum. But I do insist on installing the piece by myself. It is part of the concept that "the artist" himself puts the sign of his presence on the museum.'[5]

How do we value this action? Is it indeed a work of (jewellery) art or is it a sign of artistic poverty, laziness and arrogance? – just some of the comments that I've heard over the years. In my view, it is indeed an installation and a genuine work of art that stands in the tradition of Duchamp's signed – with his pseudonym R. Mutt – *Fountain* and Stanley Brouwn's conceptual artworks made in the 1960s and 1970s, works of art that stressed the importance of the artist as an author of a concept rather than of a 'hands-on' made work of art. Marcel Duchamp's *Fountain* was the first ready-made object that was a product of an artistic action which consequently became accepted as art in a museum, 'blowing it up as a storehouse of "eternal" values' in the meantime, as theorist Martin Damus put it.[6] Stanley Brouwn's *This Way Brouwn* series of artworks (sketches and books) focuses on mapping the artist's movements.[7] Both of these works rely on the conceptual integrity of the artist. Künzli's red dot, however, already carries this information within it – it is about ridiculing the museum as an old-fashioned art institution and about mapping the artist's presence – and, besides that, is a topical comment on the art world, including statements on the influence of the market, commercialism and the artist as an icon that sells as a brand. But beyond this, it is an interesting action in the context of jewellery because the red dot not only marks a museum but also decorates the museum's facade – a decoration attached to the building by the jeweller himself. It is noteworthy that in 1991, when Künzli was preparing his solo exhibition *The Third Eye* in the Stedelijk Museum in Amsterdam, Wim Beeren, the museum's director, refused to let him attach a red dot to the facade of the Stedelijk Museum because he 'found it not appropriate to have a jewel on the facade while the drug addicted and homeless people in the streets don't have enough food'.[8] Here the red dot is exclusively interpreted as a piece of jewellery, and in an utterly politically correct way turned down as such. Other museums proved less inhibited and allowed him to install his mark.[9]

On 20 December 1983, Otto Künzli organised a remarkable performance in the Lothringerstrasse in Munich. In a small room behind a large window, which acted as a shop window of sorts, sat a woman dressed festively in black. She wore a heavy chain made of two hundred German one-mark pieces. A man also officially dressed in black stood beside her. He wore a large gold brooch in the form of a bar of gold, complete with official stamps, made from the paper wrapping from Swiss chocolate. The jewels were entitled *The Swiss Gold* and *The Deutschmark*. The man and woman enjoyed a relaxed get-together, smoking, talking a bit, listening to music and drinking champagne, isolated in their own world behind the window. In the adjacent empty room, visitors gathered and drank beer from cans. They were watching the man and woman, who, on their part, were watching and probably discussing the visitors – there was no acoustic contact between the rooms. From the street, people passing by could watch both the audience and the performers through the large shop window.

In a document written by Otto Künzli he observes that when entering the room, the visitors had to pass close by the window where the man and woman were, which was apparently a scary experience: 'Most of them are now trying to keep their distance, lowering their voices and glancing furtively at the man and woman from afar. Four windows look onto the street from the large room. Passers-by, under the protection of nightfall, stop to observe the visitors.'[10]

What was happening here was the creation of a scene for an intricate network of people watching and being watched, while all the time the jewels only played a minor role. Of course these jewels, *The Swiss Gold* and *The Deutschmark*, enhanced the atmosphere of decadence, idleness and affluence and indeed were the clues to the scene, but, notwithstanding that, they seem to have been there more as props than as actual works on show. The work itself was not about jewellery but, in the words of the artist, about 'exhibitionism, voyeurism, fake and real, reception, consumerist behaviour, the arbitrariness of moral concepts, exploitation, vanity and illusion'.[11]

> 44

As the final stage of this installation, Künzli made a photograph of the couple (fig. 44), like an official portrait, and he showed and sold the jewels in later exhibitions. *The Swiss Gold* brooches, made from the paper chocolate wrapping, were made in an edition of around ten while the chain, *The Deutschmark*, presenting 1.2 kg of 200 genuine German one-mark coins, was made as a one-off piece. The jewellery can be observed as the relic of a performance that was the actual work of art and which is further only documented in a series of photographs, a written account and the official portrait of the couple by the artist. According to Künzli, the portrait photograph was only exhibited two or three times, and it was never acquired by a museum where it could actually belong.

Showing jewellery in alternative ways has long been Künzli's objective with respect to his own work and that of his students at the Academy of Fine Arts in Munich, where he has been professor and head of the jewellery department since 1991. German writer Maribel Königer even thinks that 'the stagings of their annual exhibitions have become […] the stuff of legend.'[12] The ideas about students' exhibitions are worked on collectively and focus on different aspects of presenting jewellery, such as jewellery and the human body, the showcase or light – all of them of vital importance. One year, the students invited ladies of a certain age to show and wear their jewellery live at fixed moments during the exhibition. On another occasion the jewellery was shown in discarded showcases bor-rowed from many different Munich museums – an idea that was later repeated in a much more elaborated form in the exhibition *Des Wahnsinns fette Beute (The Fat Booty of Madness,*

> 45

2008) in the Neue Sammlung/Pinakothek der Moderne in Munich (fig. 45). In 2006, the annual *Schmuckklasse* exhibition focused on the aspect of light through the design of a lighting system based on daylight. Elaborate cardboard pipes and constructions created a highly theatrical effect. An eyewitness account reads: 'The exhibition space was completely darkened. Conical light shafts of corrugated cardboard up to thirteen metres long led to scattered bases on which the pieces of jewellery were spread out. The light tubes mysteri-ously concentrated the sunlight, thus creating an almost surreal effect with it: daylight treated like artificial lighting.'[13]

Yet the most daring presentation of the Künzli's class took place during the *Siamo Qui* symposium in Florence, Italy, in April 2008. The symposium, organised by the Alchimia Jewellery School, involved an exhibition in which several classes from different European schools were invited to present themselves. Künzli's class was confined to one cube show-case with a heap of students' work, piled up at random. Although this presentation of jew-

> fig. 47

> fig. 46

ellery seemed quite disrespectful, both towards the audience and the participants, Künzli
argued that this was a misconception and that the decision to do it like this was made in
mutual agreement. The true value of this presentation (or installation?) is still unclear to
me. One can either interpret it as a way to evade the invitation by the organisers or as a
rather arrogant way to show that the individual work made in the Munich jewellery department is of such an outstanding quality that it remains apparent even when shown in a heap.
Either way, Künzli's class always promises radical solutions and good discussions.

In the last ten or fifteen years, Munich has become a magnet, a true jewellery centre.
Schmuck, the annual jewellery exhibition organised at the Internationale Handwerksmesse
in Munich since 1959, attracts an ever-increasing amount of international visitors. The
satellite programme, which has become increasingly popular, proves the viability of presentation as an artistic statement. The exhibitions organised by *Rebellen der Liebe*, a group
of (ex) students of the Munich Academy consisting of Alexander Blank, Stefan Heuser,
Christian Hoedl and Jiro Kamata, have been highlights in this programme for some years
now. Their exhibitions *Attacke die Waldfee* (2008, figs. 46, 47) and *Oben hart oder der Abschied* > 46, 47
vom Ösensystem (2009) showed the importance of presentation as a way to deepen the
perception and understanding of jewellery. Their 2011 exhibition in the spacious
Kunstarkaden der Stadt München was further proof of their ability to master the art of
presenting jewellery in an unorthodox way. By making use of a half-pipe in one room and
a long corridor covered in gold foil in another, which moved and made sound due to air
displacement when passing through it, they were able to evoke a sense of excitement. This
way, looking at jewellery can become a challenging experience. It reflects their ideas about
jewellery as being 'things for love and fight [...]. What we need to get close and to repel'.[14]

At the beginning of the 1990s, a growing number of art jewellers began making special
installations to show their jewellery, either in a gallery or in specific surroundings. These
installations became as important as the jewellery. One of the main advocates of this idea,
as a teacher, guest teacher and influential figure, was the Dutch artist Ruudt Peters.[15] Peters
is opposed to simply showing jewellery in showcases. He believes it is important that people
can touch and feel the pieces and therefore designs a new installation for every exhibition,
which is meant to present the work in the appropriate context and to make the work touch-
able and intimate. Another, more personal reason for the spatial presentations of his jewellery might be his sculptural background. As a sculptor, Ruudt Peters was used to handling
space, and over the years we can see how he continuously works with it, either as a jeweller
who creates special environments for his work or as an artist who creates 'applied' or monumental art works in architectural settings.

After his studies (1970–74) Ruudt Peters abandoned jewellery because he felt ill at
ease in the dogmatic, purist climate that dominated the Dutch jewellery scene at the time.
He began making sculptures and discovered religion and philosophy to be the driving force
in his life and work. Around 1990 he returned to jewellery. Probably due to his sculptural
background, the showcase soon proved too limited.[16]

In 1992, Peters made his first installation for his *Passio* jewellery series in Galerie
Marzee's basement in Nijmegen (then at the address Ganzenheuvel). The *Passio* series
consisted solely of pendants. The use of symbols – sawn out, engraved or attached to the
pendants – was pivotal in this jewellery. Some pendants were completely covered with
symbols – a powerful statement in Dutch jewellery at that time which was still dominated
by abstraction and whose meaning and narration were viewed as utterly suspicious. The
work, which referred to historical and biblical figures, suggested incense holders as used
in Roman Catholic ceremonies. The ceremonial and religious atmosphere was intensified

> 48

by the installation itself (fig. 48). Each pendant hung in a cylindrical tent made of transparent violet gauze, rising high up to the ceiling like airy columns. The installation transformed the gallery space into a solemn environment. Today one can hardly imagine what a thrilling experience it was to open the gauze, reach at the pendants and actually take them in one's hand – this 'touchability' was so unusual at that time that many people were hesitant to do so.

In the same year, Peters organised an event for an earlier collection, the *Interno* brooches (1990). When the public entered the room in Galerie Spektrum in Munich, there was nothing to be seen but fifteen hooks on the wall. After some time, fifteen male models entered the room, each wearing an *Interno* brooch on the lapel of their black suits. After crossing the room, each model stood in line against the wall next to a hook. The public had to walk past and get near the models to get a better look at the brooches. After an hour, the models hung their jackets on the hooks, where they remained hanging for the duration of the exhibition. As an event, in its forced and uneasy interaction between models and public, it is akin to the aforementioned *Clothing Suggestions* happening and Otto Künzli's *The Swiss Gold – The Deutschmark* event.

Ruudt Peters's unconventional installations soon became a trademark of the artist, though not always to his advantage or success. The *Ouroboros* brooches (1995), dealing with eternity and divinity, were shown pinned to the old wooden ceiling of Galerie Marzee,

> 49

high above wobbly ladders, like the gods on Olympus (fig. 49). The use of this device, the ladder, was not just a rhetorical 'trick': in alchemy – the main source for Ruudt Peters's work – the ladder is a symbol that represents reaching for the divine. The public was invited to climb the dangerous, old-fashioned ladders that stood in rows under the beams of the ceiling in order to get a closer view of the jewellery – indeed to see the jewellery at all, as nothing could be seen from ground level. This rather disturbing presentation scared rather than attracted viewers. Eventually a new solution had to be found in order to make the exhibition more accessible. This proves that the true value of an installation is to provide the proper context for the jewellery rather than make a daring sculptural installation. Ruudt Peters showed the *Ouroboros* jewellery again in 1996, this time in the National Museum in Prague, as an intervention in the antique showcases, amidst the museum's mineral collection.

Peters's next collection, *Lapis* (1998), was inspired by the alchemistic search for the 'philosopher's stone'. Inspired by an old alchemistic text – 'Grind the stone to a very fine powder and put it into the sharpest vinegar, and it will at once be dissolved into the philosophical water' – the artist created his own stones.[17] Peters ground precious minerals and mixed the grit with liquid acrylic, casting this material into moulds made of other minerals. The *Lapis* collection was presented on a white table with twelve white laboratory coats serv-

> 50

ing as a background to emphasise the artificial, alchemistic nature of the stones (fig. 50). His following collection and installation, *Pneuma* (2000), in clinical white, stressed the manipulated character even more as a reaction to scientific experiments with cloning and genetic manipulation.

In his work Ruudt Peters discovered what installations can do for jewellery: expanding the atmosphere already present in the jewellery through the right combination of materials, props, constructions and lighting. Therefore, the word installation can easily be exchanged for the word scenography, which is also aimed at provoking the correct atmosphere in order to understand the work.

Iris Eichenberg, who studied with Ruudt Peters at the Gerrit Rietveld Academy, understood this principle quite well when she claimed the academy's 'gipshok' (a shed for making plaster moulds in the school's garden) to present her final presentation in 1994. Her graduation collection consisted of knitted jewellery pieces with some moveable silver parts. It was groundbreaking work in her choice of materials and techniques, unintentionally setting a trend to such a degree that the academy was sometimes criticised for 'all these knitting and crocheting girls'. The narrative would become an important characteristic of Eichenberg's work, even though 'storytelling was a bad thing' in Europe and especially in the Netherlands at that time, as Eichenberg recapitulated later.[18] She had to find a way to present her work so that people could understand what it was about. An installation was exactly the right medium to make her point.

Eichenberg's jewellery was about life and the body, or to be more accurate, about the damage that life causes you – nail-biting, grinding one's teeth, thyroid gland defects and amputations. Her jewellery consisted of knitted sleeves in greys and browns, which referred to veins.[19] There were branches and little holes enclosing hammered silver parts. The fact that the work was knitted from wool, a comfortable, isolating and organic material, and that it slowly grew in her hands, was of much significance.

The room where the installation was built was a rather battered place. It was filled with a muffled sound, repeated in a slow and regular rhythm, originating from a pump in a water tank. The sound related to the heap of hearts on a windowsill above the tank, which Eichenberg's mother and friends in the German countryside had knitted. Every heart was different because of the individual interpretations and knitting techniques. Some looked rather realistic, others presented weird and uncontrolled growths. The atmosphere in this 'breathing' room was impressive and touching and provided a sublime context for her work (fig. 51). A review of the installation put it like this: 'Her presentation was shocking and moving: the moment you entered the room you sensed a loaded atmosphere, without being able to describe it. Here was something going on, this was a living place.'[20]

>51

The Swiss designer Christoph Zellweger needs special places to exhibit his work; he is not interested in mere presentations in galleries, although he does not escape from doing this every now and then. These special places have to provide the right context for the story that Zellweger wants to transmit. He sees human beings in the light of evolution, but it is a creation that today can be changed with the help of human intervention. Zellweger is concerned with the body and with our notions of naturalness and authenticity.[21]

An intervention in the Swiss National Museum in Zurich (2004/05), in the room which held the archaeological collection, had been a most successful way to present his *Fremd-Körper* [Foreign Bodies] as 'fossils from the future'.[22] A question Christoph Zellweger likes to pose when speaking about his work is: What kind of objects will future archaeologists find when they excavate our remnants, and what will these findings tell them about our culture? These questions were again raised in the Swiss National Museum where Zellweger's uncanny objects – combinations of bones with shiny medical steel devices, engraved with dark numeric codes and symbols – were displayed as an extra layer amidst the archaeological artefacts and reconstructed graves. The uncanny character of these objects was due to their ambiguity, halfway between imaginary implantable devices and autonomous art objects.

In the summer of 2005, Zellweger presented his new pieces, *Ossarium Rosé*, in the Salo do Veado in the National Museum of Natural History in Lisbon (fig. 52). *Ossarium Rosé* consisted of bone-like manipulated ornaments covered with a layer of soft pink flocking. Zellweger used the only remaining antique showcase that survived the 1978 fire, which had destroyed the museum. The immense room was left bare apart from the showcase and some pieces hanging on the wall in an unpretentious way. The showcase was filled

>52

with more than one hundred manipulated bones – horrifying (because of the association with remains of living creatures), alienating (because they were manipulated) and seductive (because of their velvet, soft, sweet pinkish second skin) all at the same time. This 'tomb' under cold, functional light presented a semi-scientific Wunderkammer. In the wall some very delicate, almost invisible, silver *Breath Pieces* were installed – as if these thick stone walls that survived the great fire were in need of resuscitation. Clearly Zellweger, like Eichenberg and Peters, knows how to orchestrate our emotions and reflections through his installations. The story is there in the work, but the installation, the perfect scenery, enhances the experience and reflections of the viewer.

> 53

The so-called glasshouse at Galerie Marzee is an inspiring room. Ruudt Peters and the Munich Academy students created installations here, as well as the Belgium artist Hilde De Decker, beginning with her creation *Lustre for the Eyes* (1998, fig. 53). De Decker covered a 7 m high (glass) wall with a tapestry, made of Belgian tourist souvenir tapestries, which acted as a baroque background for a mantel piled with porcelain objects. The teacups, soup terrines, breadbaskets, elegant vases and other crockery were covered with silver lustre – an old, nearly forgotten process. By transforming the light, open room into an opulent cabinet, an adorned room, all eyes were on the ultimate domain of the housewife. By doing this, she was commenting on gender issues, just as she was already doing with her jewellery. The installation had a playful undertone, confusing the visitors. Waffles cast in silver were placed between the decorative objects, about which she told anyone who wanted to listen: 'Only the waffles are fake'. Only an heir to the Surrealist Belgian tradition of René Magritte and Marcel Broodthaers would stress the difference between a cast waffle, a real computer-aided woven tapestry and industrially fabricated crockery.

> 54

A year later (1999) she transformed the same room into a real glasshouse, filled with large pots and plants (fig. 54). The tomatoes, peppers and aubergines were grown by the artist herself and were furnished with silver rings. As described in the *Marzee Magazine*, De Decker had to study in order to be able to select and cultivate plants: 'Digging, weeding, raking, ventilating the greenhouse and – not to be forgotten – watering and feeding. Studying a mass of literature (how do you grow aubergines, what do you do about tomato disease, how do you tie up your plants, etc.), listening to good advice from organic market gardeners, gaining early successes (too early), overcoming unexpected setbacks (courgettes eaten by unknown creatures, melons refusing to be re-potted, tomatoes burnt by the sun, etc.), making vegetables grow exactly as you want them, getting to know their tricks and traits.'[23] The fruits grown in the rings were then harvested and preserved in bottles of acid so that people could actually buy the pot with fruit and the ring.

A jeweller who starts gardening as an open-ended art practice is a unique proof of crafts' self-sufficiency. Inspired by a newspaper article about a wedding ring that appeared twenty years after its loss with a potato grown inside it, De Decker embarked on a project that was far bigger than jewellery but never turned its back on it. The installation was a living objects environment, bearing the fruits of her work. Reality provoked imagination and resulted in ambiguous ornaments provided by nature, tickling our ideas about the natural and artificial.

Her next installation, *Silver Leaf-ed* (2000), was another impressive project. The effort was tremendous: selecting a massive oak tree in the forest and moving it to the gallery with the help of workmen, machines and a heavy truck, putting it up in the glasshouse and then exhibiting hundreds of fine silver oak leaves among the slowly growing carpet of fallen leaves on the floor. This muscular effort resulted in a very poetic installation about a dying tree, the silver leaves emphasising the beauty and magnificence of the tree.

In 2010, De Decker was appointed the third Hanauer Stadtgoldschmiedin [City Goldsmith of Hanau]. Since 2004, the city of Hanau, a German centre of jewellery, has appointed an international jewellery artist to be their city goldsmith who will live in the city for six weeks while working at the famous Staatliche Zeichenakademie Hanau, culminating in an exhibition in the Deutsches Goldschmiedehaus. Because De Decker sees an installation as the epitome of her work, she decided to start to develop her ideas from the exhibition space, the Silver room at the Goldschmiedehaus. The room, very large and filled with thirty-four huge, unmovable showcases, was subjected to regulations for safety and fire among others. The academy began a huge renovation, making it impossible to work there. But working in an improvised workshop was not too bad, she reported: 'Indeed a good "blank" start for developing new ideas just from scratch. And because the concept is always my starting point – instead of the technique or the material – I didn't miss the technical advantages of the academy.'[24]

> fig. 54

All restrictions in the exhibition room made her dream of a moveable museum. The title *On the Move* came first, starting a process of associations about moving, being there and not being there, presentation and representation. *On the Move* was about the essence of things: 'How far is an object reducible? What is the least we need to imagine something? And how much material do we need to give us the feeling of the real material? In short, what helps us to create an image in our head and what do we need at least to realise this?'[25] The huge showcases were partly veiled under white sheets – as if ready for moving – while different exhibited objects referred to jewellery and other everyday items without presenting the actual pieces of jewellery.

As an artist Hilde De Decker takes the position of the involved outsider, freely choosing different media (installation and book) to reflect on pivotal issues: gender, wealth and nature. De Decker's attitude is conceptual and allows her to cross the borders of jewellery whenever she likes. At the start of her career, when she made the nipple jewels *Pap* and *Distress*, the *Cookies Chain* and the necklace *Sois belle et tais toi* [Be Beautiful and Keep your Mouth Shut], her stories dealt with femininity and gender. Later, nature and ecology became the centre of her interest, while only recently she seems to have found a new fascination with jewellery as a phenomenon. She is political without using slogans. Instead she creates complete environments that absorb the visitor.[26]

Many jewellery artists today take jewels as part of an everyday world filled with objects that have a domestic and ritual character in the life of human beings. Manon van Kouswijk, Gésine Hackenberg, Rian de Jong, Mette Saabye, Pia Aleborg, Anna Rikkinen, and Nelli Tanner all like to show their jewellery in specially designed or adapted surroundings, emphasising their ritual and daily character. To stress this connection, Manon van

Kouswijk worked with oversized furniture, Rian de Jong with dressing tables and Anna Rikkinen and Nelli Tanner with furniture and photography.

Manon van Kouswijk combined chains and pearl strings with textile collars to be observed as daily objects, usable and functional like the ceramic plates, ceramic spoons, knives, tablecloths and mirrors that she also designed. In the installations for her *Horizon: Table* and *Re:place* exhibitions at Galerie Ra (2001 and 2003), all objects were in a transitional stage, with floating borders between usable and non-usable, decorative and functional, object and product, jewel and cloth, offering the viewer an idiosyncratic world of everyday objects (fig. 55). Gésine Hackenberg's interest in the ritual character of daily objects started with instruments for feeding: spoons. Ceramic or silver spoons were transformed into rings, pendants and other jewellery. She made an installation consisting of a large table with plates hollowed out in the wood and silver spoons with porcelain grips (like the handle of a cup). In 2004, Hackenberg made a collection based on antique urushi cups, pastry moulds and other kitchen utensils. Small circles were sawn from second-hand domestic china, which were then threaded onto a long chain – the different elements all having individual forms according to the curves of the cup or plate from which they were cut. The pastry moulds and other small aluminium kitchen moulds were treated with many layers of black or red urushi lacquer. Urushi is a complicated, age-old technique, dependent on a rare material and specific climate conditions, which was used in Japan to make cups but also to restore and beautify cracks in porcelain. Gésine Hackenberg learned the technique from a Japanese urushi master living in the Netherlands.[27] Her show *Somethings* at Galerie Ra (2004) provided the appropriate context to let the audience reflect about the preciousness of everyday things. The plinths were painted 'urushi-lacquer' red and one of the walls was painted with the contours of a cabinet, also in red. One part of the flat cabinet was turned into a three-dimensional showcase with a glass window left open (fig. 57), as a perfect surrounding for the refined pendants and brooches based on everyday cooking utensils.

Swedish Pia Aleborg is also interested in everyday objects and in the relationship between the private and the public. She has treated everyday objects, such as the mess of electrical cords and forgotten socks and T-shirts on the floor, as possibilities for jewellery. Fringes, socks and T-shirts were dipped in coloured rubber and hung as ornaments from gold-plated chains. A bunch of electrical cords was also transformed into a necklace. The collection was photographed on models in a domestic environment and published in a brochure *Apartfrom* (2005).[28] Again, scenography was used to transmit the message, bridging the gap between art jewellery and daily life.

The 'daily life' strategy became extremely popular at the Gerrit Rietveld Academy's jewellery department in Amsterdam, under the leadership of Iris Eichenberg. It culminated in the 2004 graduation show where three students, Taiwanese Mina Wu, French Amadine Meunier and Finnish Anna Rikkinen created their own explicit mini worlds. Mina Wu literally built a small room decorated with the aid of pencil, textile and thread (fig. 56). The wallpaper and power sockets were decorated with elegant flower patterns hand drawn in pencil. Different scattered objects, like a pair of socks or a dishcloth, were embroidered with silk in an 'Asian' style. Amadine Meunier graduated with an installation of small unidentified objects – although not wearable they could fit in your hand and were somehow identifiable as daily, usable, ritual and moveable. Anna Rikkinen showed her body-related jewellery for nose and eyes on a three-dimensional dressing table built from cardboard.

Some of the presentations described above gave the impression of nervous and cramped attempts to stress a connection between jewellery and life that seemed to originate

> 55
> 57
> 56

from a lack of jewellery awareness. As in the 1980s, when there was a short but fierce tendency in the Netherlands to overlook jewellery in favour of small autonomous objects, the same things happened again at the end of the twentieth and the beginning of the twenty-first century. This period saw an increase of objects that had a highly confusing ambiguous character. Some were not made with the intention to be worn at all. They had no connection to the body and were not made to move around and be confronted with other people – which are all important characteristics of jewellery. There were also objects created which were both autonomous and wearable, and at the same time crippled and meaningless because of their highly dualistic nature. At the same time, the installation began to change from a way to display one's jewellery into a work of art of its own, including a collection of objects. Therefore, the situation came under pressure. Instead of reconciling author jewellery and life, a new class of objects was generated that was impossible to determine or classify.

In the 1980s, the short-lived movement of trained jewellers making objects, such as Onno Boekhoudt, Iene Ambar, Adri Hattink and Gabriël Barlag, was inspired by investigations into different metals, like iron, lead, copper, brass and zinc. The most recent object revival was inspired by similar investigations into soft materials, such as textiles and paper. While the first objects were strongly related to the human scale, personal expression and a fetish-like attitude, the later objects related more to our domestic surroundings. Both short-lived tendencies can be interpreted in the light of an uncertainty about jewellery's use and destination, and the latter was certainly influenced by the new fashion of creating installations. Jewellery artists were struggling with the freedom that caused them to cross boundaries but left them and the public alone in confusion.

The increase in object making by jewellers, which took place not only in the Netherlands but also in Scandinavian countries, was noticed and questioned within the jewellery world. For some years Filippine de Haan, a Dutch artist who immigrated to the United States, offered an inspiring alternative for these confused jewellery objects. She herself made objects that were kind of weird and ambiguous, made of textile, silver and other combinations of flexible and solid materials. Some of these objects were wearable but most often they were not. De Haan's rather big and soft textile object *Branch with Five Brooches* alludes in a confusing way to wearing. It is a typical example of the kind of objects being made at that time (fig. 58).

> 58

In the United States, Filippine de Haan created a website, *hotel275*, that offered rooms for 'homeless jewellery objects'.[29] It was meant as a kind of shelter for undetermined objects and for ideas and photos – jewellery makers from all over the world could join the concept. Simple animations, designed by De Haan, invited the visitor to enter the site. The site was changed completely several times in the period between 2002 and 2006. The hotel was a rather worn and home-like place, where every visitor could enter the virtual reception, corridors, bathrooms and other rooms. The visitor was invited to look around carefully, looking for strange scattered objects that could be clicked on and enlarged. The intimacy of these odd stray things and jewellery scattered around on beds, chairs, washbasins or on the floor was increased by the idea of nosing around in a space that wasn't yours.

De Haan's website conquered the ultimate new space and offered a new context for jewellery that has infinite possibilities. Her project, which ended in 2006, showed that the Internet can offer a creative space for jewellery with unlimited possibilities. It offers an alternative exhibition space where interdisciplinary connections are made, which would be achieved with great difficulty in the traditional art and craft circuit. Unfortunately virtual projects are also finite.

Above, we have seen how jewellers have successfully used installation or events to transmit the story of their jewellery. For some it is almost a must, a matter of principle (for instance, for Ruudt Peters and Hilde De Decker). It can also be inherent to the way of working, such as French jeweller Frédéric Braham's performance *Inner Beauty*, where the public is invited to drink a specially made solution of gold, silver or copper from a specially designed spoon.[30] For others, it is an incidental way to present a special collection of jewellery. However over the last ten years, the focus on the presentation of jewellery has become more important than ever before, resulting not only in installations but also in small interventions that transform an 'ordinary' gallery space into an adapted context.

It took some time for jewellers to overcome their natural inclination to show their work in the safe environment of a gallery and the showcase, but today we can see more jewellers looking for alternatives. Of course there is no necessity to do so, and the average jeweller will be happy to show their work in a jewellery gallery. It is also questionable whether alternative 'non-showcase' ways of presenting jewellery really do lead to the broadening of the field as is sometimes suggested. What they do achieve, when done well, is creating a better understanding of the jewellery.

1   Donald J. Willcox, 1973. *Body Jewelry: International Perspectives*. Chicago: Regnery, p. 221.

2   In the Dutch Newspaper *Het Vrije Volk*, 10 Feb. 1974.

3   Allan Kaprow, 1993. 'The Legacy of Jackson Pollock (1958)', in Jeff Kelly (ed.), Allan Kaprow, 1993. *Essays on the Blurring of Art and Life*. Berkeley and Los Angeles/London: University of California Press, p. 7.

4   Leonor D'Orey, Emilia Ferreíra, Rui Santos, 2005. *Mais Perto/Closer*. Lisbon: Instituto Português de Museus, p. 109.

5   Ibid.

6   Martin Damus, 1973. *Funktionen der Bildenden Kunst im Spätkapitalismus*. Frankfurt/Main: Fischer, p. 44.

7   Stanley Brouwn is a rather mysterious figure in the Dutch art world. Born in 1935 in Paramaribo/Surinam, he refuses to give any further biographical information, interviews, photographs, written texts about himself or his work. In the 1960s and 1970s, he published several artist's books about movements and distances, taking himself as point of reference. In 1962 he started his famous series *This Way Brouwn* showing raw sketches from one point to another, made on request by passers-by with felt pen on paper. In 1971, he published a book under the same title, with drawings and texts by himself. König in Cologne published it in a limited edition of 500. He participated in exhibitions such as *documenta 7* in 1982. In 2005, the Van Abbemuseum in Eindhoven made a retrospective of his work, also showing new work especially made for the museum rooms.

8   Email from Otto Künzli, 3 Dec. 2008. This is how he remembers it, and it sounds authentic with respect to the political discourse in Amsterdam at that time.

9   The first one was installed permanently at the Städtische Galerie im Lenbachhaus in Munich, where it stayed for years. Later it was removed from the facade and is now in the museum's collection. The second red dot was installed on the facade of the Kelvingrove Art Gallery and Museum in Glasgow and the third one on the facade of RAM Galleri in Oslo – according to Otto Künzli both should or could still be there. The last one was installed temporarily on the facade of the Museum of Ancient Art in Lisbon.

10 Otto Künzli, 1991. *Das dritte Auge/The Third Eye/Het derde oog*. Amsterdam: Stedelijk Museum, p. 40.

11 Otto Künzli, interview with the author, Munich, 15 Mar. 2009.

12 Maribel Königer, 2008. 'A Class of its Own', in: Florian Hufnagl (ed.), 2008. *The Fat Booty of Madness*. Stuttgart: Arnoldsche, p. 48.

13 Ibid. p. 48.

14 Alexander Blank, Stefan Heuser, Christian Hoedl and Jiro Kamata, 2011. *Rebellen der Liebe*. Munich: Kulturreferat der Landeshauptstadt München (unpaginated).

15 Ruudt Peters taught and teaches at different schools, among them: Gerrit Rietveld Academy Amsterdam (1990–2000), Konstfack University of Arts and Crafts Stockholm (2004–09), Alchimia Contemporary Jewellery School Florence and Opere jewellery summer school.

16 While working as a jeweller, Ruudt Peters also started making sculptures again. These sculptures, which are all related to architectural projects, concentrate on the same themes as his jewellery. An impressive example is the wall sculpture created in 1997 for De Vinkhoek, a complex of renovated social housing apartments in the centre of Amsterdam. They are derived from the *Lapis* jewellery and based on the same alchemistic principle. The rocks – one rock under each window, three rows of twenty windows in total – made of differ-

ent metals (iron, brass, lead, tin, silver and gold, in this case gilded brass) are cast in moulds from a large
amethyst.

17 Ruudt Peters (ed.), 1997. *Lapis*. Amsterdam: Uitgeverij Voetnoot.

18 Liesbeth den Besten and Mònica Gaspar, 2007. 'The Afternoon Talk', in Mònica Gaspar (ed.), 2007. *Christoph Zellweger: Foreign Bodies*. Barcelona: Actar, p. 142.

19 The work of Iris Eichenberg is also discussed in Chapter VI.

20 Liesbeth den Besten, 1994. 'Eindexamens Rietveld Academie – ziel en zaligheid', in *Bijvoorbeeld*, vol. 26, no. 3, pp. 14–7 (translation by LdB).

21 Zellweger's corporeal work is discussed further in Chapter VI.

22 Mònica Gaspar (see note 19), p. 102.

23 Bart Geurts, 1999. 'For the Farmer and Market Gardener', in *Marzee Magazine*, no. 9, October, p. 5.

24 From an unpublished text by Hilde De Decker, *About being Stadtgoldschmiede*, dated August 2009.

25 The quotation is an adaptation from a Dutch text by Hilde De Decker about her exhibition *On the Move*; it is not published, or dated. The exhibition *On the Move* in the Goldschmiedehaus in Hanau was from 15 Apr.–6 June 2010.

26 The work of Hilde De Decker is also discussed in Chapter II.

27 Gésine Hackenberg does not pretend that she is a skilled urushi master now. The technique is far more complicated than she was able to learn. You could say that she uses the technique in a rather metaphorical way to emphasise the preciousness of everyday things.

28 The collection was exhibited at the cooperative Sintra in Gothenburg in a semi-domestic environment. See also: *www.piaaleborg.com*.

29 Although the full address of the website is still accessible, for many years now it has been in use for another purpose.

30 Exhibition *Cosmetic Attitude*, Galerie Biró, Munich, 10–14 May 2005. The performance was repeated in the Villa Bottini in Lucca on the occasion of the opening of the exhibition *Lucca Preziosa 2006: No Body Decoration*, 22 Sept.–22 Oct. 2006.

IV. Reading Jewellery

The wearer of a piece of jewellery can be a completely different person to the preferred wearer the maker of the piece had in mind. But when looking at jewellery pieces in a gallery or museum, one can often wonder if the maker was concerned at all with the wearer when the work was created.

Since the days of the New Jewelry, it is almost as if thinking about the wearer is a taboo. After all, the emancipation of contemporary jewellery proclaimed a new artistic self-awareness and a new positioning in the market, irrespective of clients, conventions, fashion or economics. The jeweller became an artist, acting with the assumed freedom of an artist. Finally, after some forty years of struggle, their work was recognised as a new 'species' called art jewellery or author jewellery. With this notion, a kind of jewellery is described that is not only there to adorn a person for the sake of the wearer's enjoyment or to show their wealth, but that wants to transmit meaning or content similar to the way that fine art does – with one difference: that it is worn by a human on the body.

Paul Derrez's jewellery is in a category of its own: affordable, democratic, wearable. In 1975, when Derrez started working as a jeweller, Dutch jewellery was all about formalism: geometry and Constructivist severity prevailed. Paul Derrez's attitude was rather loose, although his vocabulary did fit in with the formalist style of the day. His first silver rings and bracelets with replaceable coloured acrylic elements firmly placed him midway between the stern Minimalists and the playful Experimentalists who tried to gain a foothold in the Dutch jewellery scene. The design, made in 1975/76, is still selling today, and according to his own statement Derrez must have sold more than a thousand of these rings. The idea behind his jewellery at that time was that the person wearing it should become involved with it by being able to do something with it (for instance, to change the colour) or to play with it – a rather democratic way of thinking that answered the general political and social issues of the day and one which became rather popular in jewellery within a relatively short period of time.[1] Wearers are exactly what Paul Derrez is concerned with when designing jewellery. From 1976 onwards he regularly performed as a model for his own designs. In doing so he wanted to stress the corporeal aspect of jewellery (fig. 59).

> 59

Derrez's designs are characterised by simple, undecorated forms; acrylic, also suitable for making clear shapes, is applied as a contrasting element. In 1996, Derrez presented aluminium and acrylic jewellery, which had obvious erotic connotations. They were tool-like with pierced phalluses and crosses. The *Risky Business* collection interacted with social cultural phenomena, homosexuality, and youth cultures. Titles such as *Hurts so Good* and *Dick* (fig. 60) were shameless signs of a personal inclination. But how do you find a wearer for these erotic objects? And is it possible to wear this kind of jewellery without coming under the suspicion of being overtly sexual?

> 60

Experience showed that this jewellery was purchased and worn by both men and women. These ornaments do not get stuck in their subcultural origin and inspiration. One of the reasons must be the harmony between forms, material and content; the shiny white metal being the perfect transmitter of references to instrumental sex toys and play. There is no ambivalence, no hesitation, but there are wit and guts in each piece. For the wearer, even decent elderly ladies, these jewels work like signs. They show the person for who they are: not an overtly sexual person but someone with a special kind of humour and taste. The fact that this jewellery when worn is provocative even adds to its attraction for some buyers, especially for those who are used to wearing contemporary author jewellery and enjoy answering questions from complete strangers.

Author jewellery, whether it is erotic like Paul Derrez's, narrative or geometrical and abstract, can never be worn naively. It will always demand some understanding, involvement and commitment. When the maker of a piece of jewellery is an author, the work is loaded with a meaning that is neither commonplace nor middle-of-the-road. Even if the work in question is a completely abstract piece of jewellery it can still be confusing and confronting. Gijs Bakker likes to tell stories about the formative years of his career, when he and his wife Emmy van Leersum were acquainted with Constructivist fine artists who were at that time making sculptures, paintings and wall reliefs. Emmy and Gijs were trying to apply the same Constructivist principles in their jewellery, and in their view: 'It didn't make any difference to us if you did it on the canvas or on the body. But in our view it was much easier for our friends who did it on the canvas, than for us. Because people can easily be emotionally released from a work of art. It doesn't affect your personality like a jewel does, because you wear it on your body. Wearing a piece of jewellery of ours demands much more involvement from the wearer. We thought that what we were doing was much more difficult.'[2] Decades later, Melanie Bilenker, whose work will be discussed further on in this chapter, would say the same: '… I see jewellery as a confrontation by its very nature. If I wear a brooch on my body I am making a larger commitment to it than if I were to hang a painting in my home.'[3]

Dutch jewellery between 1967 and 1980 was Modernist and abstract. The object was an entity, autonomous, referring only to itself. There was the material, preferably aluminium or steel tubing, and there was an intervention in the material, a rationally reasoned incision or fold. No emotion was involved – at least this was purported. The carrier of expression (i.e. the line, the incision) was exactly the same as that what was expressed – at least this was their ideal. In reality, the makers knew from the outset that such a work of art acted like a sign when put on the body. At that time, they were not interpreted as neutral at all by the wearers and viewers; on the contrary, these ornaments were signs of a revolutionary attitude, symbols of good taste and for some years were favourites among the cultural avant-garde elite in Amsterdam.

Through the 'objectifying' of the jewel (the notion referring to the phenomenon that all focus is on the 'objecthood' of the jewel, its independency and autonomy), a new relationship with the wearer was established: you had to agree with the jewel. Under the influence of changing tendencies in the visual arts, the jewel as art object could gradually become a medium for storytelling. Today the relationship with the wearer is less directive than was the case around 1970. In 2011, it is not about 'having to agree with it' but rather 'having to connect with it'. As in contemporary fine art (e.g. painting, installation and video art), storytelling in jewellery is a broad and complex process of layering which needs 'close reading'. Furthermore, meaning and content are only partially controlled by the maker and at the same time significantly influenced, imposed and constructed by the wearer. In this chapter I will try to unravel the relationship between the maker, the wearer and the viewer.

In the standard communication model, we distinguish between the *addresser*, the *message* and the *addressee*, or as some theorists put it the *speaker*, the *message* and the *hearer*. In fine art, this model can instead be the *maker*, the *message* and the *viewer*. If we consider jewellery, there is a fourth element, which complicates the relationship between the *addresser* and the *addressee*, the *maker* and the *viewer*; this element is the *wearer* because the viewer and the wearer are not necessarily one and the same person. The moment the wearer wears an ornament, they become an intermediary between the maker, the piece and the viewer.

Where should we position this fourth element in the series? Perhaps the best position is between the maker and the wearer, but it can also be positioned between the wearer and the viewer because the wearer is often the 'trigger' to a piece. This observation brings us to the core of the discussion: jewellery is quite different from fine art as it is mobile, wearable and therefore semantically changing according to the context and conditions under which it is viewed. Whereas a painting is dependent on how, in which context and where it is exposed, a piece of jewellery has to deal with even more circumstantial influences, not only with the showcase, the juxtaposition, the light and the room but also with the wearer, the personality of the wearer, the clothing and the situation where the wearer is moving, sitting or standing. The wearer is another kind of display, a moving display, a living display, a display that can answer and look back and also a briefly experienced display because the viewer normally cannot gaze at a brooch that is pinned on a woman's breast or a necklace that is hanging in a woman's décolletage. Highly reflective jewellery in particular, for instance, Elizabeth Callinicos's *Mirror Brooches* (2009) or Dinie Besems's *Small, Medium, Large* shiny 24 ct gilded silver pendant (2004), carries an ambiguous message: it is attractive and repulsive. Who dares to look properly at a jewel that reflects one's own face? A jewel like that is frightening. And who can perceive all elements in a complicated composition when the wearer or the viewer passes by? The process of viewing is very short; the narrative is often beyond reach. It is the wearer, the owner, who has the advantage of enjoying the jewellery under the most perfect circumstances, that is, in their hands. This intimate relationship between object and subject is unique in the visual arts.

In her book *Looking in: The Art of Viewing*, co-founder of the Amsterdam School for Cultural Analysis at the University of Amsterdam Mieke Bal argues that 'viewers bring their own cultural baggage to images', meaning 'there can be no such thing as a fixed, predetermined, or unified meaning'.[4] Bal supports her theory by describing and interpreting allegorical paintings of Vermeer and Rembrandt. She talks about the nature of signs having many meanings because, in allegory, the mythical story can refer to something other than itself. Yet she concludes that the production of meaning is not a supplement to the work of art but that it is something already inscribed in the semiotic status of the work.

The question is now how a jewel, that as an object seems to have a foremost decorative function and resists coherent figurative readings, can tell stories? And what kinds of stories are being told in jewellery? Up until now, not much attention has been paid to the narrative in jewellery, which is not unusual, and we may even wonder if a thing called 'narrative jewellery' actually exists and how we can find out what narrative as a genre in jewellery means. Narrative in literature or texts is an idea we can get hold of, but how can we use it in a broader sense? Mieke Bal points out that you can employ visual images as other, non-linguistic, sign systems. She defines a text as a 'finite ensemble of signs'; there is a beginning and an end, a first word and a last word. This can also be applied to visual art, film or painting, she argues: it is the first and last image of a film, the frame of a painting.[5]

In her view, an artefact can also be observed as a text. Although she is not quite clear about this, it is an intriguing and important assumption. While it is clear that stories are told in jewellery by the use of figurative elements, it is also clear that the manner in which these are presented is completely different than in a text. Within the small framework of a jewel, the picture can hardly be viewed as a story because mostly there is no action or event, no sequence of time, no hero, no plot and there are no actors (maybe sometimes just one). In jewellery, as in fine art, images and titles can evoke stories in the mind of the viewer – whether we call this narrative jewellery remains a point of discussion. In my view, the fact that a jeweller consciously uses figurative images and a title points to the fact that they want to tell us something – whether a story or something else – or wants to entice us to find our own meaning and make up our own stories. Which leads to the question of how to define a story. Is a story the same as meaning? And whose story is it actually that is told when analysing a jewel? We should be aware that what we see is a subjective view, an interpretation. Different viewers read images, text and events in different ways, and it is through this agency that jewellery can gain narrative and associative meaning that goes beyond art history's usual search for facts of origin, materiality and iconography. The content of a piece of art or jewellery (whether constructed by the maker or the viewer) therefore might be called the story of the work in question. I will try to explain this with the help of some examples, inspired by the theory of narratology.[6] My main question is: What does the piece say to me and in general? And how is this content transmitted to the wearer and the viewer?

GROSS-SCHNEEN

> 61

If we focus on the brooch *Gross-Schneen* (2004, fig. 61) by Iris Eichenberg we cannot call it figurative, although there are some recognisable elements in this abstract composition, a collage of various materials. At a first glance the structure looks quite undefined; the outline is sharp though at the same time blurred by threads and other protruding elements. Looking closer, we can recognise two architectural structures: a house with a gabled roof on the right side as the underlying silver structure and another structure in the front as the top layer. This house looks like a traditional German countryside *Fachwerk* [timbered] house. In between these layers is another, which is the most puzzling: stretched out we see black paper filled with small white buttons sewn together in twelve rows of six and an imprint which tells us in German that these textile-covered buttons are durable and are from 'Beste Marke', which translates as best brand. In contrast to the other layers, this one is not representing something but is instead presenting objects. Objects from the past, this much is clear. And as Mieke Bal pointed out in her book about Louise Bourgeois's *Spider*, the use of objects from one's own past can evoke the individual's life in the past. In other words, this layer is the key element in the brooch. The functional distinction between the constructed houses beneath and on top of this layer is clear: they contain, protect and emphasise. The function of protection is even enforced by the use of small pieces of grey canvas within the same layer – a material that is used to cover cargo when being moved or stored outside. The three layers are sewn together with black cotton thread, and this stitching carries through independently in the underlying silver ground.

In this brooch, the use of material creates meaning, which is also especially true of the hand-sewn black threads that hold everything together, the construction of the assemblage and the different compositional elements. The title of this brooch directly alludes to either the name of a house or the name of a village, also telling us that this piece of jewellery is about a memory of the maker, not necessarily of a certain event in the past (a story) but to an atmosphere, an impression of time and place. So although nothing actually happens in this brooch, the viewer can construct its story, or better, make up his own story.

From the above description arises an atmosphere of homeliness. Here the imagination of the viewer can take over. Mieke Bal points out that there is a similarity between found objects and memories: 'Memories are found objects that we routinely integrate into narrative frames derived from the cultural stock available to us'.[7] On a psychoanalytical level, the house can represent mixed feelings: family-life, home as a place of repression and restriction for women. When looking at this brooch you can imagine grey-haired women doing their never-ending needlework, the buttons, the seams, the holes and the hems. In this sense the brooch becomes an emblematic representation of family-life: rest and warmth on the one hand, suffocating hopelessness and unsatisfied ambition on the other.

Iris Eichenberg, the maker of this brooch, was born in Germany in 1965 and lived and worked in the Netherlands from 1990 until 2007 when she moved to America to become the head of the Metalsmithing Department at Cranbrook Academy of Art in Bloomfield Hills, Michigan. When she made the brooch as part of her collection entitled *Heimat* (2004) she was still living in the Netherlands. *Heimat* is a German word loaded with emotion and referring to notions of native country, home and native region. It is also a word with a rather negative connotation because of its (mis)use by the Nazis. In Eichenberg's work various connotations can be found. In other brooches of the *Heimat* collection, the theme of stitching and women's needlework returns. In a few other brooches she depicts the subject of Germany, portraying the outline of the map of Germany as the profile of a girl. *Deutschland ist ein Mädchen* [Germany Is a Girl] she calls them (fig. 62).

> 62

As we have learnt, seeing is a process and implies knowing. In Bal's view there is 'no sequential narrative, no development, no life story. But the eye is compelled to travel even if it chooses its own itinerary, and thus time unfolds in the act of viewing.'[8] Not only time but also the story unfolds in the act of viewing. This kind of viewing takes place when analysing a brooch such as *Gross-Schneen*, deducing every layer and every element in the image in order to construct a story. However, the fact that the representation is also a brooch makes the viewing complicated. How can a viewer who sees someone wearing such a brooch possibly understand what it means at a glance? Much of its narrative will stay hidden from the eye of the beholder. And this is what I would like to call 'the ensnaring ambiguity' of contemporary author jewellery, the reason for a lot of misunderstanding and contempt. There is still a wide gap between the intended and attached meaning of a piece and its presumed decorative function.

POINT OF VIEW

Manfred Bischoff prefers figuration, applied first and foremost in brooches and occasionally rings. However, his brooches are not conceived as sculptural three-dimensional objects. A piece of jewellery always comes with a drawing or a collage with a hand-written text, created in strong aesthetic coherence; sometimes the jewel is pinned through the drawing. Titles form an integral part of his work. The materials he prefers – paper, charcoal and paint, fine gold and coral, the gold always vibrantly yellow, the coral pinkish – have their own semantics: gold referencing the divine and universal, coral referencing the human. Bischoff uses gold to represent bodies, animals and heads, while the coral is used

1   Stefan Heuser, necklaces *Das Hüftgold Projekt* (The Haunch Gold Project), 2008, human fat, gold, various dimensions.   ///   2   Emmy van Leersum, bracelet *Folded Circle*, 1968, stainless steel. SM's – Stedelijk Museum 's-Hertogenbosch.   ///   3   Tone Vigeland, neckpiece, 1990, silver, inner Ø 14 cm, outer Ø 31.5 cm. The Helen Williams Drutt English Collection, Philadelphia.

4

5

6

4 Warwick Freeman, brooches *Fern, Fish, Feather, Rose*, 1987, 925 silver, stainless steel, various dimensions. The Auckland Museum.   ///   **5** Warwick Freeman, brooch *Green Face*, 1998, greenstone (nephrite), resin, 925 silver, Ø 4 cm. Te Papa Tongarewa Museum of New Zealand, Wellington.   ///   **6** Mette Saabye, *The Brooch Collection: Guldbroche* (Golden Brooch), 2008, 24 ct gold leaf, metal, plastic, 8 × 8 × 0.5 cm.

7 Noon Passama, *Extra Button (Edition 2011)*, 2011, electroformed copper, silver and gold plating, car paint, acrylic, readymade button pin, various dimensions.

8

9

10

8 Philip Sajet, ring *Coupé en Deux*, 2006, glass, gold, enamel, 3.5 × 2.5 × 2 cm. Private collection. /// **9** Philip Sajet, ring *Dubbel Diamant* (Double Diamond), 2005, gold, yellow quartz, rose quartz, 3.5 × 2.5 × 2 cm. Private collection, Vienna. /// **10** Atelier Ted Noten, rings *Haunted by 36 Women, Avondvlinder (Nightbird)*, 2009, black titanium, 18 ct gold, ca 2.7 × 3.5 × 0.8 cm.

11   Kim Buck, inflatable *Guldarmbånd* (Golden Bracelet), 2003, metallic plastic foil, 14 × 14 × 3.5 cm (inflated).
/// 12   Kim Buck, cufflinks *Floral Shade*, for Georg Jensen Company, 2003, silver. /// 13   Gijs Bakker, brooch
Cool Green, series: *REAL*, 2004, white gold 585, peridot, tourmaline, glass, metal, 3 × 4 × 2 cm.

14

15

16

14 Lisa Walker, necklace, 2008, plastic, wool, 48 × 20 cm. Private collection. /// **15** Mia Maljojoki, necklace *Explosive: Frozen Fireworks*, 2010, plaster, pigment, paint, strap, gold, pearl, 7 × 40 × 8 cm. /// **16** Felieke van der Leest, brooch *Super Freak Zebra*, 2007, textile, plastic animal, gold, glass beads, cubic zirconia, 15 × 6 × 3 cm.

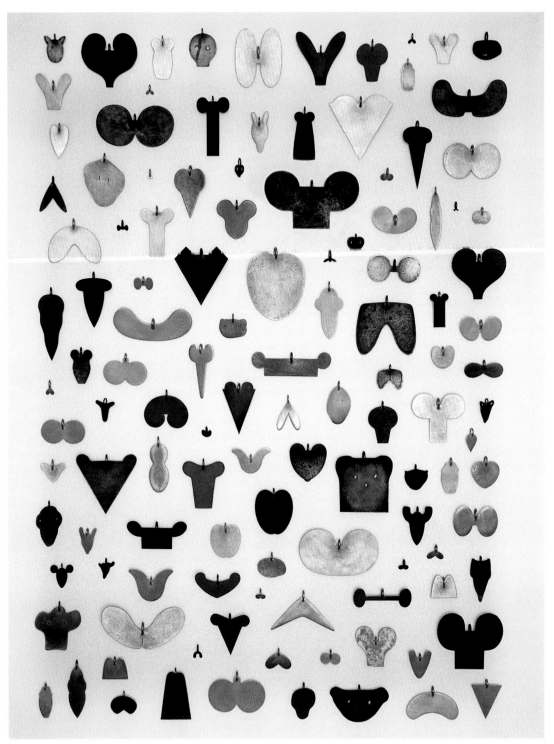

17   Otto Künzli, pendants *Cozticteocuitlatl*, 1995–1998, gold, silver, various dimensions.

18

19

20

18 Liv Blåvarp, necklace *Sundance*, 2010, amarello, peroba rosa, amboina, whale tooth, Ø 25 cm. /// **19** Sari Liimatta, necklace *Hopeless*, 2007, glass beads, pins, thread (polyamide), plastic toy, 106 x 20 x 8 cm. /// **20** Mirjam Hiller, brooch *Syspera*, 2011, stainless steel, powder-coated, 14 × 13 × 5 cm.

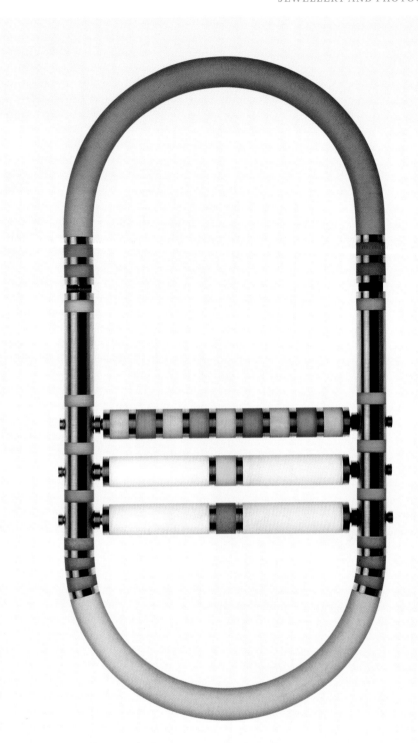

21

21   David Watkins, *Hinged Loop Neckpiece with Three Bars*, 1974, acrylic, sterling silver, 26.7 × 13.3 × 1.3 cm. The Museum of Fine Arts Houston; Helen Williams Drutt Collection, gift of the Caroline Wiess Law Foundation.

22

23

22   Annelies Štrba, photograph *Sonja mit Hirnsäge*, 1986, vintage print, gelatin silver print on Baryta paper, Model: Sonja Schobinger. Bernhard Schobinger, necklace *Hirnsäge*, 1986, steel, orange paint, chromium steel wire. Danner-Stiftung, Die Neue Sammlung – The International Design Museum Munich. /// 23   Ruudt Peters, *Symboolarmband, Canelure* (Symbol Bracelet, Cannelure), 1986, gold-plated brass, ca 11 × 6 × 0.3 cm. Model: Liesbeth den Besten. Photo: Michel Szulc-Krzyzanowski.

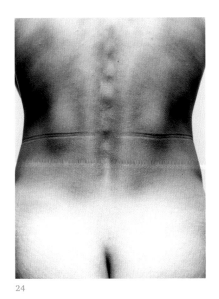

24

25

26

24 Gijs Bakker, *Schaduwsieraad* (Shadow Jewellery), 1973. Photo: Ton Baadenhuysen. /// 25 Gijs Bakker, bracelet *Schaduwsieraad* (Shadow Jewellery), 1973, yellow gold, Ø 7.7 × 0.05 cm, limited numbered edition (3). /// 26 Susanna Heron, *Light Projection*, 1979, photographic bromide print. By David Ward and Susanna Heron, copyright 1979. All rights reserved DACS.

27

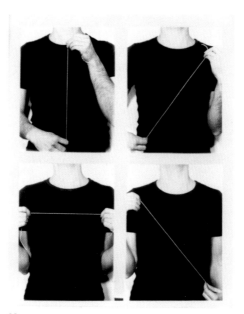

28

27 Robert Smit, Polaroid project *Everyday Adornment*, 1975, 70 Polaroid photos. The Stedelijk Museum, Amsterdam. /// **28** Otto Künzli, *Automatenphotos*, 1976, photographs, 12.5 × 9.4 cm. Collection of the artist.

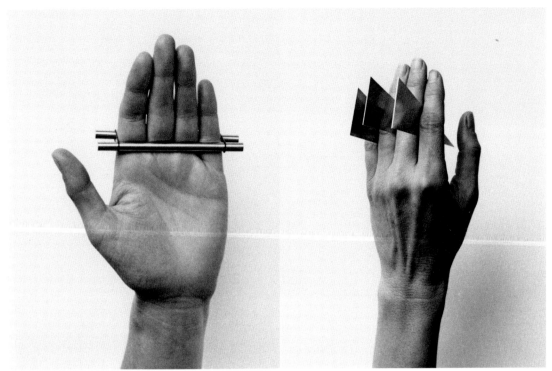

29 a   29 b

30

29 a, b Otto Künzli, *Arbeit für die Hand* (Work for the Hand), 1979–1980, pieces: stainless steel, rubber, photographs: 12.5 × 9.4 cm. Pieces: The Asenbaum Collection, Vienna, photographs: The Stedelijk Museum, Amsterdam (part of a series of 12). /// **30** Otto Künzli, brooch *Centifolia*, 1983, wallpaper, hard foam, 13 × 8.8 × 6 cm.

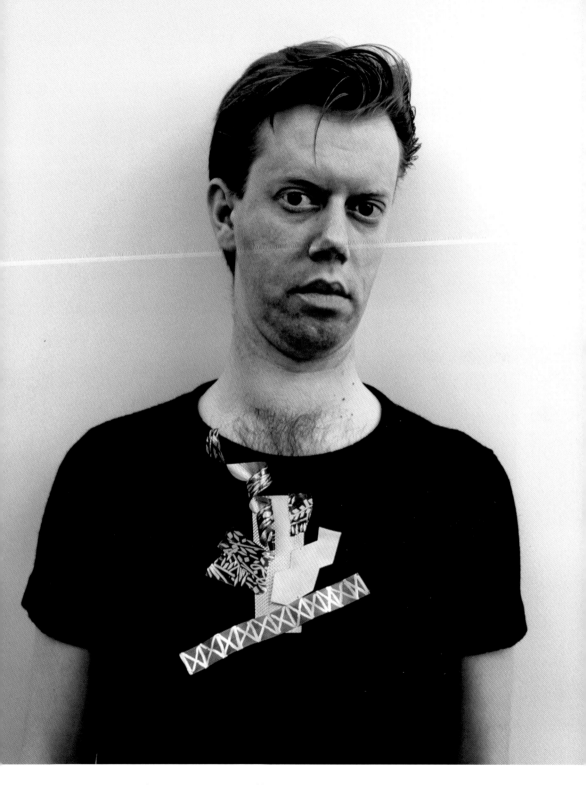

31   Otto Künzli, *Catoptric Ring*, 1988, gold, mirror.

32   Robert Smit, brooch, 1985, gold, 20 × 17 cm. SM's – Stedelijk Museum 's-Hertogenbosch.

33

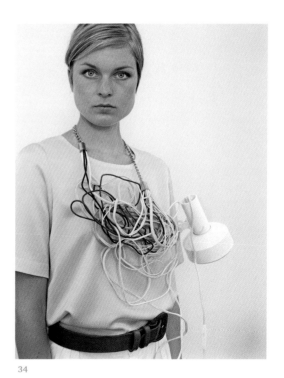

34

35

33   Hilde De Decker, *Eva's Kussen: Washand* (Eve's Cushion: Washcloth), 1995, fine silver thread, textile, 15 × 12 × 0.5 cm. Photo: Kari Decock.   ///   34   Pia Aleborg, necklace, series: *Apartfrom*, 2005, electric cord, gold plated brass, Ø 25 cm. Photo: Michael Grenmarker.   ///   35   Octavia Cook, brooch *Off with Her Head,* 2010, acrylic, 925 silver, 6.5 × 9 × 0.6 cm. Studio La Gonda, *Off with Her Head Brooch Portrait*, 2010, Fuji Flex print on diabond, 59 × 40 × 0.6 cm.

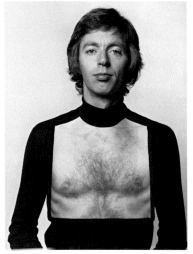

36

37

36 Gijs Bakker, bib *Slab (Bib)*, 1976, linen, cotton, 33 × 32 cm. /// 37 Gijs Bakker, brooch *Waterman*, 1990, white gold, diamonds, PVC, photograph, 15 × 9 cm.

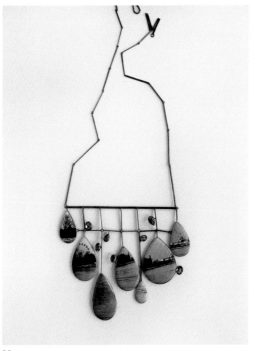

38

39

40

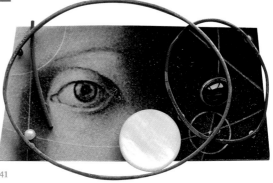

41

38 Bettina Speckner, necklace *Os Argonautas* (The Argonauts), 2010, enamelled photograph, silver, amethyst, ca 13 × 11 cm (lower part). /// **39** Bettina Speckner, brooch, 2003, ferrotype, 925 silver, raw split diamonds, 8.5 × 6 × 0.5 cm. /// **40** Suska Mackert, brooches *Augen* (Eyes), ongoing project since 2005, newspaper, cardboard, metal, Ø 1.8 –3.5 cm. /// **41** Ramón Puig Cuyàs, brooch *Nº1227,* series: *Utopos "Aspice me"* ('Look At Me'), 2008, 925 silver, plastic, photo on paper with epoxy resin, oxidised nickel, silver, onyx, pearl, mother of pearl, painted acrylic, 7 × 5.5 × 1 cm.

42

43

44

42 Gijs Bakker and Emmy van Leersum, *Kledingsuggesties* (Clothing Suggestions), 1970, knitted polyester, nylon. Manufacturer: Tiny Leeuwenkamp. /// **43** Gijs Bakker and Emmy van Leersum, sketch for *Kledingsuggesties* (Clothing Suggestions), 1970. /// **44** Otto Künzli, photo *Das Schweizer Gold – Die Deutsche Mark* (The Swiss Gold – The Deutschmark), 1983, brooch: paper wrapping from Swiss chocolate; necklace: 200 German one-mark pieces (1.2 kg), 24 × 8.5 × 4.3 cm (brooch). Collection of the artist.

45

46

47

45 Exhibition display *Des Wahnsinns fette Beute (The Fat Booty of Madness)*, Die Neue Sammlung – The International Design Museum Munich, Pinakothek der Moderne, Munich, 2008. Design: Department of jewellery, Academy of Fine Arts, Munich, Prof. Otto Künzli, and Die Neue Sammlung Munich, Prof. Dr. Florian Hufnagl. /// **46** Rebellen der Liebe, exhibition *Attacke die Waldfee*, Galerie Wittenbrink FUENFHOEFE, Munich, March 2008 (neckpieces by Christian Hoedl). /// **47** Rebellen der Liebe (Alexander Blank, Stefan Heuser, Christian Hoedl, Jiro Kamata), invitation card for the exhibition *Attacke die Waldfee*, 2008.

48

49

50

48 Ruudt Peters, installation *Passio*, Galerie Marzee, Nijmegen, 1992, cotton, steel, jewellery. /// **49** Ruudt Peters, installation *Ouroboros*, Galerie Marzee, Nijmegen, 1994, used wooden ladders. /// **50** Ruudt Peters, installation *Lapis*, Galerie Spektrum, Munich, 1996, cotton, steel, lab coats, jewellery.

51

52 a

52 b

51   Iris Eichenberg, body objects *Wollen Harten (Woollen Hearts)*, 1994, wool, various dimensions. Private collection.   ///   **52 a, b**   Christoph Zellweger, installation *Ossarium Rosé*, the National Museum of Natural History, Lisbon, 2005.

53

54 a

54 b

53 Hilde De Decker, installation *Luster voor het oog* (Lustre for the Eyes), 1998, silver-lustred ceramic objects, tapestries, 700 × 800 × 60 cm. /// **54 a, b** Hilde De Decker, growing exhibition *Voor boer en tuinder* (For the Farmer and Market Gardener), Galerie Marzee, Nijmegen, August–October 1999.

55

56

57

55 Manon van Kouswijk, exhibition display *Horizontafel* (Horizon table), Galerie Verzameld Werk, Ghent, 2001, wood, paint, cotton, 175 × 220 × 220 cm. /// 56 Mina Wu, graduation show, Gerrit Rietveld Academy, Amsterdam, 2004, used materials, wood, paint, ball point drawings, textile, embroidery, paper. /// 57 Gésine Hackenberg, exhibition display *Somethings*, Galerie Ra, Amsterdam, November 2004, oak wood, glass, wall paint, wall cabinet: ca 200 × 300 cm.

58 Filippine de Haan, object *Branch with Five Brooches*, 2001, silver, textile, wool, ca 2.5 × 8 cm. Private collection.

59

60

59 Paul Derrez, pendant *Face*, 1994, aluminium, resin, rubber, 7 × 6 × 2.5 cm. Collection Paul Derrez and Willem Hoogstede, Amsterdam. Model: Paul Derrez.   ///   **60** Paul Derrez, pendant *Dick*, 1994, aluminium and rubber, 10 × 5 × 2.5 cm. Collection Paul Derrez and Willem Hoogstede, Amsterdam. Model: Paul Derrez.

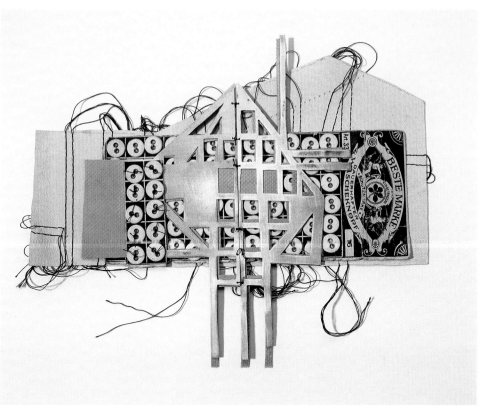

61

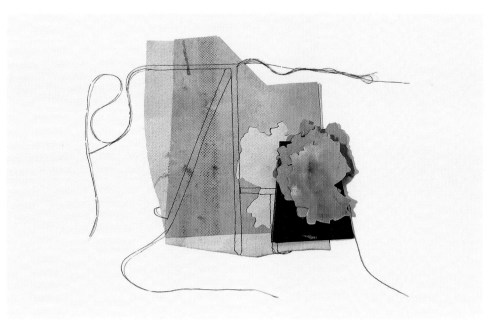

62

61   Iris Eichenberg, brooch *Gross-Schneen*, 2004, 925 silver, leather, canvas, buttons, paper, h. 14 cm. The Stedelijk Museum, Amsterdam.   ///   **62**   Iris Eichenberg, brooch *Deutschland ist ein Mädchen* (Germany Is a Girl), 2004, 925 silver, leather, canvas, hardboard, h. 17 cm.

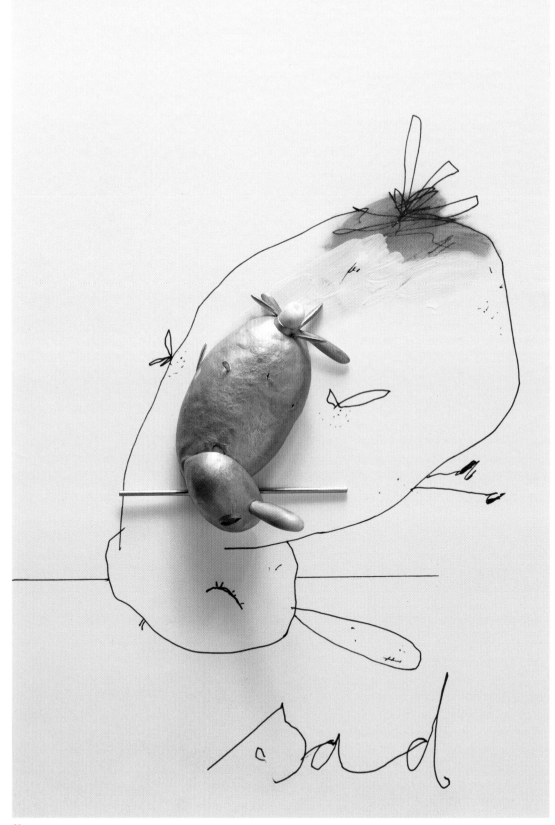

64

65

66

63 Manfred Bischoff, brooch *Sad*, 2005, gold 920, coral, 10.44 × 8.24 cm; drawing: paper, ink, ca 29.4 × 20.8 cm. Schmuckmuseum Pforzheim. /// **64** Manfred Bischoff, brooch *Esel der sich selbst trägt*, 2005, gold 920, 11 × 9 × 3 cm; drawing: paper, ink, 29.25 × 21.6 cm. Brooch: The Helen Williams Drutt English Collection, Philadelphia. /// **65** Bruce Metcalf, two brooches on stand *Catcher for a Young Icarus*, 1994, 925 silver, copper, 14 ct yellow gold, Micarta, birch, pine, basswood, aluminium, brass, 19.05 × 20.32 × 5.7 cm. Private collection. /// **66** Bruce Metcalf, brooch *Love Grown Bitter*, 1993, sterling silver, wood, paint, steel pin, polyester resin, 9.53 × 10.46 cm.

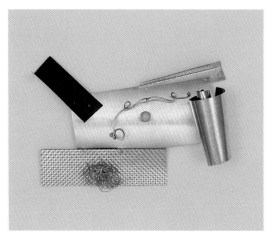

67

68

67   Robert Smit, brooch *Bello als Stilleven* (Bello as a Still Life), 1992, 18 ct, 21 ct and 24 ct gold, 1 × 7.5 cm.
///   68   Robert Smit, necklace *Cwrt from Bryn-dafydd*, 2004, gold, paint, 13.5 × 12 × 1 cm. The Helen Williams Drutt English Collection, Philadelphia.

69 Melanie Bilenker, brooch *Still in Bed*, 2004, gold, silver, ivory, resin, hair, 2.1 × 2.9 × 1 cm. /// 70 Melanie Bilenker, brooch *Undress*, 2007, 18 ct gold, silver, ebony, pigment, hair, 4.2 × 4.7 × 1 cm. /// 71 Esther Knobel, brooch, series: *The Mind in the Hand*, 2007, 925 silver, iron thread, 7 × 4 × 0.7 cm. /// 72 Esther Knobel, kit *My Grandmother Is Knitting Too*, 2002, bear, pliers, brooches, thimble, enamel on copper, various dimensions. The Israel Museum, Jerusalem.

73

74

73   Lucy Sarneel, neckpiece *Zeebauw*, 2002, 925 silver, thread, textile, zinc, epoxy filled shells, 35 × 18.5 × 2 cm.
///   74   Lucy Sarneel, brooch *Pronkstuk* (Showpiece) with saucer, 2003, porcelain, red gold, silver, brooch:
12 × 8 × 4.4 cm, saucer: Ø 15 cm. Private collection.

for skulls, vaginas, anuses and navels. There are human beings and animals functioning as heroes in his compositions, while human artefacts such as antennas, walls, ships and instruments form part of other jewels. Moreover, many birds and rather undefined mammals, mostly just their head, plus numerous beaks, ears and tails occupy Bischoff's vocabulary. You don't need to be a psychiatrist to understand that some of these are visions from dreams. You could say that this jewellery is therefore typically narrative, but it seems to me that the attribution narrative is too easy and goes beyond what Bischoff wants us to feel or experience. A narrative or a story adapts to a certain logic and structure, whereas Bischoff's work withdraws from any logic. His work is full of symbols; a beak, antenna or skull is not just a mere representation. Bischoff's work nestles in the subconscious, and he is unwilling to give us any clues about his themes, inspirations or sources – although some have been unveiled in rather general terms, such as mythology or art. Although words play such an important part in his work – rousing a certain atmosphere (*Sad*, fig. 63), stimulating your imagination (*I Want a Sailor Who Comes and Goes*), mystifying (*Nichts als meer*) or expressing humour (*pleh! pleh!*) – Bischoff is notorious for not wanting to talk about his work. Perhaps he feels that common language is too sleek or too undefined: 'Real talking doesn't exist very much', he says in an interview, 'most talk is just conversation, which I don't really like. You can't force real talk – and sometimes it can be overwhelming. Real talking is when *language* comes. It's not guided by you. You might feel it, but only later do you recognize that it was there.'[9]

> 63

Language, image and material are in equilibrium and only the wearer of a Manfred Bischoff jewel knows the key to this secret complicity. The viewer will have a different impression of the piece. He can, for instance, be struck by an apparently crystal-clear image of two gold animals, a bird sitting on the head of another animal (a donkey perhaps? Or a dog?). Looking closer they will notice that the bird has turned its back towards the other animal, whose coral eye stares at the pronounced coral genitals of the bird. The bird's head is turned towards the other animal's beak. For a viewer it is a funny scene, a scene in which some action is suggested by the way the bird is sitting, bending his elongated neck backwards. Only the wearer knows the image that belongs to it, consisting of a reproduction of a classic sculpture of a naked human figure bending face down and turned backwards. The photograph focuses on the heavy bare bottom. The text 'point of view' is written in such a way that it can also be read as 'view point'. Viewing is an important subject for Bischoff, as is also shown in the brooch *Esel der sich selbst trägt* (fig. 64) where two heads on each side of a body look at each other with amazement and anger.

> 64

In an interview, Manfred Bischoff points out the fact that the title and recognisable images are like a key to a deeper understanding: '… I think you must give people a horizon to find the way in, otherwise they will say that you have not addressed them immediately enough. If I make a bird, they can immediately identify with it by calling it "a bird". They accept it as their own object, which they themselves have seen. That's what I mean when I say "surface", or "horizon": a starting place for people.'[10] Bischoff leaves it to the 'reader' of his jewellery to find out what it means. A brooch by Manfred Bischoff can also leave you dumbfounded, feeling illiterate in the face of his intellectual and artistic versatility. It is as if these brooches and rings withdraw from intellectual reading. Words seem trivial and too restricted to interpret these forged mysteries. Their story is manifold, elusive and associative and resides beyond the reach of singular interpretation and description. Manfred Bischoff once put it like this: 'No matter how important the image or text, the synthesis of those elements always leads back to nothing.'[11] In other words: look, enjoy, reflect but don't expect any decisive answers.

With this in mind, it is interesting that Manfred Bischoff prefers the form of the brooch above the other jewellery typologies. Brooches and necklaces are the most confronting pieces of jewellery, because they are worn on the chest, mostly in the centre, and directly address the outside world. A necklace bears all kinds of recollections and references to symbols of power, not only in ethnological jewellery but also in Western European jewellery (chains of honour, mayoral chains, etc.), whereas the brooch offers a rather neutral form to work with. Apart from some flexible restrictions about size and weight there are no limitations, the pin on the rear side giving the wearer the possibility to fasten it wherever they want. A pendant on the other hand always needs a necklace, a construction to hang it from, which one way or another affects the neutrality and entity of the piece. However, Bischoff also seems to prefer the brooch simply because it is such a remarkable statement on the body. As he pointed out, he loves to see people wearing his jewellery and calls them 'courageous'. The artist trusts the wearer as an ambassador of his jewellery.

LOVE GROWN BITTER

The American jeweller Bruce Metcalf applies a different figurative imagery than the Europeans discussed above. His jewels present cartoon-like characters with big heads, small bodies and enormous eyes. The action that takes place is small but nevertheless evokes stories, memories and associations. Metcalf exclusively makes brooches, which sometimes present architectural structures as the setting of a scene. These settings mostly consist of vaults or arches and classical tympana. A landscape background or curtains intensify the impression of looking at scenery. His brooches remind one of the miniature worlds we used to play with as children: doll's houses, snow globes, train sets and peepshows. Yet Metcalf's worlds are not sweet at all: the bodies and limbs of his cast silver figures are distorted in agony or perforated with holes. These characters are suffering, they are losers trying to get hold of their own little world.

> 65
In *Catcher for a Young Icarus* (fig. 65), a running character tries to catch a falling creature with the aid of a hand net, and in an untitled figure pin (1997) a primrose-headed figure with its right-hand fingers substituted for the leaves of a Canadian burnet is holding a pair of scissors in its other hand ready for cutting. Metcalf, himself a writer, thinker and critic in the field of crafts and jewellery, never makes a secret of his sources of inspiration or of the meaning of his jewellery. His themes are inspired by his own life, his concern
> 66
about how we see the other and by society. *Love Grown Bitter* (fig. 66), a brooch depicting a creature with a cactus for a head sitting stubbornly on the ground, arms and legs crossed and looking at a soft little worm-like form which is pierced with a nail, is indeed about Metcalf's own failed love affairs. The brooch also has a humorous quality and it comes as no surprise to learn that, as a student, Metcalf was a cartoonist for the university's journal.

His direct vocabulary has the potency to attract the attention of passers-by, which is exactly what Metcalf hopes for: 'But what can jewelry do? It seems powerless in the face of world events. In fact, all art is in much the same position. It's doubtful that jewelry is an effective agent of change. It may, however, get out in the world and make a few people think.'[12]

CRWT

One artist who is always conscious about the negotiation between maker and wearer is the Dutch jeweller Robert Smit. In an unpublished essay, Smit writes about the fact that the opinions of the maker, the wearer and the viewer of a piece of jewellery can be sharply divided. In his view, the influence of the wearer is bigger than most people think: 'A worn jewel presents a complete image but it also supposes, in fact, a new meaning.'[13] Smit thinks this is telling about the extent of (in)dependency of the jewel. In fact, his essay is a kind of plea for the liberation of the jewel, or more precisely, for 'the imagination it provokes and brings about'. Therefore he thinks it is necessary to describe the meaning of the decorative function of the jewel in order to set this apart from what the jewel wants to say. Only then – independently from the influence of place, context or wearer – are we able to really understand its meaning. In his essay, Robert Smit presents himself as an artist who believes in the complete and absolute autonomy of art, passing over the fact that there is a difference between a jewel and a work of fine art because a jewel will never function at its best without a wearer. This can be a frightening thought for a maker, as Robert Smit testifies: 'As a maker, you don't have any influence on the final manifestation which makes visual the functioning of the jewel. There starts a situation, an incredible substance for the maker, which affects, changes or possibly even cancels any intention the maker attributes'.[14] Actually, in my view the situation is not as bad as Smit thinks; most wearers 'connect' with their worn piece, especially when the piece of jewellery goes beyond mere decoration. This is exactly what makes jewellery so interesting compared to an artwork, which is hung on the wall and does not ask for personal commitment. Jewellery is more demanding and more complex. The wearer knows about this.

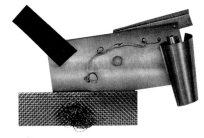

> fig. 67

Robert Smit is one of the few artists who have been both successful as a jeweller and as a fine artist, though not simultaneously. He exploits his artistic ambiguity. This can be exemplified with a golden composition put together from bits and pieces (fig. 67). One piece is rolled up; the other pieces are flat and all treated in a different way. The different parts are fastened with the aid of tiny rivets. In the centre are some gold threads, in a seemingly random tangle, and one pearl painted blue. This strange composition speaks to us; although it is not clearly figurative, the bits and pieces do mean something, so the eye starts looking for something recognisable, in the same way we gaze at clouds. And if we read the title *Bello as a Still Life* (1992) we recognise the head, paws and tail of a recumbent animal, a dog, captured from a bird's-eye view. Bello the dog is the alter ego of Robert Smit and a frequently returning character in his jewellery around 1992/1993. The narrative is expressed in the titles: *Bello at Sea*, *Bello as a Falling Cow*, *Bello as a Rocking Horse* and a collection entitled *Bello in Padova*, in which even *Bello's Presence* became the title of several brooches and pendants. Bello turned out to have family, a sister, who performs 'with a black hat' or 'dressed for the ball', and hence we even encounter such works as *Bello's Sister Undressed* and *Bello's Sister in a Nightie*. The story continues with other characters such as the innocent young girl Lilly on the threshold of adolescence, her doll, the working woman and the fat man, each of them depicted in separate brooches (around 1997). Each of them

> 67

is a strong image with no unified meaning. They can be viewed for what they represent, a dog, a fat man or as allegories referring to something entirely outside of them. It is up to the viewer.

These brooches are of special interest because together they represent a peculiar sequential narrative mode. They could be considered an illustration of an ongoing story, as bits and pieces from this story, as stills from a film or sketches from a storyboard, as actors in a play or fragments from a comic. They can be read as a story about a man of a certain age with all of his childhood memories, hopes and desires. A theme which in turn was depicted in a comic book by another artist, Boris Claassen, who was inspired by Robert Smit's work.[15] Yet this interpretation of the work is not sufficient because there are many more layers – in both senses of the word – in Smit's jewellery. Robert Smit's jewellery offers us a view on the plurality of meaning. There is no fixed meaning. Meaning is a constellation of autobiographical and cultural attachments provided by the maker and the viewer, even if the image is figurative.

The *Crwt* series (2004) is Robert Smit's final work in a series of sketches and photographs he made in the surroundings of the Welsh village of Crwt in the year 1978 (during which time he did not make any jewellery). The 1978 *Crwt* sketches showed intuitive divisions with crossing horizontal, vertical and diagonal lines and dots. *Crwt* was a metaphor for a desired place, full of expectations and fantasies. The self-enforced assignment was not just to visit Crwt but to approach it step by step from different directions. During his three-week journey in 1978 he made 'automatic' sketches, notes and photographs with the aim to work them out in drawings, which would give a credible expression of a place or a landscape without being a literal representation of it. Twenty-five years later, while preparing an exhibition in the Stedelijk Museum in Amsterdam, he came across these unfinished sketches in his archives and so decided to work them out in jewellery.[16]

In Robert Smit's view, drawing and jewellery are complementary, one not better or preferred more than the other. He made the square brooches and pendants out of gold, his preferred material, covered with little plates of painted gold, silver and lead attached with rivets. The abstract jewellery compositions with rhythms and structures are similar to the lines and dots in the initial sketches on paper. The brooches and pendants do not represent landscapes as such, but titles like *Crwt from Bryn-dafydd* (fig. 68) or *Cwrt from Allt Bryn Llywelyn* definitely point at geographical specifications, an extra bonus for those people who do not know the history behind the work. However, for the viewer who sees a person wearing a pendant like *Crwt from Bryn-dafydd* it will appear like an abstract composition. Perhaps the interested viewer does recognise a panoramic perspective, each piece like a focused detail of a much bigger world that continues outside of the framework of the jewellery. It may appear even bigger than it really is because of its exceptional right-angled and flat form. As a jewel this piece does not fit with the body – more that it is imposed on the body, as it were, the simple form reminiscent of a sheet of paper or a canvas. It is more pictorial than sculptural, more autonomous than decorative. Worn on the body, a jewel like this acts as an impressive expression of the cultural superiority of the wearer.

> 68

A jeweller who adopts more obvious ways of storytelling in the first person is American Melanie Bilenker. Bilenker creates jewels with drawings made from human hair, applied in layers of a slow-drying fluid resin. She depicts daily scenes as if keeping a diary: *Still in Bed*, *Chocolate*, *A Day for a Bath*, *Lunch*, *On the Second Floor* and *Sunday Night* are all titles that indicate certain moments in time and daily events. In all of the daily scenes we see a young woman, for example in *Still in Bed*, which depicts her shoulders and two arms on the sheets (fig. 69). In other brooches we see the woman, full size, complete with fringe and long hair, leaning on her bed while eating chocolate, filling the bath, making tea or looking in the bathroom mirror. The surface of the jewellery consists of ebony painted white. Bilenker treats this surface as if it were a canvas: the neutral carrier of a pictorial layer which is applied in a special and significant way. With reference to antique memorial jewellery, Bilenker renders her sketches in lines using her own hair. But unlike sentimental jewellery, which was made to remember a loved one, these hair drawings commemorate moments in the present life of the maker. By recording mundane and everyday moments in hair, they gain another value: Bilenker talks about 'securing' her memories. The very fact that Bilenker seems only interested in 'the quiet minutes, the mundane, the domestic, the ordinary moments' is significant.[17] By isolating these moments, or rather recreating these moments, and by meticulously rendering them in hair, combining them with costly materials like gold, ebony and ivory and applying them in jewellery, she makes these moments as precious as diamonds.

> 69

The narrative of these jewels is small and intimate; there is no sequence of events, but there is sometimes a small frozen action, comparable to a snapshot photograph of undressing, pouring hot water from a kettle or fastening a button. This similarity to snapshot photography is not unfounded: at home, where she also has her studio, Bilenker carries a tripod with her all day, camera at the ready. Bilenker says: 'It influences your way of looking. You become more aware of what you are doing and how you are doing it.' But it is more about gestures and positions than about emotions or psychology: 'For instance, you see someone sitting in a certain position and you think: I have to record this. Then you try to repeat it yourself later for the photograph.'[18] Melanie Bilenker has made her own and daily life the object of her art, like Tracey Emin, Sophie Calle and other, mostly female, artists do, but in a different, rather subdued and harmless way. Her position is more formal than emotional. Bilenker is interested in gestures and positions, which somehow connect to our concept of beauty. She does not want to present to us the sour and raw version of life, the disappointments, setbacks and struggles but rather wants to highlight the everyday beauty of a moment or a gesture. Her world is in the house, it is a female perspective, as stereotypical as the violent worlds of Sophie Calle or Tracey Emin but without the psychological drama and confrontational intimacy. Is this the difference between fine art and jewellery? Is jewellery, as is commonly thought in the world of fine art, indeed just a pale shadow of visual art, a weak infusion without balls or guts? I do not think so: if we take adorning and beautifying as one of the main functions of jewellery, the subject and form of Melanie Bilenker's jewellery is absolutely challenging. As she states: 'I see jewelry as a confrontation by its very nature. [...] It engages the viewer and makes them get very close to examine it, making it a very personal interaction'.[19]

Human hair is a very private, to many even a creepy, thing. Making your own life the subject of your jewellery and depicting the scenes with recycled material from your own body can be interpreted as an act of extreme intimacy and exhibitionism. The viewfinders that she also makes emphasise the role of the viewer as a voyeur. This shift in the role of the viewer from a rather neutral observer or a committed believer to an uncertain voyeur watching the first-person narrator while taking a bath or undressing herself is new in the history of jewellery (fig. 70). Bilenker's jewellery may be compared with antique erotic miniatures, hidden in lockets and made especially to be seen by the male gaze, but the difference lies in the fact that it is the first-person narrator who exposes herself voluntarily and on her own conditions.

THE MIND IN THE HAND

Throughout her career, which began in 1982, Israeli jeweller Esther Knobel has used narration and figurative imagery in her work. Representations of nature, flowers, branches, snakes, leaves and also humans are recurring themes. Her series *The Mind in the Hand* consists of a range of brooches with images depicting the hand at work, carrying a clothes basket, kneading pastry, handling machines, playing with a thread and cutting – all based on schematic images of working hands (fig. 71). She also depicts the techniques she used to make the jewellery itself, sometimes in an obvious 'do-it-yourself', instructional way. The brooches are made with an unusual technique, consisting of iron thread embroidery on plain silver or enamelled copper. This technique immediately refers to the hand that made it; in fact the stitches can be interpreted as traces of the handwork. In some cases the silver shows cracks near the edges, traces of the maker putting the material under high pressure.

Technique has always been an important issue in the work of Esther Knobel. She feels attracted to the rather primitive but very direct 'craftsmanship of outsiders', like embossing tin or aluminium with wire. *The Mind in the Hand* reveals that Knobel herself is a technical anarchist, inventing new techniques in order to shake off the strict traditional goldsmith's repertory. Knobel: 'The embroidery work [...] was born out of a dialogue with the splendid tradition of the cloisonné technique. Instead of the meticulous cloisonné method of creating a pattern and delineating areas of color by means of metal wire, I tried to embroider the demarcating outline with a simple stitch into a perforated plate. The motivation to liberate jewelry design from a rigid technical tradition – to refresh a field and update it – that has always been with me.'[20] In the same way, some years earlier, she started knitting with electrical wire for the series *My Grandmother Is Knitting Too* (fig. 72). This collection of jewellery and objects included a pair of pliers with knitted handles, teddy bears, spools of thread and wearable rings and brooches. The works were knitted in thin plastic-coated copper electrical wire found on the street, which was fired to burn off the plastic. They were then recoated with enamel and fired at high temperatures.

> fig. 71

This kind of jewellery is a rare and significant statement about craft. Knobel, who is interested in the theoretical debate about crafts, feels that there is a voice missing from within the field. She wants to enrich the debate, not by words or theories but by her own work: 'I'm bothered by the fact that theoretical commentary is left to theoreticians who control the words, whereas the artists themselves tend to be inarticulate, locking themselves up in their mute fortresses. But despite the muteness embedded in us, I feel that we have a duty and a responsibility to think, to formulate, to teach. I am attempting to clarify the (Hebrew) term *milekhet mahshevet* (work of craftsmanship), which actually has a poetic equivalent in English, namely 'the mind in the hand.'[21] The *Mind in the Hand* brooches express the creative process in a rather illustrative way. By presenting a sort of vocabulary of working hands carrying out basic domestic tasks, handling complicated machines or doing creative work, she shows how the mind and the hand are working together. At the same time, her use of knitting and embroidery can be interpreted as a comment on the new interest in handicrafts and crafts within the world of art and design. Her work offers an insider's statement about crafts that can be appreciated and understood by the wearer and viewer because of the charm of the imperfect handmade object and the directness of the imagery. On the body they can be read as a political badge.

ZEEBAUW

There are also less evident examples of imagery in jewellery, as seen in the work of Dutch designer Lucy Sarneel, who is a real storyteller. She evokes stories through her combination of materials and reduced but clear imagery. I would like to concentrate on one of her older neck ornaments called *Zeebauw* (fig. 73) to examine how the mind is compelled to combine all different signifiers (material, form and colour) in the piece in order to extract its story.

> 73

We see a broad band of colourful textile sewn in a rectangular form. The band is composed of two different ribbons, the inner band having an oriental floral pattern in red, the outer band being narrower and with a more geometrical pattern of pale blue diagonal stripes and flowers. The inside edge is decorated with twelve small shells set in silver casings. Six blue-grey zinc flowers are also scattered over the band.

This ornament has a highly decorative character, yet it is also a composition, balanced with precision, every element having a specific place and meaning. The work looks like a still life rather than a story. You can simply enjoy the material and formal qualities of this piece, the flowers, the shells and the textile patterns. The one thing that is perhaps troublesome is the square outline of the necklace, quite unusual for a piece of jewellery, which is normally worn on the breast.

The story behind the piece cannot be unravelled without any knowledge of Dutch folklore and history. Mieke Bal pointed out that 'perception is a psychosomatic process, strongly dependent for example, on the position of the perceiving body in relation to the perceived object. A small child thus sees things totally differently from an adult, if only because of their difference in size. The degree of familiarity with what one sees also influences one's perception.'[22] People who are acquainted with traditional Dutch costumes will recognise the coloured fabrics once worn by fishermen's wives in small coastal villages – maybe people in other European countries, too, will recognise the folkloristic origin of this piece.

The theme of this necklace is historic, dealing with the harsh life of fishermen and their families at home. The necklace refers to the small fishing island of Marken, near

Amsterdam, once home to an isolated community. The special domestic and clothing habits on this island were abandoned soon after the opening of a dyke at the end of the 1950s, which reached to the mainland. Until then women had spent a great deal of their time with needlework and the ongoing process of embellishing their costumes with exotic ribbons and fabrics, embroidery and hand-knotted ornaments. In their small wooden houses, they took pride in the furnishing of one special room, the best room (*pronkkamer* in Dutch). This room would be lavishly decorated with ceramic plates, hand-painted wooden boxes, embroidery and brass ornamental objects, together with neatly folded pieces of their costumes and other textiles. It was not in use as a living room; its only purpose was to display the family's valuable belongings. This passion for decoration is recognisable in Lucy Sarneel's necklace, composed of original ribbons used in Marken. Through these pieces comes the thought of the loneliness of these women, who often had nothing else left but to decorate their house after their husband had 'stayed at sea', as people on the island put it. Yet the narrative unfolds in the mind of the beholder, it is not inscribed in the piece. To stimulate this story, Sarneel made use of a couple of signifiers.

The title is one of them: *Zeebauw*, which is impossible to translate. *Zee* means sea, but the second part of the word, *bauw*, is a typical word from the island, unknown to other regions in the Netherlands and therefore impossible to translate into modern Dutch or English. It refers to the colourful square piece of fabric worn on the breast. Each day it was pinned on to the undergarments, and as such was an important decorative and signifying part of the traditional women's costumes of the island. The colour and pattern of the fabric showed whether someone was in mourning and at what stage. For special occasions, such as marriage, Pentecost and Queen's Day, special fabrics were used, white, multicoloured and orange respectively.

The square outline and antique textile of Sarneel's necklace are an immediate reference to the original part of the costume. The zinc flowers and the shells are direct references to the sea. Other necklaces and brooches of Lucy Sarneel's from this period also depict this theme (fig. 74). However, the narrative of Sarneel's pieces is avoidable, because it is foremost referential. Comparing Sarneel's jewellery with that of Melanie Bilenker in a sharper and literary analysis, one could say that in the latter's jewellery the story is told in the first person, whereas in Lucy Sarneel's jewellery the story is told by a narrator who is not necessarily the maker but can be the viewer of the piece.

> 74

In this chapter I have presented different modes of the narrative through eight different stories. These modes can be summarised as autobiographical, comic or cartoon, voyeuristic, philosophical, sequential, iconographical and historical. It is significant that the brooch is a favourite type of jewellery in the realm of storytelling. The brooch is considered a neutral surface, with a pin on the rear side, which is usually attached in an interesting position on the chest of the wearer. This position is crucial and a wearer knows this. The wearer knows they are a display of sorts and is willing to wear a statement on their body. As Mieke Bal pointed out, there are two moments when meaning is created: 'The first involves the author, but is no more "original" or "primary" than the second, whose subject is the reader.'[23]

We can conclude that perception depends on many factors. A piece of jewellery is not only charged by both the deliberate and unconscious intentions of the maker; the wearer also influences a piece of jewellery with their personality, clothing and movement, as well as the viewer who dares to perceive and takes his or her own perspective. The narrative is there in the piece, but it has to be stirred up by the viewer, who will complete it. Therefore the maker, the wearer, the viewer and the message are entangled in an indefinable and ongoing discourse with one another.

1 Françoise van den Bosch made several bracelets, necklaces and objects that consisted of two (or more) parts that could be joined together. Bruno Ninaber van Eyben designed a steel wristwatch with changeable Perspex parts (1975). A design by Antoinette Vroom consists of bracelets and rings in Perspex and alpaca of different parts that could be combined (1983). Others, like Lous Martin, created 'do-it-yourself' kits for jewellery in the mid-1970s. Bernhard Schobinger in Switzerland made rings on the same principle, without knowing of the Dutch and likewise without the Dutch knowing his work. His *Box with Multi-Ring* – 7 coloured acrylic rings and 1 in white gold (1970) – and his *Elements Ring* (1976) are based on the same geometric form vocabulary and the same principle of joining different parts.

2 Gijs Bakker, interview with the author, Amersfoort, 25 Oct. 1984.

3 Email from Melanie Bilenker, 6 June 2009.

4 Mieke Bal, 2001. *Looking in: The Art of Viewing.* Amsterdam: G + B Arts International, p. 71.

5 Mieke Bal, 1985. *Narratology: Introduction to the Theory of Narrative.* Toronto/Buffalo/London: University of Toronto Press (reprinted 2002), pp. 4–6.

6 In March 2005, I attended the *Maker–Wearer–Viewer* symposium at the Glasgow School of Art, organised by Jack Cunningham. I presented my paper *Tall Stories*, based on the text for the catalogue of my exhibition *Sterke verhalen, hedendaagse sieraden uit Nederland* at the Erasmus House in Jakarta, Indonesia. Bringing contemporary Dutch jewellery to Indonesia, at the request of the director of the Dutch cultural institution in Jakarta, was a challenging task. How should you present this typical Western European work to a public that was not acquainted with anything known as author jewellery? From my knowledge of Indonesia, the country has a rich mythological tradition. Combined with old colonial family stories and artefacts, Dutch literature and some personal visits to Indonesia, the country seemed to me to be a place where stories are valued. Storytelling just seemed to be the perfect way to introduce Dutch jewellery to this culture.

7 Mieke Bal, 2001. *Louise Bourgeois' Spider.* Chicago/London: University of Chicago Press, p. 27.

8 Ibid. p. 54.

9 Exhibition catalogue *Manfred Bischoff*. Vienna: Schlebrügge, p. 10. Exhibition at the Isabella Stewart Gardner Museum, Boston, 6 June–22 Sept. 2002.

10 Ibid. pp. 12–3.

11 Gert Staal, 1993. *Manfred Bischoff 'üb ersetzen'*. 's Hertogenbosch: Het Kruithuis, p. 17.

12 Bruce Metcalf, 2009. 'Five Chapters in a Life of the Imagination', in Bruce Metcalf and Signe Mayfield, 2009. *The Miniature Worlds of Bruce Metcalf*. Palo Alto: Palo Art Centre, p. 25.

13 Robert Smit, 2001. *De maker, de drager en de toeschouwer.* Amsterdam, Sept. (unpublished document, translation by LdB).

14 Ibid.

15 Boris Claassen and Robert Smit, 1998. *Kortsluiting.* Amsterdam. Published on the occasion of Robert Smit's exhibition *Kortsluiting* at Galerie Louise Smit, Amsterdam, Jan. 1998.

16 Robert Smit, interview with the author, Amsterdam, Aug. 2004. The exhibition referred to is *Geel metalliek – Goud voor Robert Smit/Yellow Metallic – Gold for Robert Smit*, Stedelijk Museum Amsterdam, 5 Nov. 2004–30 Jan. 2005.

17 Quotation from her website *www.melaniebilenker.com*. Accessed 15 June 2009.

18 Melanie Bilenker, interview with the author, Philadelphia, 2 June 2009.

19 Email from Melanie Bilenker, 6 June 2009.

20 Esther Knobel, 2008. *The Mind in the Hand.* Jerusalem: Carmel, p. xxiv.

21 Ibid. pp. xxii–xxiii.

22 Bal (see note 7), p. 42.

23 Ibid. p. 76.

V. On the Fringe

In 2008/09 Natalya Pinchuk resided for two months in Ted Noten's temporary studio in Amsterdam's red-light district: the oldest part of the city, where prostitutes, tourists, fast food and alcohol determine the street scene. In an attempt to give this run-down, corrupt part of the city a better image, the City of Amsterdam bought several of the brothels and renovated them as temporary live-in studios for designers. Ted Noten used his extra studio space to invite young artists for short residencies.

Natalya Pinchuk asked people who lived or worked in the immediate area to give her an object that they found ugly and on which they would not mind if changes were made. She recruited candidates through advertisements; seventeen collaborating jewellers carried out interviews with the candidates in order to find out the stories behind the objects and about how their owners defined the beautiful and not so beautiful. They then took the ugly things home to work on them. In collecting these stories, people were urged to look back and see for themselves just why they came to this conclusion. In this way, Pinchuk hoped for deeper insight into the powers that govern our aesthetic and social values. The transformed ugly objects were exhibited in the public library in Amsterdam at the end of 2009. One could also read the stories of the artists and owners, watch videos and see photographs of the transformation in progress on the website *www.uglyobjects.com*, which had been set up at the beginning of the project.

It is an interesting thought that jeweller Natalya Pinchuk took Amsterdam's idea of beautifying this part of the city by infiltrating it with art and design a step further by actually stepping inside the houses. It is also not without significance that a jewellery artist would be the one to initiate such a project: they are in the favourable position to think about beauty and to talk about the attachments people have to objects, souvenirs or jewellery. But what can we call such a project? And where does it belong? It is not about jewellery but rather initiated by a jeweller and carried out by jewellers who are confronted daily, through their work, with choices that consider beauty.

In her *Ugly Objects* project, Pinchuk turned the question of beauty around: instead of 'what is your most cherished' or 'what is the most beautiful that you own', it became 'give me your ugliest object', an interesting reversal that actually allowed people to think about beauty. Pinchuk's project is a typical example of work 'on the edge': it is created in collaboration with other artists and relies on the participation of people from outside of that world. It cannot be pinned down to a certain artistic discipline, even though many jewellers are involved; instead it makes use of a variety of techniques and media (interviews, photography, Internet) meant to evoke stories and be shown outside the realm of the regular jewellery gallery or museum.

Many jewellers like to temporarily straddle the boundaries of jewellery, design and art. In this sense, they are not unlike visual artists and designers. In a no-man's-land without any obvious rules, everything can be questioned and researched. It is also here that artists can freely meet the people – their audience – and work with them. Here it is not so much about the individual artist and his/her particular genius or about the artist as the loner who works in his own secluded space, cut off from society. Classic authorship becomes extended with other practices and collaborations: Japanese artist Yuka Oyama worked together with residents in a neighbourhood in Berlin to create artworks, whereas Natalya Pinchuk shared her ideas with other artists who created different works individually but shared their progress and thoughts on a website. Ted Noten swaps his rings with visitor's rings, resulting in open-ended artwork. Jeweller Suska Mackert worked with photographer Uta Eisenreich for some time; together they formed Atelier Puckie, which organised 'tinkering courses' for workers at a printing business in Amsterdam.[1] Here, there are no expectations of selling, people can be interested and participate in the work of an artist without being a potential client. Through these practices, artists (including jewellers) can resist today's consumerist idea that 'anything that cannot be marketed will inevitably vanish'.[2]

Jewellery galleries have a rather limited audience; art jewellery is a subject for insiders. At best, jewellery galleries manage to attract lovers of visual art and design. Sometimes they become collectors, sometimes they just buy a piece of jewellery directly from the showcase without further knowledge and without wanting to become involved. The reward of having your piece appeal to someone is not always enough and can even be scary. What if 'the lady in the mink coat who bought the most expensive piece in your exhibition' misunderstood it completely? How do you deal with the fact that 'your thought, your very important statement has been given a price'? The woman sees your piece as a nice decoration 'that would perfectly match her Versace blouse'. She tells her friend 'that she thinks your brooch looks like an orchid'. But you... 'you thought of intestines'. This story and these quotations are borrowed from a brochure made by students and teachers at Ädellab, the jewellery and silversmithing class at Konstfack in Stockholm.[3] The brochure raises questions about the viability of art jewellery by reflecting on the many questions young jewellery makers are confronted with. There is a rebellious tone. These young jewellers will not easily adjust to the current system, which somehow seems so obsolete.

Jewellers are constantly aware of their ambiguous position in the realm of art, design, fashion and the everyday. Their work is preferably worn on the body, but their story or intention mixes with those of the wearer. They know about beauty, the treatment of materials, size and the body, and they want to address these issues not only to 'believers', those who belong to the inner circle, but also to others.

This is why jewellers have a growing need to step off the paved path and turn directly to the street to find new sources of inspiration, sometimes combining the new conceptual or reflexive practice with that of a regular jeweller. Over the last ten years, this practice has become relatively wide spread and well accepted. In visual art this tendency to interact with the public and to stage interventions in public space is known as 'relational aesthetics' or 'relational art'. French philosopher Nicolas Bourriaud, who first used it in 1996 and published a collection of essays entitled *Esthétique relationelle* in 1998, coined the terms. Bourriaud's explanation of relational art is 'a set of artistic practices which take as their theoretical and practical point of departure the whole of human relations and their social context, rather than an independent and private space.'[4] However, pinning relational art down to only dealing with inter-human relations is too restricted. It also refers to a new artistic practice distancing it from the traditional ideas about creation and singularity: the artist as a researcher, the artist working in a team and making use of the specialities of others, the artist working with every possible technique or material, the artist becoming a copyist. It is not surprising that these tendencies have also touched jewellery making, because jewellery, as with any other artistic practice, is part of society and in one way or another reacts to cultural changes and social demands. Today's society sees a change from the specialist to the generalist and from the professional to the layperson, who are involved more and more in all kinds of decision making – even museums turned to the vernacular. In 2010 James Beighton, the curator of crafts at the Middlesbrough Institute of Modern Art (MIMA), invited three artists, Lin Cheung, Laura Potter and Atelier Ted Noten (ATN) to create wearable objects in consultation with residents of the city. The initiative was part of Museumaker, a national project involving sixteen museums aimed at stimulating an interchange between cultural heritage and contemporary crafts and thus developing new audiences. The initial idea was 'to create pieces of jewellery that will reflect the individuals' interests, ideas and ambitions. The resulting pieces will each be made in editions of two: one piece will enter the Museum's collections while the other will be fitted to the commissioner to be worn in the real world.'[5]

> 75

> 76

Cheung and Potter worked collaboratively with selected residents, responding to their drawings, suggestions and ideas. The participants chose objects from different museum collections in the region, and Cheung and Potter created new ornaments based on their choices and conversations. Instead of creating a piece of jewellery for a handful of Middlesbrough residents, ATN designed 300 ornaments for taxi drivers (fig. 75). A taxi driver is like a modern-day Greek Hermes, talking about everything that is going on in society, passing on the latest news. ATN designed car ornaments and badges for Middlesbrough taxi drivers, echoing the wings Hermes wears on his shoes. An ATN text about the project reads: 'During a one-day "drive-thru" event, each participating taxi driver received a wing-shaped badge together with a windscreen ornament. Their photographs were taken and these portraits form the "wall of fame" in the gallery [fig. 76]. The taxi drivers have also been given flyers that they can hand out to their fares. The fares in turn can then return to MIMA to post these flyers on the Hermes wall with their comments. This provides MIMA with an invaluable archive that will enter its collection for posterity. It will represent a snapshot of attitudes and opinions in Middlesbrough at this moment in time, 2011.'[6] Whether the museum will indeed succeed in attracting a wider audience for the future is difficult to predict. However, the efforts of this museum (also in regard to earlier projects) are innovative and challenging.[7]

It is not easy to define the moment in which the tendency for participation or relational art in jewellery exactly began, nor can we tell where it started or through which artists. However, in the early 1990s there were already signs of a conceptual attitude in jewellery that breached the borders of accepted ways of jewellery presentation, therefore attracting a wider, or at least different, audience for jewellery. The conceptual propensity in jewellery, which was rather strong during this period, gradually ended in a relational approach in the work of the two Dutch artists Dinie Besems and Ted Noten. Both artists have been called 'conceptual' in the past and they both combine an interest in jewellery with a constant need to question it. In their hands, jewellery became an object for research.

DINIE BESEMS, BREACHING THE SYSTEM

Dinie Besems worked as a jewellery artist from 1992 until 2006, when she withdrew from the jewellery scene convinced that she had said everything in jewellery she wanted to. Since then she has been busy creating conceptual magazines and 'one day salons', focusing on different themes including clothing, growing vegetables, cooking and selling (fig. 77). However, nobody should be surprised if she returns to jewellery in one way or another in

> 77

the future. Her work and ideas have been vital to the field and to its break with conventional thinking.

In 1992, Besems made a video of *Ice Necklace* for her graduation show at the jewellery department of the Gerrit Rietveld Academy. It showed a necklace composed of ice cubes slowly melting and making new patterns in the fabric of the dress below. It was a statement expressing her desire to take a different position. Her video of a vanishing jewel remained for some time a lonely exercise in video of an artist who felt, one way or another, 'condemned' to jewellery.

In an interview she once said: 'Actually I don't think jewellery is really interesting. I don't want to make a chain or something else. It is just that I have an idea, an image, something I want to explore. And then it turns out that you can reach people by adapting it to the body. So therefore I work on the skin, but also under the skin.'[8] Most of Besems's pieces are about wearing or the impossibility of wearing and constitute new relationships between jewellery, space and people. Her 'conceptual jewels' are in fact jewels for the mind; once you have seen them you carry them with you as an imprint on your memory. She has designed unforgettable pieces such as *Chalk Chain* (1994), which left traces of chalk on the clothing, *Ring with Tearbucket* (1995), an ephemeral idea recorded in a photograph, and *Sundial* (1994), to be stamped around the navel with which you could read the time by using your finger.

Another proof of her independent character and her ambition to look beyond the borders of the jewellery scene was her cooperation with product designer Marcel Wanders in 1994. Wanders, then at the beginning of his career, still made jewellery occasionally. They worked together on a pearl project, the outcome of which was a collection of identical hand-knotted strings of pearls comprising ninety-nine pearls and one red coral bead. The title of the project was *Geheim Verbond – oesters & zwijnen – Besems & Wanders* [Secret Pact – oysters & swines – Besems & Wanders]. In this work, context and object became one as different kinds of contexts, such as a carving board, a musical composition or a bar of chocolate, were designed for the different strings of pearls. One string referred to a specially written musical composition, another to a murder weapon or a piece of chocolate, one string could have even been made by Gijs Bakker and was furnished with a label with holes in and Gijs Bakker's signature. The title of the project referred to the bond between the context and the wearer of the string of pearls – the meaning of this string would be clear for no one other than the wearer. The idea was that in the end even the makers would become detached from the jewels. Because of the collaboration, the detachment of authorship and a creative process that goes beyond jewellery techniques the project can be observed as one of the first jewellery projects that introduced elements of an approach that would later be labelled 'relational art'.

Besems was also highly independent in her choice of gallery. She worked with all the jewellery galleries in the Netherlands at that time – Marzee in Nijmegen, Ra in Amsterdam, Louise Smit also in Amsterdam and Ademloos in The Hague – only to find that she felt too restricted and too isolated. From that moment on she started organising her own shows in different venues. On the 1 June 1997 between 1 p.m. and 2 p.m. in her own apartment in Amsterdam, she organised a one-hour exhibition under the title *Nooit meer naakt* [Never Naked Again]. Here she hung metres of tight, thin silver chain at eye level along the walls of her apartment from corner to corner, from room to room, which linearly represented the 1:1 floor plan of her entire house. Special hooks, pins and eyelets indicated doorways, windows and corners. In this way, she could describe space with a minimum of material. By wrapping the chain around her neck, her body was partially

> 79

covered, and she was literally dressed in her own house like a snail. A life-size portrait of the artist wearing this irregular bundle of chains and a collection of bobbins with chains of each separate room of her house is what remains of this event (fig. 79). At the end of 1997, she used this same idea for the exhibition *For Sale: Galerie Louise Smit*, where people could bid for a similar representation of the gallery with a form especially provided for the occasion. Projects like these illustrate how Dinie Besems easily moved between adornment, body and space.

Soon after her graduation at the beginning of the 1990s, she became a pioneer in the endless virtual space of the World Wide Web. Long before it became fashionable among jewellers to have one, Dinie Besems made her own website, not for selling or advertising her work but as a space for research. On her site she could circulate ideas about virtual jewellery, such as the *Wunschring* [Wish Ring] composed of 1 g of fine gold, 1 dead hamster, 4 mg stolen silver and one cup of magical rice. One of the questions she posed on her site was: 'How do you fill a virtual space when we are hardly able to think virtually?' She found the Internet a 'virtual wasteland' and therefore her first website looked more like a working space, a place where ideas circulated and were tested; it had nothing to do with the two-dimensional catalogues most artists' websites look like today.[9]

In 1997, *Art Magazine Downtown Boston* (vol. XXXII, winter 1997) published a four-page article dealing with 'Dinie Besems's Overview in the Fog Gallery, Boston'. The magazine was a gimmick, a fictitious article in a fictitious art magazine about a solo exhibition that might have taken place in a fictitious gallery. The project, initiated by Dinie Besems and carried out in cooperation with graphic designer Thomas Widdershoven and writer Gert Staal, again showed how Besems was eager to broaden her own horizons by creating a conceptual work of art in an equal collaboration with specialists from other fields. Books such as *The Magic Square*, glossies and other magazines such as *Gebakken Lugt* were also important mediums for Dinie Besems to express her ideas.[10]

Besems's projects often explore context and space: the space surrounding the object, the open space inside of it or the space it actually occupies as an entity. Eventually context and object occupy a space in your mind while the actual object seems no more (and no less) than a cause for a set of thoughts, associations and fantasies. A particularly strong example of this is her necklace *This Space is Mine* (1996). The object consists of a chain with four little posts, a miniature replica of the ones that are often used in museums to keep the public away from the artworks. The piece doesn't need to be worn for it to trigger associations. Indeed, pieces like the *Bracelet Wanting to Become a Ring* and the *Ring Wanting to Become a Bracelet* (1998) are so strong as an idea (of unfulfilled longing) that you do not even need to see an image of the work to have an understanding of it.

In 2002, Dinie Besems declared with astounding determination that in the near future she wanted to make five exhibitions 'on location' and then stop making jewellery. She succeeded in realising this plan, independently but in collaboration with a team of like-minded people comprising a writer, a photographer and a graphic designer – all outsiders to the world of jewellery. The first exhibition, *Epifyt*, took place in 2002 in the Oude Kerk, Amsterdam's oldest church, where she exhibited her work in thirteen glass cubes on the age-old tombstones in the floor. All of the exhibited silver objects and jewellery pieces were based on a cube of 10 × 10 cm, calling to mind the obsessive nature of her *Magic Square* book. In 2003, she organised her second show, *Jewellery for Men*, a one-hour show in Amsterdam's Museum Van Loon, an old seventeenth-century patrician mansion. A colour poster depicting a group of eight men wearing her sturdy new pieces, such as silver balls to be worn as boxing gloves of sorts, in the sumptuous surroundings of the mansion's marble floors and gilded floral wallpaper is what remains of this ultra-short exhibition (fig. 78). The third exhibition, *HERE*, took place in the same year in the old stock exchange building in Amsterdam, a monumental building constructed around 1900 by the famous Dutch architect H. P. Berlage. The jewellery was displayed in showcases designed by Besems. She showed some older work together with new work, such as *Notations*, a string of beads accompanied by a translation in sound of the sequence of the beads. Most of these exhibited objects dealt with the awareness of time and place. The fourth exhibition, *Epibreren*, took place in 2005 at Galerie Binnen, a gallery for interior architecture and product design in Amsterdam. In the minimalist gallery space, Besems created an atmosphere of chaos by making an astounding installation of hundreds of cardboard boxes. The size of each new exhibited object was 10 × 10 × 10 cm and had the possibility of being multiplied. Her last exhibition, *LoloFerrari, laatste tentoonstelling van Dinie Besems* [LoloFerrari, Dinie Besems's Last Exhibition], in October 2006 was made in the so-called Rietveld pavilion De Zonnehof in Amersfoort, an exhibition space for contemporary art designed by architect Gerrit Rietveld. In this famous brick and glass cube, Besems built her own pavilion – a cubic cage-like construction of steel, elegantly juxtaposed within the Modernist cubic building of Rietveld's. The construction was designed by Besems in cooperation with architect John van Rooijen and built on site. Upon Besems's request, graphic designer Luna Maurer developed a digital tool that enabled Besems to design jewellery with the aid of mathematic formulas. Maurer used the Voronoi-Delaunay system used in mathematics and created a digital worm to interfere with these fixed patterns. Thus Besems's final jewellery was produced with up-to-date computer technology, such as three-dimensional printing and laser cutting, resulting in highly wearable and inviting, refined decorative forms.

It seems contradictory that this conceptual jewellery artist who never cared much about wearability finished her career at the very moment she presented her most wearable and affordable jewellery collection. Yet at the same time she seemed to be encapsulated in a systematic thinking. It made no sense to stay in the jewellery scene anymore; she wanted to explore further and leave jewellery behind her. The practice of Dinie Besems is a unique example of an out-of-the-box thinker who is 'borderless' by nature. Her current artistic practice is determined by collaborations with like-minded artists in different fields and aimed at presenting in alternative locations.

TED NOTEN AND THE OPEN-ENDED ARTWORK

Although their work is quite different, Ted Noten and Dinie Besems have often been compared with each other. This is not without good reason: they studied at the same art academy at the same time – Noten graduating in 1990, Besems two years later – and both explore the concept of jewellery in such a way that their creations have been labelled 'conceptual jewellery'. Both work with ideas of using prefabricated jewellery materials and searching for solutions beyond the confines of jewellery in general, aiming to reflect on every possible aspect of the field. They turned away from the regular jewellery gallery circuit and became independent curators for their own exhibitions, organisers of events and distributors of their own jewellery or other work. In the 1990s they represented a new generation of jewellery artists that combined a strong artistic autonomy with groundbreaking ideas, and a willingness to collaborate with other people and companies and to investigate new digital techniques.

Ted Noten began his jewellery career as a searcher, unsure of his artistic direction. *Brooches for a Blue Man* (1994) seemed to belong more to the wall on which they were presented than to the human body. During this period he also made poetical jewels like the *Chess Rings* (1992/93) and the *Profession Rings* (1991/92). Even at the beginning of his career, he stated: 'I want to broaden the field rather than narrow it, which is what is happening at the moment with so many well-behaved jewellers.'[11] A case in point is *Thoughts on La Gioconda* (1993), a series of ten black-and-white reproductions of the *Mona Lisa*, all wearing a brooch in the form of a coloured rectangular cut-out from a reproduction of the portrait's chest; the brooch could then be taken off, worn and returned after use to the place from which it came. It is the first Ted Noten project that involves the idea of making a piece of jewellery in a series, while each piece differs from the other, like a customised design. Everything fell into place when he started using acrylic in 1994, first enclosing fragments of jewellery, stones and computer chips, then a dead mouse wearing a tiny string of pearls in *Princess* (1995), and later weapons in the *Superbitch Bags* (2002 onwards). Around the year 2000, serial projects became more important to him. The *Chew Your Own Brooches* (1998) and the *Mercedes-Benz Car Brooches* (2001) were serious and successful attempts to find a new market.

Noten developed into an entertainer, organiser and storyteller, accomplishing everything on a large scale. He does not hesitate to hire machines or to amuse people with a play-and-win fairground attraction in a museum. He is one of the few jewellery makers who have succeeded in bridging the gap with their audience and who are recognised in the fine art world as well as in design and fashion. His work has been reviewed in reputable magazines, such as *Frieze, Frame, Kunsthandverk, Crafts* and *l'Officiel*, and in international newspapers, such as *The New York Times*.[12]

The *Chew Your Own Brooch* contest in Museum Boijmans Van Beuningen in Rotterdam attracted hundreds of school children (figs. 80, 81). The idea started in 1998 when people could buy a piece of specially wrapped chewing gum with a return box. They had to chew a form (the buyer thus being the maker), put it in the box and send it to the artist. Ted Noten then cast the little object in silver, plated it in gold, attached a pin and returned it to the sender. The project was multifaceted; it was about inviting people to be creative, about transforming a worthless material into gold and about public participation. In collaboration with a video artist, he made a short film of a woman chewing a brooch. To this day hundreds of people have participated in this jewellery project.

> 80, 81

Other participatory projects included the *DNA Suitcase*, a project that invited people to swap one hair, which would later be enclosed in an acrylic suitcase, for a silver-painted commercial pin (2004). Recently he organised *Wanna Swap Your Ring?* in the Museum of Contemporary Art in Tokyo in Japan (2010), involving 500 *Miss Piggy* rings presented on the wall in the shape of a gun (fig. 82). Here people could swap their own ring for a 3-D printed pink ring and in so doing gradually changing Ted Noten's wallpiece. It is a risky open-ended work of art, which plays with ideas of ownership and trust. The event was repeated at other venues, such as Platina gallery in Stockholm: 'The shape of a gun on the wall, known as an icon of Ted Noten's work, will gradually change into a jewel jungle as a result of the stories told by the rings that are left behind. Jewellery reflects the soul of a city!'[13]

> 82

The *Silver Dinner* project came into being after he was invited by Galerie Louise Smit to exhibit his work in the gallery stand at the KunstRAI art fair in Amsterdam in 2000. Wanting to do something special, he installed a table and brought along a bar of silver. As an event, part of the bar was sawn into pieces from which he made brooches by fitting them with a pin. The silver brooches, in all different sizes and forms, were sold by weight, using scales to determine the price. Within the context of a luxurious modern art fair, it made the public aware of the mechanisms of making, choosing, buying and selling jewellery.

Apart from its obvious mocking character, the event showed once again how Ted Noten is capable of making customised jewellery that meets the individual needs of the buyer (an ongoing issue in product design). A like-minded project is *The Smit Collection*, a collection of 100 different brooches cut from the body of a white Mercedes-Benz 210 E-Class, later to be recreated as the (Ferrari) red *Droog Collection* in 2003. By doing this, he wanted to provide 'a little piece of status' to everyone. His dream to have a robot cutting brooches out of a car within the context of an automobile fair and so making instant jewellery unfortunately failed.

Other ideas deal with guns, bullets and the *Mr Claw* playground machinery, a device which picked up a gold bar which was shown at the *Metallic Yellow* exhibition in the Stedelijk Museum in Amsterdam in 2006. A removable tiara, cut from a ready-made polo helmet, was Noten's winning entry in a tiara competition for Princess Maxima on the occasion of her marriage to Crown Prince Willem Alexander of the Netherlands in 2002. He also designed a trophy in the form of a 1 kg bar of silver attached to a chain as the annual award for the Amsterdam Art Foundation (2001) to symbolise the heavy burden of receiving an award.

The presentation of his jewellery is a subject that keeps Ted Noten busy. Since finishing with the usual showcase presentations, he has invented some unforgettable events: *A Robot and a Ring* at Arti et Amicitiae in Amsterdam (2004) involved a robot arm that opened a wall safe, taking out a simple acrylic ring with an enclosed paper hat and moving it around to show it to the audience. On another occasion, he had a video camera recording the hand movements of the cashier selling entrance tickets to the Stedelijk Museum in Amsterdam. She was wearing his *Golden Pig Ring* (2001), and the real-time video was projected in the jewellery exhibition *Display* that was being held in the museum.

In November 2008, during the award ceremony for the Françoise van den Bosch Prize, Ted Noten and his companions at Atelier Ted Noten (ATN since 2008) together with the Amsterdam Fashion Institute organised a stylish and flashy catwalk show, *Tedwalk*, in the Museum of Modern Art in 's-Hertogenbosch. Once again, the show was born out of a feeling of uneasiness with regular museum exhibitions. However, the setting for this show was still a museum. One year later ATN installed a vending machine in the middle of Amsterdam's red-light district, under the title *Be Nice to a Girl, Buy Her a Ring* (fig. 83). > 83 Clients to the brothels could buy a red painted ring here for their favourite prostitute: the more popular she was, the more rings she accumulated. Although the machine was a true magnet and attracted many buyers who could now afford to buy a real Ted Noten ring for only € 2.50, it did not work according to Noten's initial idea. The red-light clients were not interested and the prostitutes were not pleased with a cheap metal ring; they claimed they preferred diamonds and gold.

> fig. 83

Dinie Besems and Ted Noten were pioneers who explored the fringes of autonomous and applied art. Today there are many more jewellery artists who make use of this freedom to create whatever they want. Yet their crafts background succours their work and at the same time determines the content. No matter how free the work may be – in the sense of non-functional or merely conceptual – it is usually best understood in a jewellery context, even though the street is an alluring 'playground'. Their work does not often look like jewellery, but it makes jewellery understandable as a language. It is the result of a reflexive, post-studio practice. In the rest of this chapter, some more relational art projects will be discussed as well as material artworks that take a different shape than that of jewellery.

SUSKA MACKERT AND THE MAPPING OF BRILLIANCE

By meticulously copying in graphite all of the logos and lettering on jewellery shop windows, tattoo shops, piercing salons and jewellery studios on one street in the heart of Amsterdam onto the white walls of a shop space, Suska Mackert succeeded in creating an image of merchandised jewellery and its various codes. In this bare inner space, Mackert created a concentrated environment concerned with the meaning that jewellery, body decoration and adornments have in our lives. The idea was adopted in the video *To Be On Display* (2002) in which, with the patience of a saint, the artist painted the logos of the multinational jewellery companies Bulgari, Chopard, Piaget, Tiffany & Co. and Van Cleef & Arpels in silver, gold and black letters. Mackert explained that the goal of this transformation is a statement on the 'symbolic and behavioural formulas of contemporary society [...]. The result is not a singular criticism but a stripping away of the old and worn out codes.'[14] The logos and lettering are restored to being information, which through Mackert's manipulation attain another value.

For the last ten years, Suska Mackert has been one of the artists who, from a jewellery perspective, move in the territory between the applied arts and visual art. She uses all kinds of materials and techniques, of which printed paper and books are her favourites. Although she is fascinated by the phenomenon of jewellery, she seldom makes any. Mackert is interested in the signalising, conditioning and ranking function of jewellery. In her work she tries to unmask hidden messages, codes and conventions by working a comprehensive project that she calls *Eine Ordnung des Glanzes* [A Structuring of Lustre], 'an *atlas*/a *two-dimensional museum* for and about jewellery'.[15] This illusionary atlas or encyclopaedia is an outline in which she can place all her subjective observations about the phenomenon of jewellery in an attempt to come to her own definition of 'what jewellery is or could be'.

She was already dealing with this question during art school. For her graduation in 1998 from the Gerrit Rietveld Academy's jewellery department (of which she has been the head since 2010), she made a booklet that was wrapped in a broad orange and white ribbon, the same as those used for the sash of certain offices.[16] The book contained photographs that Mackert had taken at Madame Tussauds in Amsterdam. Details of important political and religious people and royal dignitaries wearing their medals, decorations and fine jewels are portrayed in these photographs. In the middle of the book is a double-page scan from a newspaper photograph, showing the rehearsal on a broad stairway for an official delegation. The men and women are wearing rather large name tags around their necks that identify them as the president, vice-president, president's spouse, president's daughter, vice-president's spouse and vice-president's daughter. A man in uniform gives instructions. The scene certainly has a hilarious character, and it becomes even funnier when one finds the fold-out colour photo in the back of the book: in a similar group picture,

Mackert photographed her friends on a stairway wearing the same cardboard tags, pointing out the importance of this typical place for jewellery (the breast), even though the thing being worn is absolutely not jewellery. Also in the back of the book is an old newspaper photograph of a group of Russians dressed in winter clothing and proudly looking into the camera lens. On their chest is the reason for this stature: a hand-sewn badge with Lenin's portrait on it. Codes and conventions come in to play here once more for the badge must have had the equivalence of a jewel for these revolutionaries; it was at once distinguishing and classifying and a sign of belonging to a new political elite.

Another book for her graduation thesis was called *Juwelen* [Jewels], a minimalist brochure about the world of commercial jewellery. It is made from only twelve pages of glossy white paper showing captions from a jewellery catalogue, minus the photos. Descriptions such as 'A TRIPLE ROW CULTURED PEARL NECKLACE strung as three uniform rows of cultured pearls to an emerald and diamond clasp set with three rows of square-cut emeralds' read like poetry and tell the reader much about the jewel. The words alone evoke an image. By subtracting something an even stronger image is created: the image reveals itself through a system of codes and conventions. It appears that Suska Mackert, à la Roland Barthes and his ideas about 'writing-clothing', poses a philosophical question through a work of art. In Barthes's vision, words (descriptions) are stronger than reality, the very thought that underlies Mackert's *Juwelen*.[17]

Juwelen distinguishes itself by the precision with which it is made; the choice of paper, the text placement on the pages, the quality of printing and the hand-sewn binding all add to the choice effect of this object. Mackert has a sharp eye for details and the work has undoubtedly been made with a 'jeweller's hand'. On the relationship between hand and head, concept and skill, she has a definite opinion: 'The process of making, the craft, is very important; otherwise the work would be dead. Many people say I am a conceptual artist, and, in a way, they are right because I work with concepts. On the other hand, I am not a conceptual artist in the sense of Donald Judd or Sol LeWitt, although also in Judd's work you can see an enormous skill and craft. For me a concept is also emotional. I never think something up. A concept grows and it is hard work to find the precise form.'[18]

Book, paper, text and image are important elements in Mackert's conceptual work. Her outstanding archive of newspaper photographs as well as her exceptional capacity to recognise the most poignant images is hereby instrumental. She screens images, so to speak, by the details that no one else would even notice but which in Mackert's hands become valuable when placed in the correct context. An example of this is her work *Affiches* (1999), five manipulated newspaper photographs printed in offset type in poster format.[19] Printed on these five posters are pictures of presidents such as Chirac and Pinochet pinning medals on other important men. By erasing the decorations by retouching methods (a way of manipulating photos in the pre-digital era, especially under totalitarian and communist regimes) she creates an estranged image of powerful men softly touching other men, thus showing the real 'power play'. The grainy offset technique and the purposely clumsy retouching add to the secretive and voyeuristic atmosphere.

Reworking existing material is a common thread in Mackert's work. For instance, she has manipulated postcards from the so-called Schmuck Madonna or Gnaden Madonna [Jewellery Madonna or Madonna of Mercy], a statue of the Madonna in the Cathedral of Cologne that is draped with jewellery, by cutting small medallions from them. From antiquarian books about eighteenth- and nineteenth-century sentimental jewellery, she has cut out texts in the form of sentimental platitudes about love and trust (fig. 84). And in a book on precious stones she carved the text: 'die Farbe der Berge ist auf Grund ver-

> 84

schiedener Mineralien- und Edelsteinvorkommen unterschiedlich' [the colour of the mountains is different based on the mineral and gem deposits], a strange text that she picked up from a television programme. These 'super-texts' that are superimposed on top of the original text and images in a book thereby have the effect of intervening and strengthening the content of the work.

The Andy Warhol Collection (2008/09) is a book adapted from another typical 'Mackert find'. From an auction catalogue of Andy Warhol's jewellery collection, all the images have been cut away and the remaining pages painted. What remains is a fragile construction where the exposed pages of abstract cut-outs reveal a three-dimensional, browsable composition (fig. 85). This work reminds us of our fascination with hidden treasures. To most people it was a complete surprise that Andy Warhol possessed such an enormous collection of fine jewellery and watches.[20] It is also a story that quickly disappears into the recesses of our collective memory. The book is a jewel of workmanship and has an intimacy that is comparable to that of illuminated handwriting or miniature work.

> 85

Suska Mackert ascribes great importance to skills and highly values objects that are handmade, laborious and time consuming. Her work methods are neither cynical nor criticising; rather she confirms and strengthens existing codes and conventions with small interventions, like the annotations in the margins of a book. By doing this, she wants to make us partners in her fascination with jewellery.

SCHMUCK2: INTERDISCIPLINARY PROJECTS

While Suska Mackert generally shows her work in the context of a regular jewellery gallery, there are also jewellery artists who deliberately look for new settings. One of the most outspoken in this field is the German artist Susan Pietzsch. In 1997 she founded Schmuck2, which demonstrated her curator's capacity in interdisciplinary collaborations and exhibitions and as such is a typical relational art initiative. In an interview, Susan Pietzsch explained the goal of Schmuck2: 'Actually the name/logo focuses on the multiplication of the concept of jewellery (Schmuck [Jewellery] squared). My aim was the enhancement of the term and the consideration of Schmuck as a phenomenon. Besides, I also wanted to focus on reaching a wider audience for new jewellery.'[21] Within the context of Schmuck2, she regularly works with artists from other disciplines. Her first project Anprobe [Fitting] was organised in 1998/99 in a public space in Heiligendamm, an old seaside resort in north-east Germany. On this occasion, four participating jewellery designers worked together for two weeks, their goal being to make jewellery. The jewellery was then presented to the public on the street; those interested could try the jewellery on, and they could exchange it with a piece of their own jewellery on the condition that they would wear the jewellery for three weeks and afterwards fill in a questionnaire about their experience. On the Schmuck2 website, one can read several of the reactions to this project. One person wrote: 'It was a therapeutic aid, the therapy was: come out of your shell, dare something new.' This project can be seen as reconnaissance, experimental research in the field of experimental jewellery. The public were not only offered a real piece of jewellery to try on and to wear temporarily but were also asked to give up something of their own. With this, two basic assumptions of jewellery were posed for discussion: 1) people have a special, emotional bond with their jewellery and 2) 'art' jewellery is under glass in a gallery or museum showcase.

Since Anprobe, Susan Pietzsch has, either of her own initiative or commissioned by others, organised ten projects and exhibitions.[22] They are all remarkable projects, including, for example, *Immaterial Jewellery – Jewels of the 3rd Millennium* in Schloss Plüschow and the Stadtgalerie Kiel (2004).[23] In comparison to the exhibition *Les Immatériaux*, curated by the French philosopher Jean-François Lyotard in 1984, jewellery as such was absent from the *Immaterial Jewellery* exhibition (with the exception of *Belly-Chain*, a chain especially made for and hung around a round, oriental wooden table from the location's inventory by the Italian sculptor Johannes Gamper). Instead photographic work, collages, videos and installations were shown. The exhibition was a twenty-first-century answer to the immaterial jewellery of the previous generation who began to work with this theme in the 1970s and 1980s. Gijs Bakker's *Schaduwsieraad* [Shadow Jewellery] from 1973 and Manfred Nisslmüller's mini tape recorder from 1984, which was hidden in a breast pocket of a man's sports jacket and played the word 'brooch' repeatedly, were referred to in the accompanying catalogue text as immediate reference points in jewellery.

Commissioned in 2005 by MIMA, which at the time was still under construction, Susan Pietzsch, along with Schmuck2, organised an exhibition in public spaces in Middlesbrough. Under the title of *Wrappinghood*, eight artists of differing nationality created installations that dealt with wrapping or applying a new surface and the idea of decorating or adorning the city. The Japanese artist Tsukioka Aya presented clothing with the image of a soft drink vending machine printed on the inside. In an emergency, this piece of clothing can be unfolded and used as city-camouflage so that the wearer can hide. Valentina Seidel in collaboration with Susan Pietzsch took the automobile, in this case the Mini, as the starting point for personal adornment (fig. 87). Their posters entitled *Miniskirts*, depicting a woman posing with an automobile body-part in front of her, held as if it were a skirt or a jacket thrown over her shoulder, were spread throughout the city. Suska Mackert set a text in gold leaf on the pavement in front of cheap jewellery stores. The shiny text was a commentary on the glittery sale items in the shop windows and read: 'Materials with a shiny surface reflect light while elsewhere the light is fully absorbed'. Spanish designer Martí Guixé designed a pink printed tape that was used to wrap various architectonic places in the city, such as facades, railings, posts, etc., according to a 'taping protocol' (fig. 86). Ines Tartler was also among the eight artists who exhibited; she wrapped a car in gold foil and installed it at the museum's construction site.

Through these street presentations, *Wrappinghood* reached a very different viewing public than a normal jewellery exhibition would attract. The exhibition was also important because it created a bond between visual art and jewellery, making that 'in-between zone' a central focus. Schmuck2 tries to address the audience in a different and unexpected way. The various projects show that an open and associative approach to the phenomenon of jewellery in the broadest sense is possible. Schmuck2 demonstrates the power of the philosophical, the interdisciplinary and the disordered by turning expectations upside down and breaking through set routines while placing visual arts, design and jewellery alongside each other as equal partners.

RELATIONAL PROJECTS: YUKA OYAMA

Yuka Oyama found yet another, more direct way to connect with her audience. Since 2003 the Berlin-based Japanese artist has been organising performances in which she spontaneously makes jewellery on the spot for whoever may want it (fig. 88). Every element counts, from the carefully chosen location to collecting the materials, making up the kit, initiating contact with people, making the jewellery and documenting the performance in the form of photographs. When Oyama was studying at the Art Academy in Munich,

> 87

> 86

> 88

she experienced the city as tidy and grey and her own area – the art school – as far too isolated. To break through that isolation she wanted to do something immediate, on the street and to use this method to get in contact with people. Because she had little money, she used simple materials. The first fast jewellery literally became a form of communication, developing while talking to people, asking for their participation and ideas about the jewellery they would like to have.

> 89

She later professionalised this idea by designing a mobile workbench and a big pouch that she could wear like an apron and which provided space for materials and tools (fig. 89). She also designed a system that had her assistants collect useless items in a specially designed see-through backpack. Oyama made *Schmuck Quickies* [Jewellery Quickies] throughout Germany, Japan, England, Austria and Italy. The material was collected especially for each performance and was dependent on the idiosyncrasies of each host country.[24] In contrast to a fast portrait artist, who in a few minutes can make a quick sketch of his model without even speaking to the person, an artist that wants to make a piece of jewellery for someone quickly must get to know something about this person in a very short period. While getting to know her 'client', Oyama builds the jewellery directly on the participant's body from the directions and desires of the person in question. The constructions, often elaborate, colourful and large, portray one's deepest desires – for instance, jewellery to camouflage a big belly, jewellery as a pet that you can carry around with you or jewellery that gives the image of a strong, indestructible person.

It may seem paradoxical that Oyama would use the bizarre and blatant to portray the inner feelings of someone, but even though her jewellery constructions are extravagant, she sees them as servicing designs. Oyama claims her *Schmuck Quickies* are a service because she is not actually concerned with her own preoccupations and thoughts but rather with those of the person for whom she is making the piece. According to Oyama she works in the same way as a classic goldsmith would: 'I dig deep and add',[25] with the fundamental difference, of course, that a goldsmith creates for eternity while Oyama's creations are based on and aimed at recycling. The *Schmuck Quickies* are kindred in spirit to relational art pieces: they bring art to the people or people to the art, they bring people together in conversation and they allow one to think about themselves and others.

The step towards a different method, in collaboration with passers-by, families and neighbours, was obvious. Yuka Oyama also made decorations for rituals in the home and by doing so gave a new face to the accompanying feeling of unity. With the *Invasion of Privacy* projects, she created rooms filled with decorations for Christmas, Halloween, Easter, birthday parties and weddings. In 2007, she worked for months on *Berlin Flowers*, a project in which a Modernist high-rise block of flats from the 1950s in the Berlin Hansa quarter was decorated for an entire week with garlands made by the residents themselves

> 90

(fig. 90). Every balcony received one of these garlands, for which Oyama had provided the materials and an aesthetic pattern. Oyama sees this as a utopian project because it brings people closer to each other. Neighbours who would otherwise never have met each other worked together in a free and cheerful atmosphere.

From a design point of view, the project is interesting because it makes us see that handwork and applied arts, which by nature are small and manageable, can still achieve a monumental result. In addition, this type of art and craft participation project is accessible and attractive to everyone because it appeals to the needs and the creativity that lie hidden in many people. For Oyama, this project reflects her definition of jewellery: 'This is jewellery for a building. Jewellery is something decorative, something that that is added somewhere in order to make it better and more personal.'[26] As such, this work undoubtedly deals with the main functions of jewellery – decorative, signifying, distinguishing and signalising – on a significant scale. The idea that the relational art of Yuka Oyama is related to the development that has been going on in the visual arts for some time does not take away the fact that Oyama's art, which is deeply rooted in art jewellery, is representing a new approach in the crafts.

JEWELLERY IS LIFE: MAH RANA

British artist Mah Rana has also worked closely with people for some time. She is using *Jewellery is Life* (also available on badges) as an umbrella title for her work that is about the close relationship between people and jewellery.

Meanings and Attachments, an ongoing work initiated in 2001, arose from her discovery of how important inherited jewellery is to people. Invited by a guest organisation, which asks people to come with their favourite piece of jewellery, Mah Rana photographs them standing against a neutral background; she then asks them to write down their story about the piece of jewellery on a standard-size piece of paper (fig. 91). In Middlesbrough, where Rana was invited by MIMA to work for a two-week period, she photographed people in their own social environment. As a self-taught photographer, Rana takes her role as photographer seriously: 'It meant that I applied a different way of photographing them. I am a big fan of photography and cinema photography and the narrative within an image. So, I decided that the images should have a cinematic quality to them. So part of my research was to study film stills from different film genres. And I knew I wanted images that had a narrative quality.'[27] Since beginning her project she has portrayed hundreds of people and archived their stories in booklets, on a CD, on her website and also in a calendar for MIMA (2007). *Meanings and Attachments* is an infinite project that could go on for years in different places and different settings and one which taught her a lot about the meaning of inheritance and how memory affects our judgement and taste: we are prepared to wear something we would never buy for ourselves were it an inherited piece.

In 2004, triggered by the idea of inheritance, Mah Rana embarked on a project called *Every Piece of Jewellery is its Owner.*[28] In this project, photography, research, text writing and study replace jewellery. According to Rana 'remembering often exists in the photographs we have of our relatives'.[29] The physical piece of jewellery may be gone but lives on in an image. She began researching who she is when she started her university studies in psychology. Genealogy research brought her back to the days of the explorers, the slave trade and colonialism. The history of her family, however extreme (her research led her to such faraway places as Bermuda in 1600, Virginia and British Guiana), is exemplary for European and world history with all its emigration waves. Up until now she has only shown bits and pieces, which only partially reveal how she envisions this project ending up in a portrait gallery. Her fictional creation of the *Worthing Observer* from 31 March 1901, exhibited together with a brooch in the Library of Worthing in 2004, exemplifies her approach. A short article inserted on the front page of the 'antique' newspaper read: 'In one hundred and three years from now a piece of jewellery will be found on display at Worthing Library. The brooch made in that year by Mah Rana is dedicated to the sister of her great-great-grandfather Sir Joseph Garnett (born c. 1861 in British Guiana), who resides today at 59 Marine Parade. The brooch features a round gold disc coated in blue paint, covered with glass. By the time the jewel is exhibited the apartment that is rented by Mary Garnett will be replaced by a municipal car park.'[30] A portrait of Mah Rana wearing the brooch was also shown with the *Worthing Observer* and the actual brooch (figs. 92,

> 91

> 92

93). Rana's integrated historical, textual and conceptual approach also involves the craftsmanship of jewellery making and photography. It is an extreme example of the blurred
boundaries of the artist's practice, resulting in not only relational artworks such as
Meanings and Attachments but also in work that needs the art gallery or a similar place as
the most preferred context for perception.

THE CORPORAL EXPERIENCE: NAOMI FILMER

Naomi Filmer calls herself a jewellery artist but consciously works on the boundaries of
fashion, design and art. Milan-based Filmer trained as a goldsmith at the Royal College of
Art but never felt at home in the world of author jewellery. She has collaborated on catwalk
presentations with fashion designers Hussein Chalayan, Alexander McQueen and Valerie
Hash as well as for the 2003 Swarovski Runway Rocks catwalk event in London. She is
interested in where the object is placed on the body and in doing this tries to subvert our
conventional understanding of jewellery.

The jewellery that she designs for fashion catwalk shows is, one could say, extremely
non-functional as jewellery. Yet it reveals a lot about movement and the body, and therefore she also experiments with moving images, such as film loops or lenticulars (high-tech
holograms). For an Alexander McQueen Spanish-flavoured catwalk show in 2001, she
designed large bulbs, half silver and half glass, which required the models to hold their
arms in the posture of a flamenco dancer (fig. 94). In 1994, Filmer designed a silver *Ear to
Mouth Piece* for Hussein Chalayan, a simple reference to contemporary communication
apparatus. Also for Chalayan she designed a silver *Mouth Bar* (1995) that kept the mouth
wide open. For most of Filmer's jewellery, what matters is the influence that it has on the
movements of the body, yet as an object that is not being worn it also notes its absence.

Filmer searches for the forgotten places (or as she calls them 'negative spaces') on
the body with her jewellery: in between the fingers or toes, the palm of one's hand, under
the arm, around the elbow or behind the ear. By doing this she looks for the relationship
between the body and the object and is mainly interested in how it feels to wear it. For this
reason she has also experimented with ice and chocolate, liquidness, solidification and
melting. She does not make this work for a performance, more for the physical experience
of the wearer: 'I am not comfortable with my work under the title of performance, because
it suggests that you are a spectator to the work. But I want my work to be a physical experience, not a passive one. That goes for my early work too. The pieces were never made for
an audience, but for the wearer.'[31] In the video *A Sensual Shiver* (2000) that she made for
her *Ice Jewellery*, a flat slice of ice that hangs over the shoulder and upper arm, gives a real
life sensation as the viewer watches; one actually feels the shiver that runs through the
body when the ice touches it. The slow melting and the jewellery's eventual dripping create
another sensation: that of time and loss.

She finds that author jewellery dominates the wearer too much: 'Contemporary
jewellery wears *you* rather than you wearing the jewellery'.[32] Therefore her work should
be seen as a critique, and she is never too tired to explain her position.[33] By approaching
jewellery from a conceptual instead of a beautifying point of view, she makes use of the
possibilities that catwalk performances offer as a theatrical stage for new and outrageous
ideas. In her various projects Naomi Filmer works together with skilled craftsmen and, as
a designer, is interested in seeing these skilled craftspeople translate ideas into material
objects. If necessary, she will also influence the process herself. For this reason she finds
it important that she has had a good technical education. Filmer is one of the few jewellery

designers who prefer to work as a designer and director-producer to working as a 'hands-on' artist. Because of her style of work she is able to infiltrate different worlds and reach a broader audience than the usual gallery visitors.

HANS STOFER'S WORLD OF THINGS

While all of the artists above relate to jewellery in their own way, this artist, goldsmith professor and author of a publication on wire jewellery seems to divert from jewellery in his own work. Hans Stofer's exhibition *Walk the Line*, which took place at Gallery S O London in 2010, was again proof of his intriguing 'design wilderness' (fig. 95).[34] Walking > 95 the line referred to the line between art and design, a grey area that over the years has become more and more his domain. With the help of a built-in corridor with doors, filled with and surrounded by a mass of absurd and Surrealist objects, Stofer created a world of things that needed to be investigated and experienced. The show contained halfway tools and tools that were halfway jewellery pieces (like nails with sculpted heads), an odd and crude silver cup pierced with screws in *Stofer's Mug (Voodoo)*, a small sculpture built from metal wire and mandarin peel, a *Hunting* chain with keys ending in thorns, candlesticks, wall ornaments, a spider's web with a gold wedding ring in the centre and the three-tiered trolley in *Off My Trolley*, full of a bizarre collection of useful things found in an artist's studio (fig. 96). Rings and other jewellery could also be found amongst cans, brushes, > 96 paint tubes, cups, cigarettes and a crucifix made of Swiss cheese. Although the trolley looked like a jumble, the artist had made every item. As Stephen Knott in his review for *Art Jewelry Forum* points out, 'Stofer deceives the audience into thinking he has only used ready-mades, when actually he has employed craft skill to make things look like ready-mades. There is a deception at play, showing how makers can exercise magic on materials to trick viewers – an exploration of craft as "crafty", or cunning.'[35]

What drives a highly qualified jeweller such as Hans Stofer, who was trained as a precision engineer and toolmaker before he gained an MA in jewellery and design at the Zurich School of Art in Switzerland, to cheat – that is to say from a craftsman's point of view – the viewer? One possible answer may be that Stofer does not want us to take his work for granted. He forces the viewer to look intensely and to be engaged, offering the viewer a world that is more about enchantment than about rationality. Jewellery is part of this world of everyday objects. The pieces look like characters in a play: the funny nails beside the fragile mandarin and wire portrait, the sturdy pierced cup beside the elegant spider's web. His objects and jewellery try to resist any law of design or 'good craftsmanship'. By emphasising the imperfect he makes room for thoughts about beauty and virtuosity and for our own ideas and stories. He succeeds in interpreting jewellery as an everyday utilitarian phenomenon, comparable to a cup, a candlestick, a tin or a screw – as an object that is deprived of any economical, symbolical, ornamental or magical value and that dwells in the realm of the personal and sentimental.

The art of goldsmithing is no longer just a skilled craft but also a manner of artistic and reflexive expression. During the last decade of the twentieth century a 'jewellery language' that can be expressed in various mediums such as photography, video, installations, animations, books and digital media has developed. As such, a middle space was developed, still within the context of jewellery but outside the known framework and exhibited in both public and virtual space. It is important to see these types of projects and events within the context of jewellery; they enrich it and intend to remain in proportion to it. This type of work endeavours to build another form of contact with people while at the same time tries to relate to a new audience. Quite often the work is temporary, open ended, changeable, ephemeral, a work in process – just the opposite of the characteristics of jewellery as wearable, stable, permanent. These character traits do not make it easy to appreciate this work. All too often this work is seen as an attempt to make visual art, which is then labelled as 'bad' visual art by criticasters because according to them everything in jewellery occurs years later than in the visual arts and therefore is nothing more than a pale echo of 'real' art.

But no, these sorts of boundary-breaching projects are the offshoots from the stem of applied art. A development that also raises its head in other fields of the applied arts, for example in the work of the British ceramicist Clare Twomey's installations and outside sculptures, the Belgian ceramicist Anne Ausloos's video installations, the British textile artist Freddie Robbins's textile sculptures, the American textile artist Anne Wilson's video installations and the American textile artist Dave Cole's installations in public spaces, to name a few.

Artists who work in this way breach the borders of their trade, yet at the same time their work is rooted in their craft, its history, usage, codes, conventions and bigotry. It appears that other mediums in particular offer the possibility to reflect upon the different phenomena of jewellery, ceramics, glass or textile. Non-craft-based techniques (such as photography or video) in the hands of a jewellery artist should be seen as an extension of the goldsmith's material rather than as the end product itself; the jeweller does not want to become a photographer or a visual artist. All of these expressions contribute to a new kaleidoscopic view of jewellery in which all aspects of jewellery are present: decoration, memory, emotion, power, distinction, wearability and physicality.

Clearly a kinship exists between the art jeweller and the visual artist: both work autonomously on work that is generally not made for a specific person, situation or place and both make use of the expertise of companies and skilled professionals for the realisation of their ideas. However, the working methods of a jeweller are also related to those of the designer: both are in search of innovative material, of techniques and production processes, and they both must take into consideration the demands of function or use. As designers, jewellery artists take up an interesting transitional position between visual art and design.

In the twenty-first century, it has become more and more clear that jewellery, although autonomous and independent, remains isolated. Despite the growing number of jewellery galleries in the world, the scene remains small and known only to insiders and aficionados. The jewellery galleries seem unable to bridge the gap to include other persons interested in art, whereas the design world has found a way to reach the cultural elite, a path that is paved with glossy magazines, newspapers and television exposure. Money seems to be of the essence within this system: the more extravagant and expensive, the more interesting as a 'Brad Pitt buys chaise lounge from Joep van Lieshout at Art Basel' newspaper headline proves.[36]

Since the late 1990s, this appears to have been an unsatisfactory situation for the young generation of jewellery makers. They observe that, in general, jewellery has meaning in the lives of people, and beginning with this idea they search for another strategy to develop a new relationship with the public. They are more interested in jewellery as a relational and societal phenomenon than as adornments and merchandise. Sometimes, with the precise eye of the goldsmith, they may approach it as being another implement; at that point it becomes more about the associative ideas of jewellery and adornment.

Sometimes the experience of the jewellery piece is central even though this is achieved with what appears to be contradictory means.

There was a time, in the 1980s and 1990s, when jewellers aimed at an art status. That time is now gone. Jewellers today find this no longer necessary; they have discovered the power of their own trade. Suska Mackert clearly explained how she sees her position in an interview. In answer to the question of whether her work should be seen as art or as craft she answered: 'I don't want to fit in this old hierarchy. I see there are differences between design or craft and art. I don't consider myself a designer, I prefer to consider myself a jeweller. I use jewellery as a source, but what I make is in a sense autonomous, although it is linked to something which is not autonomous.'[37] Her view reflects that of many art jewellers today.

1   Their workshops *Plezier met papier*, workshops with waste newspaper, were held at PCM, a newspaper print-ing company in Amsterdam, in 2001. See: Claudine Hellweg, 2001. 'Atelier Puckie, eigenzinnig en lichtvoetig', in *Kunstlab*, October, pp. 20–3.

2   Nicolas Bourriaud, 2002. *Relational Aesthetics.* Dijon: Presses du Réel, p. 9.

3   *In the Mind of Ädellab*, Stockholm 2011 (home printed, not officially published brochure).

4   Bourriaud (see note 2), p. 113.

5   Post on *www.museumaker.com/projects/modern-jewel* from 25 Mar. 2011.

6   Text 'Art Rehab, 2010/11', from Ted Noten's website. Accessed 13 Apr. 2011.

7   The collaborative commission was part of Museumaker, a national partnership between makers, museums and visitors and involving sixteen museums across the UK. In Middlesbrough the project started May 2010 and ended March 2011 with the exhibition *The Modern Jewel in Time and the Mind of Others.*

8   Dinie Besems, interview with the author, Amsterdam, Nov. 1995.

9   The website is now inactive.

10   *Magisch vierkant Deel IX* [The Magic Square Part IX] is an obsessive book completely based on the number 9, published on 9.9.99, consisting of 99 pages, 999 words, 9 mm thick and size 18 × 18 cm (1 + 8 = 9). The cover was printed with a sequence of 9 numbers in 9 different rows, the sum of these being 369 (3 + 6 = 9), also the number of copies in the edition. The nonsensical content was a sequence of randomly chosen words. Studio Gonnissen en Widdershoven, a young, innovative and brilliant design couple with whom Besems had collaborated before, carried out the graphic design work.

11   Ted Noten, Liesbeth den Besten (text), 1996. *Verplaatsingen, Shifts.* Amsterdam: T. Noten, 1996.

12   *FRAME, The International Magazine of Interior Architecture and Design* (NL), no. 28, September/October 2002; *Kunsthandverk* (NO), no. 103, 1/07; *Crafts, The Magazine of Contemporary Crafts* (UK), no. 219, July/August 2009; *Frieze, Contemporary Art and Culture* (UK), no. 67, May 2002; *l'Officiel, de la couture et de la mode de Paris* (NL), no. 7, September 2008.

13   From the press release by the Platina gallery in Stockholm for the *Wanna Swap Your Ring?* Event on 9 Apr. 2011.

14   Suska Mackert, 2002. *Display: gemeentelijke kunstaankopen 2000–2001.* Amsterdam: Stedelijk Museum (unpaginated).

15   Press release by Galerie Louise Smit in Amsterdam for the presentation of *The Andy Warhol Collection* at Collect in London, May 2009.

16   The book has no printed title but is called *Juwelenboek Madame Tussaud*, 1998 (edition of 200).

17   See: Roland Barthes, 1983. *The Fashion System.* New York: Hill and Wang, p. 9, in which he differentiates between 'image-clothing' and 'writing-clothing', thus photographing clothing and describing clothing. In his view, words take over the position of the real article of clothing; words become a 'super code'.

18   Interview in Zandra Ahl and Päivi Ernkvist (eds.), 2005. *REAL Craft in Dialogue.* Gothenburg: Röhsska Museet, p. 13.

19   The Department of the Applied Arts at the Stedelijk Museum in Amsterdam bought the series.

20   The story surrounding the discovery is too good not to mention: 'The recent discovery of jewelry in a storage room in Andy Warhol's townhouse came as an enormous surprise to everyone. After all, prior to the auction last spring of the Andy Warhol Collection, the principal rooms of the house had been completely emptied. Everything had been thoroughly and exhaustively searched. We were certain that nothing had been over-looked. But Andy outwitted us. Despite the extensive procedures put in place by the Andy Warhol Foundation for the Visual Arts, all it took to conceal the jewelry was one of the most inventive, brilliant, and fertile imaginations of the era and two old metal flat filing cabinets, stacked one on top of the other. Andy had used them for years to store his own unframed drawings and prints and those of other artists. It was a perfect

hiding place. The jewelry would not be visible when the drawers were opened, as he had hidden it in the self-contained space underneath the drawers, between the two cabinets. It would never be found unless these cabinets were separated for some reason. And, as Andy knew that these cabinets would be moved only under extraordinary circumstances and only by the very few people he trusted, he could be sure that no stranger would stumble on this hiding place…' (Preface by Frederick W. Hughes for Sotheby's New York catalogue 1988).

21 James Beighton, interview with Susan Pietzsch in 2005, in: *Wrappinghood: An Exhibition Curated by Schmuck2 for MIMA Middlesbrough Institute of Modern Art.* Middlesbrough: [Schmuck2 e.V.] (unpaginated).

22 See: *www.schmuck2.de.*

23 It is noteworthy that Pietzsch organises many exhibitions in her own region, the rather secluded north-east of Germany where she lives in the countryside. Pietzsch is a good networker and she knows how to transfer her exhibitions to other places; she has also exhibited in Japan.

24 Information from a lecture given by Yuka Oyama, Gerrit Rietveld Academy in Amsterdam, 30 Oct. 2007. In this way Oyama found that the Japanese materials, for instance, are more careless and colourful than the Austrian materials.

25 Ibid.

26 Ibid.

27 Email from Mah Rana, 6 Jan. 2008.

28 Mah Rana, interview with the author in London, Feb. 2008, in which she told me extensively about the project and showed me her photographs and ideas.

29 See: video portrait made for the Jerwood Applied Arts Prize 2007, directed by Tim Crowie and Martin Banks and produced by Annie Kwan. *www.timcowie.com/jerwood-mah-rana/.* Accessed 22 May 2011.

30 See: *http://navigating-history.net/projects/mah_rana.htm.* Accessed 22 May 2011.

31 Interview in: Laurie Britton Newell (ed.), 2008. *Out of the Ordinary: Spectacular Craft.* London: V&A Publishing, p. 79.

32 Glenn Adamson, 2008. 'The Spectacle of the Everyday', in Britton Newell (see note 31), p. 23.

33 In a recent book about fashion jewellery, she tries to position her work by pointing to the openness of the fashion world, her jewellery having been used for shoots in many glossy magazines: 'Each stylist who works with a piece of jewellery has a different perception of the work, thereby giving it a new life. Its context can be reinvented each time which is something that doesn't happen in a gallery or museum […] I would refer to the pieces I create for the catwalk as couture accessories, or simply jewellery.' Furthermore: 'Art jewellery celebrates ideas and craftsmanship regardless of fashion trends and does not necessarily see the body as the initial source of inspiration.' Maia Adams, 2010. *Fashion Jewelry: Catwalk and Couture.* London: Laurence King, p. 127.

34 Hans Stofer and Linda Sandino (text), 2006. *Hans Stofer's Design Wilderness.* Solothurn: Edition Galerie.

35 Stephen Knott, 2010. 'Tooling around', in *Art Jewelry Forum,* 19 July.

36 See: 'Brad Pitt buys Van Lieshout Chair', in *NRC Handelsblad,* 11 June 2009, p. 9.

37 Interview in Zandra Ahl and Päivi Ernkvist (see note 18), p. 13.

VI. The Body

In 1999, under local anaesthesia, the German artist Katinka Kaskeline had a row of seven pearls sewn into the skin of her underarm. Her body was used as a direct object for physical attachment. The operation was recorded on video and in this sense was similar to Peter Skubic's steel implant *Jewellery under the Skin* executed in 1975, which could be viewed in a photograph or seen by X-ray (fig. 97).[1] Through this video, Kaskeline's pearls are exposed to the public and solicit reactions. The viewer battles disgust and fascination because this jewellery refers not only to surgical intervention and to a conscious assault on the skin but also to the intimacy of a piece of jewellery that has become a symbiotic part of the body. Furthermore, Kaskeline makes use of the symbolism of the pearl: it is a most conventional bourgeois symbol of status, adulthood (young girls tend not to wear pearls) and credibility (professional working women are often seen wearing them). Her work is also reminiscent of the far more radical French body artist Orlan, who for decades has transformed her body by undergoing various surgical procedures such as facial implants while under local anaesthetic. With her *Carnal Act* the body is actually elevated to the position of a canvas and the operation room to a theatre, where Orlan, adorned in special outfits, answers questions from a live audience viewing the performance from a museum gallery in another location.

> 97

Decorating the body is all too human. Some of the earliest signs from which the human presence can be discerned are body decorations, such as the 75,000-year-old shells found in the Blombos Cave in South Africa and the 82,000-year-old shell beads found in Morocco. The shells, with holes bored in them to make beads for wearing, and the shavings of red ochre found in the same cave seem indicative of this fact. They are seen as examples of the ability to think symbolically, an ability which separates Homo sapiens from animals.[2] Symbols that are used to give meaning to who we are, are thus symbols that presuppose the awareness of 'the self'. It is not possible though to ascertain whether this jewellery or the ochre paintings meet the expectations of a certain standard of beauty at that time.

The body is not a neutral 'bag of cells' nor just a 'material covering', a tabula rasa without inherent meaning. The body is full of meaning. The French philosopher Maurice Merleau-Ponty talks about the *corps vécu* – the 'lived body' – the body as one experiences it, the body that you not only *have* but also that you *are*. Merleau-Ponty does not want to see the body as an object but as a subject: the *lived body*, formed by the experience of our body's senses. You do not just live in your body, you are your body.

Anthropologist Ted Polhemus indicates that ancient tribes from different continents applied all the methods that humans had developed to enhance themselves visually at around the same time. That is why he proclaims that, 'body decoration is essential for our species'. The 'designed personal body' is, according to him, the core of the symbolic universe of Homo sapiens: 'By decorating it, the body finds itself in the symbolic universe. The human body is by nature special; it is the only object that we cannot do without, the only object that is a subject as well. For this reason, it is in the center of this symbolic universe.'[3]

For Polhemus, who became famous for his books about street culture, style surfing and body manipulations, the body is an empty canvas where one is free to experiment with a seemingly infinite amount of possible decorative techniques. The skin is not only the delineation between the outer world and the self, a neutral screen, a boundary; it is also a surface upon which the inner self can manifest itself. Everyone's skin is unique; it not only displays unique inner emotions as outward reactions (blushing, goosebumps, acne, birthmarks) but also carries life's history (scars, wrinkles, age spots). Piercings, tattoos and scarification are fetish-like methods for self-expression and presentation. Whereas they form a union with the body and permanently change it, jewellery is external, not integrated and is usually only a temporary addition.

In a different work, Katinka Kaskeline showed that there is another way to apply decoration to the skin. As part of her research for identity, she 'dressed' herself with a live bloodsucker, which bit into her décolletage with its many sharp teeth. The harmless insect, commonly used for medicinal purposes, sucked itself full of blood before falling dead, after which the wound continued to bleed for a while. The tiny star-shaped scar that it left can be seen as a unique piece of jewellery, just as scars are considered trophies or as proof of one's personal identity. The artistic quality of Kaskeline's decoration method lies in the concept and the making. The artist created the design for the skin decoration herself; it was not the bloodsucker that sought an arbitrary victim and a random spot on the body but the artist that allowed the creature to do its work on a specific spot. Barbara Maas correctly points out that Kaskeline's work is not meant to be provocative, no matter how shocking or disgusting it may seem to many: 'Her work is about communication, intimacy and contact. About the attempt to both take control and direct others' perception of oneself, and to bare the "Self" and lay it open. It is about transcending the skin, experienced as a barrier that separates, overcoming the border between the "I" and the world outside.'[4]

In this chapter, I will examine jewellery that takes or uses the human body as its subject. This happens, for example, when researching the relationship between the body and jewellery, where the piece of jewellery acts as an interface between the individual and the world. However, the human body as the subject of jewellery, as we will see, can also be investigated, imagined and sometimes commented upon.

It should already be clear that there is a close connection between jewellery and the body. The bracelet and ring follow the body's form the closest, but the necklace, the pendant and ear jewellery are only adapted to the body to a certain degree because they must be hung. Much of the jewellery made from the late 1960s to the 1980s looked like constructions added as an extra layer to the body. It is reminiscent of Emmy van Leersum's aluminium collars and head-pieces, of Gijs Bakker's head and body ornaments and of other Dutch jewellery makers working in and around 1970 such as Nicolaas van Beek and Hans Appenzeller (fig. 100). It also nods to the enormous painted stick constructions from American designer Marjorie Schick, the plastic *Tabards* from British designer Julia Manheim and the wood and textile constructions in the early 1980s from Dutch artist LAM de Wolf (fig. 98). There was also a general tendency towards upsizing and expanding the scale of jewellery at this time. Peter Skubic's *Jewelry Wears Me: I Am Imprisoned by Jewelry* (1982) is a steel object measuring approximately 50 × 50 × 250 cm, which can actually hold a person and looks like an enormous brooch.

In the catalogue *Fear and Fashion in the Cold War*, Jane Pavitt interprets Emmy van Leersum and Gijs Bakker's *Clothing Suggestions* (1970) as 'a concern for armouring the body', in which she, rightly so, poses the question of what the body must be protected from.[5] According to her, the answer was found in the general feeling of fear due to the Cold

> 100

> 98

War. Still, as much as this interpretation has value, it is merely a part of the reason why Van Leersum and Bakker's jewellery looked like this. It was also the 'space age', the time of the first space travels, moon landings and an unbelievably positive feeling of progress and power (on both sides of the Iron Curtain). Another explanation should be sought in the singular attention drawn to the body. At the time, the contemporary fashion world was a source of inspiration – the entire body became a playground for investigation. Van Leersum and Bakker's jewellery was made from industrial material and developed under the influence of cybernetic phenomena, such as the futuristic aluminium dresses in the cult film *Qui êtes vous, Polly Maggoo?* by William Klein (1966) and the harness-like mini-dresses made from steel plates by fashion designer Paco Rabanne (1968). Other jewellers who studied and worked in a totally different culture were inspired as well. Athenian goldsmith Ilias Lalaounis, who found his inspiration in a completely different direction, was also working on body jewellery and in 1969 presented *The Body Jewellery Collection* in Paris.[6] The 18 and 22 ct gold, life-size jewellery pieces were the antithesis of the modern image of Dutch body jewellery from the same period. Lalaounis's jewellery pieces are voluptuous and decorative, like the coverings that Mata Hari was often photographed in; they are based on fantastical, free interpretations of Minoan, Mycenaean and Byzantine art, yet they are also an expression of the exact same spirit of the times.

Whether looking back at the past or fantasising about the future, the body seems to have had a conspicuous role in the development of jewellery around 1970. The entire upper body is used, sometimes also from the feet up. Donald Willcox's book *Body Jewelry* (1973) shows the results of this development. The book, for which Willcox interviewed some fifty-odd artists, brought together bizarre, frumpy and hip body jewellery from around the world, in which there is much art and craft type work to be found, such as macramé, wool, feathers and beads (the international textile art and hippy culture was blooming at that time). At the very back of the book, there are six pages dedicated to Van Leersum and Bakker's *Clothing Suggestions* introduced carefully by Willcox as 'risky', 'provocative' and 'open for criticism'. As dated as the book may seem to our twenty-first-century eyes, it is a valuable source of information about popular and street culture around 1970. Willcox states: 'Forms began to grow larger, bolder – even "dangerous". Forms began to grow onto and into the human body as if they belonged there. The body was being rediscovered, and jewelry was being redefined. Yes, we had always considered the body, but we had too often defined it in terms of confining our forms. We didn't make a ring too large. A lady might not be able to fit her gloves on over it. We didn't dare build a bold form on the breast. A lady might not be able to fit her fur coat on over it. What had we done? We had mistakenly defined the body in a way that made it necessary to limit our jewelry.'[7]

This emphasis on the body must be seen in connection with the social and artistic developments of the time. It was the Age of Aquarius, the age of hippies and the mini-mode. At youth rock festivals like Woodstock (1969), an atmosphere of freedom, communality and anarchy reigned. The naked body was not accepted by the majority of the population per se but had become more and more visible as a subject for discussion. For example, in 1967 when a Dutch television programme for youths, *Hoepla*, released film shots of a naked girl reading a newspaper on TV it led to so much public commotion that the government minister responsible for public television was held accountable for the incident. And because the foreign press had picked up the news, the naked model received international status.[8]

In the visual arts the body became a part of performances that had a ritual, quite often physically threatening, character. Body Art became an international phenomenon around 1967. Life or the body as a piece of art was the subject of the Viennese Actionists, whose intense performances of smearing naked bodies with animal blood and inner organs confronted and shocked the audience. Other artists such as Vito Acconci, Gina Pane, Chris Burden and Ulay and Abramovic went even further in their performances, which often appeared as a marathon session: Burden shot himself in the arm (1971), Gina Pane ate rotten meat, regurgitated it and ate the vomit, and Ulay and Abramovic rhythmically sucked up each other's breath until, when the oxygen diminished, they reached the point where their breathing became more and more difficult, as can be seen in the video *Breathing Out, Breathing In* (1978). VALIE EXPORT's *Tap and Touch Cinema* (1968–71), where the artist walked on the street with a box in front of her chest and invited men to touch her breasts through the curtain enclosing the box, was about voyeurism and a man's perspective. With this performance, which is only superficially comparable to Van Leersum and Bakker's *Clothing Suggestions* (1970), EXPORT made her own body the subject of art.[9]

Ironically, there are not so many direct parallels between Body Art and jewellery. In jewellery, Gijs Bakker and Peter Skubic were the main protagonists of a short movement of anti-jewellery, influenced by Fluxus, Conceptual Art and Body Art. This work took the body as subject and departure and resulted in non-material work documented in photography and video. The performer or artist was like a sculptor who perceived his own body or that of another performer as a neutral material with which to work. Bakker's *Organic Jewellery* (1973) showed how the body could be changed and decorated temporarily through a small intervention: the tightening of a wire around the arm, leg or waist. After the wire was removed, the imprint was documented in photography before it disappeared forever.[10] Peter Skubic went to the extreme with his aforementioned silver implant and its removal (1975/1982), where the first action of introduction was documented in photographs and the removal was recorded on video. Perhaps less radical but more provocative is Skubic's action at his 1981 solo exhibition at Galerie Mattar in Cologne, where he dangerously suspended the sharp pointed tip of a sewing machine needle right in front of his pupil; it was fastened through a sticking plaster above his left eyebrow and documented in a photograph entitled *Irritation*. In 1979 Austrian artist Gert Mosettig exhibited twenty-four X-rays showing how a steel ball travelled through his body for a period of one day.[11] More jewellers continued to investigate the body and its possibilities and limitations. One work that can be regarded as a free interpretation of Body Art in jewellery even though the aspect of self-mutilation is completely absent is Gerd Rothmann's *Gold unter meinen Fingernägeln* (fig. 99), where dirty nail borders were replaced with golden ones. Frans van Nieuwenborg even used the discomforting and annoying bodily fluid sweat to produce ornaments. He did this by making a photo series of perspiration marks in clothing, interpreting the body as the producer of ornamentation. The work was never exhibited but it can be seen as a true representation of the significant role of the body in jewellery in the 1970s.[12]

> 99

Just like fashion, jewellery forms an extra layer on the body but is very rarely about the body itself. The new physicalness in the visual arts contributed to jewellery artists beginning their search for a more direct relationship with the body, for example, Emmy van Leersum's bracelets based on the cylinder as a form that came the closest to the arm, Gijs Bakker's yellow-gold ear shells (1967) that followed the form of the ear and were slipped over them and Hans Appenzeller's *Personal Ornaments* consisting of broad aluminium bands that twist around the entire upper part of the body of the wearer, starting from the middle and reaching up towards the neck (ca 1969). The individual body also became a subject of research. In 1974, Gijs Bakker designed head ornaments from the profiles of Fritz Maierhofer and Emmy van Leersum during the symposium *Schmuck aus*

Stahl [Jewellery in Steel]. In the 1960s, behind the Iron Curtain in Bratislava in the former Czechoslovakia, Václav Cigler made very unusual head and body ornaments that could literally be taken for armour. Based on the circle and fastened to the body with metal wire, some were created as open structures and some were made of a shiny material which reflected the surrounding area in a bend or on a corner of the piece. The wearer could literally spy on his surroundings. Different from Bakker's and Van Leersum's jewellery, this jewellery was meant to give the wearer a feeling of security and provide shelter while at the same time giving them power. In Austria some artists stressed the discomforting function of jewellery, taking it as a kind of prosthesis, as can be seen in the ring *Fingerspanner* [Finger Stretcher] (1968) by Conceptual artist Walter Pichler and the *Gelenkring* [Joint Ring or Hinge Ring] (1974) by Leonhard Stramitz. Both pieces look like medical accessories, the first one actually preventing movement of the finger.

Some years later, the body also became the subject of a different kind of investigation. Around 1980, jewellery makers were looking into the relationship between the body, movement and gestures and geometric forms and also dealing with the beauty and individual features of the body. With this body research, they discovered new places and new ways in which forms could be integrated, even if only temporarily as a photographic moment. In doing this, not only was the body explored but other visions of decorating and of jewellery began to develop as well.

The exhibition *Körperkultur* (1982), a collaboration between Otto Künzli and Gerd Rothmann and organised by Galerie am Graben in Vienna, was an important event in this context. Künzli and Rothmann extended the traditional places for jewellery on the body to other unexpected places. They let one see how the palm, the space between the fingers, the space between two people, the underarm or the inside of the ear could be taken in by jewellery – or something that looked like jewellery. Künzli's jewellery, conceived by him as tools or instruments, were made mainly of flat, loose, geometric forms which could be clamped between body parts. The simple square black boxes with custom-made forms to contain these tools reinforced the idea of an armamentarium. The tool collection, consisting of metal triangles, a golden bullet, steel rods and rubber bands, had to be used and adapted to the body as strange intruders from outside.

Gerd Rothmann's approach is different. He explores the body in a tactile, erotic way, emphasising the sensuality of the touch and about the individuality of each finger, hand or bodily imprint. In the late 1970s, Rothmann began a series of silver casts of body parts, such as the heel, the elbow, the nose, the chin and skull. They could be slipped over each body part as a shiny, smooth, polished shield. Only the nose cast was made of gold. This jewellery was custom-made for (and on) one person. In Rothmann's monograph, each model is mentioned by name.[13] His pewter *Bodyprints* of the arm, the nipple, the underarm, in between the fingers, the inside of the hand, the shoulder blade and more reveal the fine folds and pores of the skin.[14] His *Collection: 107 Palms of Friends and Acquaintances* (fig. 101) > 101 demonstrated a semi-scientific need to collect, classify and sort the handprints; packed in plastic sleeves, dated and named, they were filed in a special white box just like a butterfly or mineral collection.

While Otto Künzli stood for an abstract and conceptual approach, Gerd Rothmann continued to move in the direction of the personalised and the wearable; his individual ear-prints dating from 1979 to 1982 can be worn directly on the ear. Later, in the 1980s and 1990s, Rothmann created highly aesthetic, wide silver and gold bracelets with his own fingerprints imprinted into the surface. He also made some intriguing castings: his armpit (1977), the inside of Daniel Fusban's nose (1987), a golden nose of Jan Teunen (1984) and

> 102

The Balls: From Him for His Girlfriend Rosetta, a chain with silver gold-plated testicles (1986, fig. 102). The last piece of jewellery was a remarkable statement inside the world of jewellery: intimate, vulnerable and provoking. But Rothmann had evidently set limits for himself. This became clear when in the same year he decided to name a chain made with five gold and five silver nipple prints *Masculine-Feminine*. The personal for him became too intimate: 'The necklace with the nipples lay unfinished on my table for a long time. [...] People's associations took the wrong course. I do not wish to provoke people, nor do I want to intrude on anyone's private life. While rounding off and polishing the nipples, I found a solution which might reduce the awkwardness of the necklace somewhat. The shape is anonymous and therefore merely a symbol. Personalities play no role in this piece of jewellery. In mythology, the moon is feminine (silver) and the sun is masculine (gold). The necklace is to be worn symmetrically, one half on the right and one half on the left.'[15] It is a typical, rather disappointing jewellery solution that, within the context of the visual arts, could never have been found. It shows that jewellery has its own language and systems. The extra layer that jewellery forms on a body should never be too confrontational, shocking, provocative or anti-aesthetic because it would then lose its symbolical, congenial and protective function that the conversation piece normally provides.

The Italian artist Bruno Martinazzi has transformed in detail the human body into gold, silver and stone. Martinazzi is an intellectual par excellence and is a recognised artist in both sculpture and jewellery. His marble sculptures and golden jewellery appear to interact with and feed off each other. From the very beginning of his life as an artist, the human figure was Martinazzi's subject, both in sculptures and in jewellery.[16] After a brief period, in which he made abstract jewellery characterised by expressionistic forms, a fascination for texture and expensive precious stones, he concentrated on the plastic nature of the human body. In 1968, he made his first brooches using the body as subject: *Backside*

> 103, 104

(fig. 103), which shows two naked buttocks chased in silver, *Occhio* (fig. 104), which portrays an eye in white and yellow gold, and *Mouth, Economic Growth*, which shows a mouth perfectly sculpted in a rectangular sheet of gold. All three pieces are sensual and seductive, not only the *Backside* cheeks but also the secretive half-closed eye, behind which a partially visible pupil gleams, and the mouth's slightly open lips with barely visible softly shimmering white teeth.

This jewellery makes an impact because of the unbelievable craftsmanship of the maker, who allows the lips to rise up out of a square piece of gold plate in an almost natural manner. The rounding of the buttocks and the folds of the eyelid are proof of the same plastic abilities. In this way, the viewer does not take the fragment as something that is imperfect, a remnant of something that is lost and isolated, but uses the part to imagine the whole. For Martinazzi, however, it is not only about singing the praises of beauty, about the soft curves of the body and the glowing curvature of the lips. In his work the thumb begins to grow in importance, too, as weight and measure and as a symbol for understanding

> 105

(fig. 105). Martinazzi uses the human body more and more as a means to understand the world and to understand what it is to be human. He represents themes like Narcissus, Homo sapiens, convertibility, metamorphosis and chaos with the help of fingers or lips. His pieces of jewellery, such as the famous bracelet made of golden fingertips that surround the arm in a grip, offer protection or a philosophical harness of sorts. Martinazzi writes: 'If a human being wears jewellery, he is expressing symbolically his need for transforming himself; not merely superficially transforming his skin and profile but profoundly transforming himself and his life.'[17]

French jewellery designer Carole Deltenre, who works with castings of the body, is generations younger than Rothmann and Martinazzi. Her female perspective on the female body is a valuable contribution in jewellery. Deltenre is neither afraid nor cautious. When she takes castings from vaginas she asks a lot from her models, but as a woman she is perhaps more able to. These weird porcelain castings (incidentally, no organ is the same, they are like individual 'portraits') are mounted in elaborate filigree silver frames and made into medallions called *Nymphes* (2007–09). The frames enhance and glorify these sex organs that are so often deliberately maltreated, abused and mutilated in the reality of daily life and though war and plastic surgery. Deltenre makes use of the social and signalising function of jewellery by using the brooch as a badge. These brooches are not made for male pleasure; they present a strong female perspective on the body.

> fig. 103

> fig. 107

At the beginning of the 1970s, Swiss designer Pierre Degen, who has worked in London since then, researched the connection between humankind and jewellery. First, he made wearables: small abstract symbols in metal and other hard materials and pieces of cloth that could be tied around the arm that still had the character of jewellery or intimate treasures. After 1980 the investigation towards wearability demanded a more radical approach and led to life-size constructions with ladders, flags and sticks. He conceived jewellery as a personal environment, a construction that you step into before you can take it with you to wear. This is not so far from Václav Cigler's idea about jewellery being a 'landscape for the human body'. In a text accompanying one of his drawings, Pierre Degen describes: 'A person in front of a tree, a window, a railing, a cross, a shutter, a scaffolding, an animal, a boulder, a kite on a path, a container, a flag against a cloud, a tailored hedge, a sign, a door, a painting, a drawing, a poster, or behind ephemeral jewellery.'[18] From this description of a person in relationship to his or her environment, Pierre Degen proposes that one sees themselves in relationship to these environmental phenomena, including jewellery. In a pictorial sense, Degen positions mankind between a background and a foreground (jewellery). A piece of jewellery can be an extra temporary layer, behind which one can hide.

Because of the scale and nature of this work, not many people would have immediately recognised this as jewellery. Other examples include *Large Loop* consisting of a large hoop approximately 1.6 m in diameter which was attached to the body with a cord, *Square Frame* (fig. 107), a framework of rope and sticks on which drawings and a newspaper article hung, and *Brushwood*, a bundle of branches carried on one's back. All this and similar work from his solo exhibition in 1982–83 had a relatively theatrical character, a feeling that was enhanced by the setting in which they were photographed, namely a backdrop of paper painted with wild strokes. They were three-dimensional reflections

> 107

about wearability that were at most suited for demonstration but that one would never actually wear. With hindsight, it seems a weak position for work that claims to be about jewellery, but it fit precisely with the developments of the day, especially in England and the Netherlands where the whole body, the idea of wearable and the overtures to fashion and performance were central. Yet, because of its radical nature, this work was indeed a dead-end street.

> 106

The neck and shoulder jewellery made out of painted sticks by the American designer Marjorie Schick are more daring than Degen's 'personal environments' because they were emphatically jewellery; namely an aesthetic object meant to be worn, no matter how difficult that might be (fig. 106). In this respect they differed essentially from Degen's objects which were props to be used on stage. In the mid-1970s, Marjorie Schick made large, wearable papier-mâché sculptures constructed with metal wire and used in experimental dance improvisations. In the 1980s, her work became more wearable but no less sculptural. She also made 'drawings to wear' where the emphasis remained on what she called 'body sculptures'. Just like Pierre Degen, she is interested in the borders of wearability, but while Degen got stuck on the belief that everything is wearable Schick concentrated on the sculptural form that she wanted to make wearable. 'My work is about form', she claims. 'The content of my work is the form and also the scale of it, so I really work hard at the aesthetic qualities of the piece.'[19] She has been working for over forty years and it appears that her manner and approach have not led to a dead-end. For Schick, wearable means primarily to ensure that one can hang a piece on the body, even if only for a brief moment. She feels that it is important to wear her pieces, that there is physical contact and interaction, that a person should think about wearing them and about when they would wear them. Schick says, 'Obviously it makes you reconsider how you move in space – how others see you – because it takes a great deal of nerve to wear such a large piece.'[20]

In 1982, Marjorie Schick's work was introduced in Europe at the exhibition *Jewellery Redefined* in London's British Crafts Centre.[21] The theatrical achievements of her work and the physical consequences were immediately recognised. The expressive character of Schick's work contrasted greatly with the geometric, reduced and extremely controlled experiments with form on the body which were popular in Europe. The style of European body jewellery approached clothing and accessories and was literally tailored to the body where textiles and other soft, flexible materials were popular at that time. In England artists such as Julia Manheim, Susannna Heron and Caroline Broadhead worked in this field.[22] Other European artists include Anita Evenepoel, Emmy van Leersum, LAM de Wolf and Joke Brakman together with Claudie Berbee and Johanna Hess-Dahm together with Bloomer.

The 1980s were the years of 'objects to wear', the years in which the body received a greater emphasis and presence as an entire surface for jewellery. During this period jewellery tended to be large, like Verena Sieber-Fuchs's necklaces or Otto Künzli's wallpaper brooches. The wearable sculptures from the 1980s were scarcely worn, only in exceptional circumstances and special settings; they rarely appeared at public functions and instead found their reverberation mainly in photographs.

The jewellery created at the end of the 1980s and into the 1990s was used and seen in public, and although in the 1990s jewellery physically lost ground it gained in meaning on the body through its emphatic content and its narrative. The body plays a new role in jewellery now. Jewellers began to research the body as a concept. What the body means, how a person experiences their body, and how the body is experienced in public space are questions that are increasingly finding their place in society and in the arts. In this interpretation, jewellery embodies the character of an attribute or a body extension. The body is not only observed as a private subject but as a biological, medical and social object and concept.

Christoph Zellweger has been working on this theme since the beginning of the 1990s. Zellweger is interested in the smooth transition between the artificial and the natural, between false and real, of which mankind is the personification, the epitome. The human body, for centuries the subject of scientific research and human intervention, has in the twentieth century become a real object of manipulation. 'Body design' leads to body corrections, anti-aging treatments, cosmetic surgery, liposuction, sex transformations, artificial insemination and organ transplants, amongst other things. Zellweger bears no moral judgement about this phenomenon; he accepts it as a given and offers us the chance to reflect upon it. Just as we design our surroundings, we give ourselves form with the help of technology. Through his work he wants us to experience that technology belongs to humankind and that it satisfies our human needs, which continue to get closer to developments in the sciences. In Zellweger's earlier work, technology itself was the subject, some examples of which include the silver, the polystyrene (fig. 108) and the rusty steel jewellery, which looked like half-decomposed industrial archaeological finds; around the mid-1990s, his attention gradually shifted to the human body. Initially polystyrene seemed to be a good material because the structure of this man-made element has a cellular structure that resembles that of the inner bone structure of humans. This cold, 'nasty' packing material offered an interesting confrontation with the body. *Body Pieces* (1996/97) connected the consumer society with the body as a feasible object. Christoph Zellweger himself sees them as 'prostheses with a mental dimension'.[23] With this he wants to state that these objects, by their own design, are the median between medical instruments and organic forms, not only for the body but also about the body. In a lecture in 1996, Zellweger introduced his concept *homo ipsi faber* (literally, one who creates himself) where he points to the fact that we need to invent ourselves. Our identity, which we derive from intrinsic and extrinsic factors, has increasingly become a matter of discussion. With therapy and classes we can work on our personality and keep our body in condition; with surgical interventions we can make ourselves as beautiful as we would like to be. We create our own identity through our body.[24] Zellweger sees jewellery as an external prosthesis that belong to the kingdom of the imagination. Jewellery as a means of communication gives meaning to the wearer, just as cell phones, iPhones and even implants can. Zellweger's *Body Pieces* and *Foreign Objects* find themselves on this borderline. They are made of surgical steel and present themselves as fictitious body extensions. Sometimes they are combined with leather belts that accentuate their prosthesis-like duality. Because this jewellery cannot be casually worn around the neck nor can it be pinned to one's clothing, wearing it becomes a conscious deed that involves the whole body and the entire character. It derives its importance from its transitional position between prosthesis, implant and jewellery, while some of the shiny hard steel objects, such as the used artificial hip with its leather sheath, can even look like weapons. Their inherent awkwardness is their power.

More recently Zellweger moved away from wearable jewellery. In 2010 he exhibited *Incredibles*, his objects slip-cast in porcelain, some with a rubber coating, and *26 Stitches*, wall objects in leather (fig. 109), with breast surgery (aesthetic as well as reconstructive) as its point of departure. This new work shows how dedicated Zellweger is to science: 'Rather than relying on books about reconstructive surgery to inform the process of making, I work with surgeons. Their rich accounts and the opportunity to observe procedures have offered me unique insights into the physical aspect of aesthetic and reconstructive

> 108

> 109

plastic surgery. These ideas continue to evolve through discussions with surgeons and patients who generously share their experiences.'[25] The work *26 Stitches* celebrates a nipple-areola reconstruction, which can be carried out on women after a mastectomy. The operation is meant to improve the self-image of these women, but it also raises fundamental questions about what healing actually is or what we understand as natural. As a work of (jewellery) art *26 Stitches* unveils the precise and emulating potency of the surgeon's craft, the ingenious stitches meticulously copied by the artist in a leather wall sculpture, framed as an oval mirror – or, with regard to jewellery, as a giant medallion.

As discussed in Chapter III, Iris Eichenberg introduced knitting as a way to deal with corporeal themes, such as growth and decay and human aberrations. Her work reveals a pronounced medical fascination stemming from her former work as a hospital nurse in Göttingen in Germany. Eichenberg, interested in the vulnerable system of the body in relationship to the biochemical mass and the elusive human soul, turned the body inside out, as it were, and revealed a mechanism that runs but that at the same time can stop running without warning.

> fig. 109

> fig. 111

She does not choose her material for decorative or trendy reasons. Her material, whether it is wool, porcelain, felt, rubber, plastic, mirrors or items found on her family's farm, speaks in the language of its origins – a phenomenon that, as she further develops, will continue to manifest itself more clearly. Silver, deep white or hammered, is the binding element in many of her collections. After graduation, porcelain made regular appearances in her work, in which she made castings in organic forms, mostly chicken hearts. Combined with silver forms, new, manipulated organs were created. The suggestion of clotted blood is given by gluing on layers of small garnets. In later collections, such as *Blossom* (1998), Eichenberg allowed the organic forms to grow together with natural growth patterns. The body as organism and mechanism plays a great role in all this work, but the work takes on a certain aloofness as well. The body is observed, taken apart, examined and put back together again just like a do-it-yourself kit. In other work, objects obtain a corporeal presence: *Two of the Same Kind Keeping Each Other Warm* (1998) is one such object made of felt, which represents two flat hot-water bottles, joined together at the sides with a channel. With their rose-red fleshy colour and their organic form, these water bottles which referred to the human body, became an intimate ode on life and love. The sturdy, woollen double container entitled *You and Me* (1998) deals with the same subject. The total concept of the body comprises a series of 'jackets' knitted with wool or made of old blankets, with which Eichenberg 'dresses' a group of simple wooden tables (2000). These tables, some of which stand on extremely high legs, become touchingly human with these warm, homely body warmers.

Eichenberg's collection *Sunen* (2002) deals with small organisms. Cells are engraved onto car mirrors, and embroidered onto linen, wool and silver – the organism becomes an ornament, a pattern, but it misses the intimacy of the work where she considers the body as a whole. In the following years she explored memories and homesickness as themes in *Heimat* (2004), *Tenements* (2007) and *New Rooms* (2008). But in 2009 Eichenberg returned to the corporeal with new work entitled *Pink Years Later* (fig. 110). This jewellery combined girlish and sexy materials, such as shiny rose ribbons and tights with gold, rose-coloured plastic and rose quartz; it played with the sexually laden intensities of the body. She likes the transformation a piece gets when worn: 'Being placed on the body they melt into the clothes and the body at the same time … they long for a body but also long for the person standing in front of you, triggering the voyeur in the other.'[26]

> 110

Wearing Eichenberg's jewellery lets one see the body in a new light. Initially she never used standard solutions like pinning something onto clothes; according to her that leads to carelessness. This is the reason she creates hooks, edges and other solutions in order to make her work wearable. The connection with the object is more intimate and personal, wearing becomes a conscious deed. Her radical approach is the result of her choice for jewellery and to be jewellery it needs to be wearable – but Eichenberg loathes the obvious and the customary. In the presence of a body and under the influence of the personality of the wearer, jewellery acquires meaning.

In the 1990s Iris Eichenberg and Christoph Zellweger introduced a manner of working in jewellery that focused on the body in a way that had not been done previously. The perspective of the body as an empty canvas where jewellery can be displayed or that of the body as theatrical armour against the outside world was now extended with an approach that used the human body as a source, a toolbox with which one could create. Their work developed similarly to the developments in biomedical science and aesthetic plastic surgery, where not only possibilities grew but the availability for an increasing number of people as well. Characteristic of their work is the use of an organic language and evidence of a non-aesthetic, at times abhorrent, and narrative position. Anthropomorphic jewellery is a reflection on contemporary social phenomenon, such as genetic manipulation, gender and aesthetic surgery, without taking a stand for or against. At the same time they use the inner parts of the body as symbols and metaphors for human situations, behaviour, wishes and desires. Similarly, when Nanna Melland for want of a human's heart used a real pig's heart as a charm and a pendant, it was meant as a metaphor for life and death. She elaborated on this theme in necklaces that were composed of hundreds of used IUDs (intrauterine devices), the most widely used contraceptive (fig. 111).

> 111

Besides the anthropomorphic approach, a more clinical approach has been discernable in the work of Frédéric Braham since 2000. His focus is the cosmetic industry and how ideas about perfection and manipulability affect people through insidiously imposed beauty standards. He makes use of the cosmetic industry's own glossy materials and products by transforming luxurious famous brand cosmetics boxes containing eyeshadow or compact powder into precious jewels by adding a setting and a pin. In doing this, the wish to have a perfect appearance is turned into an object of desire, a precious piece of jewellery. Other works, such as the brooch in the form of a mask, are a continuation of this reflection of longing for a perfect look. In a series of works from 2000 onwards, Braham embraces a more ephemeral and philosophical approach in order to beautify the inside of the body. The stylised *Inner Beauty* glass bottles are filled with drinkable solutions of different metals and minerals, for instance gold, silver, copper and ruby (fig. 112). The jewel then becomes a ritual when during a performance the artist offers visitors a drink from a spoon full of

> 112

'precious water'. Is it irony or is it the utmost consequence of working in the beauty business – after all jewellery is as much about beauty and attraction as cosmetics – to create a drinkable jewel that is supposed to work on the inside of the body? By making jewellery and objects with a highly cultivated and aesthetical character that speaks the same language as the cosmetic and fashion industry, Braham holds up a mirror for us and wants us to think about our own objectives and ideals.

In its radicalism, the body jewellery of Australian designer Tiffany Parbs and New Zealand artist Selina Woulfe can be compared with that of performance artist Stelarc, but with a decorative and refined twist showing that it is jewellery-based. For decades, visual artist Stelarc (also living and working in the southern hemisphere) has been engaged in the development of body extensions, which deeply affected his perception of his own body. With the aid of robotic technology, he created machines which he himself became part of; for example, he learnt to write with his extended arm. He hung himself from flesh hooks on the ceiling and had a cell-cultivated ear implanted into his left arm. In Body Art, the utmost borders of the physical – pain and endurance – are explored, but this is not the objective of post-studio body jewellery, although experiencing pain can be part of it.

Selina Woulfe graduated from Unitec's contemporary jewellery department in Auckland in 2009. She is especially interested in the psychological, emotional, sensual and physiological dynamics of the jewellery object. In order to explore this field she has her own designs attached to her body by a professional piercing artist. Woulfe, who is inspired by French philosopher Maurice Merleau-Ponty, actually chose to undergo her own painful body jewellery experiments: 'Originally I was not going to do anything that was so invasive to my own body, but then came to the conclusion that the concept of the work would be undermined if the jewellery could only make reference to a kind of experience.'[27]

As part of her 2008 graduation work Woulfe developed her *Experiential Jewellery*, consisting of ready-made flesh or surgical steel suspension hooks combined with chains and rings.[28] The jewels were pierced into her back and the action and outcome was documented in photographs and in a video showing the movement of the jewellery while on her body. In a statement, she says: 'Once the body's borders are determined by the individual; cold, pricky jewellery becomes a device which challenges sensory boundaries whilst integrating the body & object with the mind.'[29]

Her new body piercing jewellery made in 2009 is more focused on the jewellery object, as such. It was made on the basis of 'graftification', a technique that she describes as 'an invasive procedure performed on the body with surgical wire and "silvergrafts".'[30] *Silvergrafts* (a word invented by the artist, fig. 113) are abstract jewellery versions of skin grafts. These jewellery 'grafts' are fastened to the skin with a surgical wire pin. However, while medical skin grafts ultimately will become one with the rest of the skin, Woulfe's silvergrafts are aesthetic foreign bodies penetrating the body. Although the forms of Selina Woulfe's grafts are inspired by the mesh and fragile pattern of the human skin, the antagonism between body and decoration was never illustrated more effectively. Woulfe sees her *Silvergrafts* as a protecting, decorative layer and being pierced as a private ritual. The fact that this protective jewellery contradicts itself by causing pain contributes greatly to that idea. After all, beauty and pain are connected in many cultures, past and present. Wearing a *Silvergraft* in public for the first time made her feel 'both exhibitionist and voyeur, witnessing people's reactions'.[31] It is Selina Woulfe's intention to learn the skill of body piercing herself so that she can attach her future designs to potential buyers. Her work is an attempt to explore jewellery's potential as a psychological and corporeal experience. At the same time it can be observed as an intellectual and creative answer to the

> 113

immensely popular subculture of piercing, where the design of the object is subordinate to the experience of the act itself.

Australian Tiffany Parbs uses her own body as a material to make work about skin changes and embellishment. Like Selina Woulfe, Parbs is unrestrained when undergoing some quite radical treatments in order to make her own very special kind of personal jewellery: by pouring hot wax onto the skin of the middle finger of her left hand she created *Blister Ring* (2005), and by letting the sun burn her she produced a body adornment that spelt out RAW in huge letters across her décolletage (2008). Both examples show how a jeweller can craft her body and the self. However, Parbs's interventions are only ephemeral and leave no lasting traces on the body.

Horrifying body augmentations such as incredibly long eyelash extensions hang over the face like a loose curtain. The action, rendered in photography, produces some highly uncomfortable images, yet photography is needed to record these temporary interventions of the artist. Nevertheless, where Woulfe is explicit, Parbs operates in general, in a more suggestive manner that can be as intriguing and terrifying as the actual modifications themselves. In one of the photographs from the series *Cosmetic* (2006), small stainless -steel pins mark the outlines of a closed mouth. In another photo, the seemingly random marks follow a wide path around the eye but also come threateningly close to it (fig. 114). > 114 Their function is unclear, they could be either preparatory or permanent embellishments of the eye. In fact, the steel pins near the mouth indicate the insertion points for Botox, while the marks around the eye are the guidelines used for eye-tuck surgery. Through these works, Parbs investigates the psychological impact of cosmetic surgery – or the cutting into a healthy body – from the perspective of the viewer. In the series of photos *Peel* (2008), a piece of skin appears to peel off the forehead, eventually hanging in front of the eyes as a 'veil'. In this case, Parbs let the simulated skin make a movement contrary to that of a facelift, where the skin is actually pulled back. Parbs explains: 'The title also references the technique of chemical peels used to strip the top layer and regenerate new growth. The simulated chemical peel used for this piece creates a similar irritation on the skin as occurs during a chemical peel process but heals in minutes instead of weeks.'[32]

The temporary work of Parbs can only exist when recorded in photography. The many years of collaboration with photographer Terence Bogue is therefore very important in this process. The real work is not the photograph but the 'piece in situ', as Parbs calls it, a piece of jewellery that is the result of a lengthy period of studio research and experimentation and one which only exists for a very short period of time. The photo should be observed as a record of the piece.

American jewellery artist Lauren Kalman uses many different media, such as jewellery, photography, video, sculpture and performance in her work. She uses precious materials to amplify those aspects of the body most people don't want to talk about and literally try to hide. *Blooms, Efflorescence, and Other Dermatological Embellishments* (2009) is a series of photographs of female human bodies showing imagined skin diseases represented by patterns of acupuncture needles embellished with pearls, precious and semi-precious stones, gold and silver (fig. 116). With the aid of jewellery, a complete horror story of warts, > 116 carbuncles, eczema and other spots is represented. Some of her digital prints from the *Hard Wear* series (2006) show a gilded tongue with a tendril of mucus hanging from it, a nose with a cluster of gold and green stones growing from the nostril and lip adornments made from gold-plated, electroformed copper and semi-precious stones that look like giant fever blisters. The *Hard Wear* collection also involved photographs, video recordings of performances and actual artefacts. Like other body artists, Kalman is her own model and subject to her own manipulations. On her website Kalman explains: 'The photographs allow me to amplify the textures of the skin and gold whereas the videos show the reflexes of the body against the discomfort of the adornment. I display the video on small LCD screens and the photographs as portraits in conjunction with the adornment and relics of the actions. The presentation of the work oscillates between commodity and medical specimen mimicking the duality of the objects.'[33] Lauren Kalman's work demonstrates how the body, when merged with jewellery (or jewellery related materials), can become an object of disgust and horror. This way it attracts our attention to the discourse about the ideal body and body aesthetics.

Boldily fluids have also become part of jewellery's domain. In 2005, Tiffany Parbs created a silicone *Tear Sac* to place under the eye and to collect tears; a touching idea that nevertheless remains empty because nothing is actually done with these human body fluids. The sac is just a device to focus our attention on the private, emotional and human act of crying (no other mammal is able to cry). In this sense it is reminiscent of Dinie Besems's *Ring With Tearcontainer* (1995), which created a place for a tear where normally a precious gemstone is mounted. German Stefan Heuser went one-step further when he collected real human matter, mother's milk and body fat, to use as material for 'wearable but unbearable' jewellery (2008/09).[34] The mother's milk was transformed into plastic beads, 'pearls' and ornaments, such as a heart and an egg – symbols referring to love and fertility (fig. 115). The anonymous human fat, obtained from a liposuction clinic, appears in his jewellery as a yellowish, amber-like plastic material, formed in simple, oval medal-lion shapes. To work with human fat must be a disgusting job, and the result, no matter how beautiful the yellow-gold colour, is horrifying as well – at least for those in the know. Heuser's initial idea to use his own fat, which was dropped because of health risks, would have made it even more significant. Yet having surplus human fat converted into a precious jewel is like merging two generally acknowledged beauty ideals, leading to jewellery that at first sight might seem appealing. Its attractiveness is a horrendous trap.

> 115

At the advent of contemporary art jewellery, the body was a thing to celebrate and protect by making large wearables. Then came a period in which the inside of the body was brought outside and transformed into wearable ornaments. In the twenty-first century, the body itself has become a material to work with and to work on. Female artists especially celebrate a very radical and experience-based attitude.

The wearable objects and wearables of the 1970s and 1980s must be understood in the context of their time. Their function was to both celebrate and protect the body. It was the period of sexual liberation and of a new awareness of the body, away from puritan taboos that seemed to be done with forever. However these wearable objects also wrapped the body as if the wearer needed protection – a paradox that can be explained by the inher-ent experimental character of these objects. These objects were about coming out, about showing a commitment to the New Jewelry; they were not about intimacy but about pro-claiming yourself to be a member of a new and controversial group within the context of jewellery and art. In reality, these wearable objects were more like mental experiments, more about thinking of oneself as 'wrapped', and were mainly manifested in photography. Other jewellery of this period celebrated the body, portrayed the body through prints, casts and sculpting. This jewellery was mostly made in silver or gold. In contrast to the 'wearable objects' this jewellery was intended to be worn.

The antropomorphic jewellery of the 1990s had an introspective character regardless of how explicit their form and content was. This kind of jewellery was the first overt reaction to the cosmetic industry, biomedical research and the adaptability of the human body. The body is now a subject of negotiation, open to any changes the owner of the body may wish to have. While in the 1970s cosmetic surgery was seen as a taboo, forty years later it has become the subject of real-life television shows. And in some countries, for example in Latin America, the cosmetically updated body has become a daily practice for both women and men and an accepted part of the culture.

As a result of these social changes, twenty-first-century body jewellery differs profoundly from that of the 1970s and 1980s. The youngest body jewellery is more radical in the methods it uses and not necessarily aesthetical in a material and ornamental respect. It really tries to get 'under the skin', not only physically but also mentally. Skin becomes flesh, jewel becomes tool, scar, bruise or blemish becomes ornament, personal becomes public, pain becomes art, while the craftsperson is 'crafting' their own body and self. It seems that in Jewellery, finally, all sacred cows have been sacrificed.

1   See also Chapter II. A video was made when Peter Skubic's implant was removed in 1982: *Extraction* by Wilhelm Graube (3' 28").

2   As a result of the discovery of the oldest beads ever found, shells with holes bored in them, found in the Blombos cave in South Africa in 2005, a Dutch newspaper ran the headline: 'Modern man is 30,000 years older'. From the fact that these shell beads, all of the same type and with traces of red ochre, are found in very remote places, scientists conclude that there existed 'an early distribution of bead-making in Africa and southwest Asia at least 40 millennia before the appearance of similar cultural manifestations in Europe'. See: Abdeljalil Bouzouggar, Nick Barton, Marian Verhaeren, et al., 2007. '82.000-year-old shell beads from North Africa and implications for the origins of modern human behavior', in *PNAS – Proceedings of the National Academy of Sciences of the United States of America*, vol. 104, no. 24, 12 June, pp. 9964–9.

3   Ted Polhemus and Uzi PART B, 2004. *Hot Bodies, Cool Styles, Nieuwe technieken in lichaamsdecoratie*. Weesp: N&L, pp. 7–9.

4   Barbara Maas, 2005. 'Berührungen. Barbara Maas über Katinka Kaskeline', in: Elisabeth Holder and Herman Hermsen (eds.), 2005. *Choice: Zeitgenössische Schmuckkunst aus Deutschland. Ein Lesebuch*. Düsseldorf: Fachhochschule Düsseldorf, p. 35.

5   Jane Pavitt, 2008. *Fear and Fashion in the Cold War*. London: V&A Publishing, p. 70.

6   I saw the jewellery in 2002 in the Ilias Lalaounis Jewelry Museum in Athens, in the temporary exhibition *From Mycenae to Yannena: Body Jewelry from the Permanent Collections*, Sept. 2001–Sept. 2002. See also: *Ilias Lalaounis Jewelry Museum Newsletter*, no. 12, November 2002, p. 48.

7   Donald J. Willcox, 1973. *Body Jewelry: International Perspectives*. Chicago: H. Regnery, p. xii.

8   The model was the 21-year-old art student Phil Bloom. She had connections with fine artist Wim T. Schippers. Schippers, who belonged to the Fluxus movement, was the founder of the so-called a-dynamic art movement, and he was one of the programme developers for the TV programme *Hoepla*. In 1968, one year after the first *Hoepla* broadcast, *Playboy* published an interview with Phil Bloom entitled 'TV's First Nude'.

9   One of the costumes from the *Kledingsuggesties* exhibition series had a peek-a-boo box that exhibited a woman's breasts, but they were not meant to be touched; the box should emphasise vital body parts.

10 The work was exhibited in a show in Groningen in May/June 1974 and referred to as organic jewellery. According the accompanying documentation, photographs and gold wire were part of Benno Premsela's collection. Later, and also in Gijs Bakker's monograph (Arnoldsche 2005, p 146–147) it is called 'shadow jewellery'. In my view the original title is much more appropriate to the idea of the work.

11 The X-rays by Gerd Mossettig were exhibited at the Galerie am Graben stand at an art fair in the Vienna Secession building in 1979.

12 The photo series is described in Liesbeth Crommelin, 1976. 'Vormgevingsprocessen', in *Scheppend Ambacht*, vol. 27, no. 6, p. 125. Recent inquiries with Frans van Nieuwenborg did not add any new information.

13 See: Margit Brand (ed.), Gerd Rothmann, 2002. *Schmuck Jewellery*. Munich: Bayerischer Kunstgewerbe-Verein, pp. 14–29.

14 Exhibition *Bodyprints*, Electrum Gallery, London.

15 Margit Brand (see note 12), p. 44.

16 Bruno Martinazzi studied goldsmithing under the brothers Mussa at the Scuola Orafi Ghirardi in Turin. From 1953 to 1954 he studied at art schools in Florence and Rome, where he concentrated on sculpting techniques. His first exhibited work was a copper and silver relief. As a sculptor he worked first in bronze and later in marble.

17 Fritz Falk and Cornelie Holzach, 1997. *Bruno Martinazzi: Schmuck, Gioielli, Jewellery 1958–1997*, Stuttgart: Arnoldsche, p. 52.

18 Catalogue, 1982. *Pierre Degen: New Work*. London: Crafts Council. Handwritten text printed on the backside of additional loose-paged exhibits list.

19 Marjorie Schick, interview with Tacey A. Rosolowski at the artist's studio, Pittsburg, KS, 4–6 April 2004, Smithsonian Archives of American Art, transcript, p. 4. Accessed 18 Aug. 2009.

20 Ibid. p. 1.

21 *Jewellery Redefined: The 1ˢᵗ International Exhibition of Multi-Media, Non-Precious Jewellery*. London: British Crafts Centre, 1982. Of the 100 plus contestants, the jury selected 80 participants.

22 All three of these artists crossed over to sculpture in the 1980s.

23 Mònica Gaspar (ed.), 2007. *Christoph Zellweger: Foreign Bodies*. Barcelona: Actar, p. 79.

24 Zellweger's lecture was held during the seminar *Savage Luxury*, Crafts Council, London, 15 Nov. 1996.

25 See: Autobiographical review: 'Christoph Zellweger, Art and Design Research Centre, Sheffield Hallam University, UK', in: *Craft Research Journal,* vol. 2, no. 1, 2011.

26 Email invitation from Ornamentum Gallery for SOFA exposition in Chicago 6–8 Nov. 2009.

27 Email from Selina Woulfe, 17 Aug. 2009.

28 These hooks are used in fetish rituals called hook or flesh suspension. They are the same as used by Stelarc.

29 Email from Selina Woulfe, 17 Aug. 2009.

30 Peter Deckers and Hilda Gascard (eds.), 2009. *Handstand: Unfamiliar and Innovative New Zealand Jewellery*. Wellington: handSTAND, 2009, p. 70.

31 Email from Selina Woulfe, 13 Aug. 2009.

32 Email from Tiffany Parbs, 4 Nov. 2009.

33 Fragment from *www.laurenkalman.com*. Accessed 17 Nov. 2010.

34 Laura Bader. 'Kunstprojekt. Hüftgold um den Hals. Fettabsaugungen mit kreativen Folgen – Der Künstler Stefan Heuser kreiert Schmuck aus menschlichem Fett', in *Focus Online*, 11 July 2008. Accessed 18 Nov. 2010.

VII. Jewellery and Ornament

Imagine an oversized brooch, 20 × 20 × 8 cm. It has a flat ornate base of linoleum and a three-dimensional, hand-painted silicon animal's head protruding from it: a white cat, sweet and smiling like a cuddly toy (fig. 117). Gold-plated brass chains hang from it as if to give this strange XL ornament a final jewellery touch. The head is perfectly made and looks like shiny glazed porcelain. This funny and impressive brooch was made by Korean/Swedish jeweller Aud Charlotte Ho Sook Sinding (Charlotte Sinding), one of the big talents in Swedish jewellery who passed away way before her time. Sinding gave her pieces of jewellery a truly ornamental character – she needed to because she wanted to challenge people to actually wear them. Hanging on a wall, these remarkable brooches featuring dogs, cats and rabbits are beautiful but can easily be mistaken for visual puns on hunting trophies or cuckoo clocks. Worn on the body these brooches become powerful, playing with the idea of jewellery as a new type of ornament. One of the reasons for me to introduce this brooch as an example of ornament is the flat linoleum base with its baroque scrolls – this is ornament in the sense of 'art we add to art'.[1] If this layer had not been there, the cat's head would have had a different meaning. With this layer its meaning increases; the linoleum ornament functions as a beautifying frame that enhances the value of the head and signalises that this is something special. Other pieces by Charlotte Sinding show how she made use of the effect of oversized objects (fig. 118): floral corsages as (latex) sculptures that cover the entire chest, a ring with a bird and flower covers the hand completely, hindering everyday movement – this jewellery wears you. She must have loved to see people wearing them; only then are they done justice to as independent wearable objects, as ornaments to man.

> 117

> 118

While we are able to observe a piece of jewellery as an ornament, at the same time this ornament is characterised through its own ornamentation, by motives and patterns, with the help of filigree, gemstones, and so forth. This double predestination of a piece of jewellery as ornament makes it a complicated phenomenon in a cultural and aesthetical sense. Twentieth-century Modernism made ornament suspect, and even today there are people who hold severe, Minimalist, undecorated style as a sign of good taste. Ornament came to be observed as something additional, as a frivolity without any reason, function or other meaning, and as purely decoration. And even worse, ornament also came to be observed as a deceptive act of dressing up, of illusionism and as transforming a shape, object or product into something other than what it was. This general rather moral point of view on ornament had quite some consequences with respect to jewellery: jewellery, with its inherent additional character, became to be seen as a 'mere decoration', as something redundant and marginal.[2]

Today ornament is back. We can find it in design, architecture and art and in the streets on a warm summer's day when we can observe a multitude of ornate and simple tattoos on the bodies of people, young and old. Tord Boontje's *Chandelier Light* and *Blossom Chandelier* for Swarovski, both made in 2002, can be understood as milestones in post-

Postmodernist design, which set a trend for decorative design. In 2003, young Dutch designer Joris Laarman presented *Heat Wave*, a highly decorative concrete radiator based on a lush and baroque floral repeated pattern, which converted a non-object into an object of desire – a victory on the rationality of a long unnoticed appliance. Droog Design soon took this new domestic ornament into production. Alongside Tord Boontje, designers such as Marcel Wanders, Studio Job and bernabeifreeman are now famous for their ornate designs, while Spanish designer Jaime Hayon and fine artists such as Lilly van der Stokker from the Netherlands and Beatriz Milhazes from Brazil are praised for their imaginative decorative style that is often related to either street art (graffiti) or folk art. Ornament is also a theme for Belgian artist Wim Delvoye. In his series *Gothic Works* he laser-cuts impressive neo-Gothic ornate sculptures, such as *Caterpillar* (2002), *Cement Truck* (2008) and *Tour* (2010), from Corten steel. The texts accompanying ornament and decoration in design and fine arts such as these express a certain feeling that stands worlds apart from the serious tone in design and art reviews that is so well known to us. It is now a matter of joy, happiness, fairy tales, light-footedness, enjoyment, sweetness, lucky art and feel good design, and – one level higher – the romantic and the sublime.

Ornament in jewellery is back in the shape of garlands, festoons, leaf patterns, flowers, scrollwork, arabesques, filigree, arcs, loops, drops, bows, animals and geometry, with or without mounted stones, in silhouette or three dimensions, in any conceivable material. Ornament is composed of motifs, mostly repeated or combined in such a way that they result in a pattern, but a motif can also be used in its own right. Ornament is enjoyed as a very personal statement, in the words of James Trilling, 'as an art of intense if elaborately veiled emotion …'.[3] In fact, ornament has become a theme. It is not simply a matter of surface decoration; it has become a subject of research and a means of artistic expression. Jewellery as ornament is also back in the sense that artists are taking pleasure in making pieces that have a highly ornamental character, in expressing their skills and historical knowledge and admitting their delight in doing so. For the Australian jeweller or contemporary goldsmith (as he calls himself) Robert Baines, his ongoing scientific, stylistic and chemical research of historical jewellery has brought him the vantage of artistic play.[4] He created groups of jewellery, such as *A Brooch from Saaremaa* (2004), referencing historical examples of filigree ornament with the inclusion of 'impurities' like metal car toys or plastic car windows. In other groups of jewellery, such as the *Bloodier than Black* (2001–02), *Meaner than Yellow* (2002), *Redline* (2003) and *Whiter than Red* (2004) series, we can find a clutter of filigree wire that reads like an intricate ornamental composition alongside highly stylised compositions built from tracery spheres, cubes, unfolding cones and other ambiguous geometric forms.

The mimicry or popularisation of classical, historical ornaments is a way of working that is broadly accepted. Jewellers draw from history, from all classical and historical ornaments that are part of our collective memory. The following jewellers are just a few of those currently embracing ornament to create attractive, contemporary pieces as tokens of our time: Uli Rapp transforms Renaissance jewellery into textile prints on T-shirts or rubber jewellery; Emiko Oye created a *My First Royal Jewellery Collection* from Lego pieces; Evert Nijland draws inspiration from floral Baroque and abundant Rococo architectural ornaments like garlands and putty for his exquisite glass and porcelain jewellery that expresses an atmosphere of opulence (fig. 119); Vera Siemund transposes nineteenth-century industrially produced eclectic ornaments into lush ornaments in copper or iron; and Iris Nieuwenburg creates small decorative stages, which broach the subject of interior adornment.

> 119

The history of twentieth-century art jewellery is imbued with a need to reveal jewellery's *raison d'être*, along with a strong inclination towards fine art and a concentration on formal and plastic qualities. Therefore throughout the twentieth century, beginning with the period of Art Nouveau, the use of classical jewellery ornaments (bows, flowers, festoons, leaves, stars and sculpted floral or natural rims) had been eschewed in favour of ornaments that were considered more up to date and in line with visual arts and design. The form canon was Modernist.

In some extreme cases abstract forms were observed as 'functional', as being dependent on and determined by the forms of the body or as being the result of material or technical properties. When speaking about these examples of abstract jewellery, we cannot pass by the work of Emmy van Leersum, whose ideas had such a tremendous influence on and reverberation in Dutch jewellery. Van Leersum struggled with the idea that jewellery was observed and used either as a mere decoration or as a status object.[5] She therefore liberated herself from traditional ideas about the making, craftsmanship and material values. Her bracelets were based on rational interventions in aluminium tubing, which made the cylinder of the tube appropriate to wear on the conical form of the arm. Yet these straight foldings and incisions can be observed as ornaments as well – they were 'the sense-giving detail' and therefore had a symbolic function besides their functional intention.[6] This applies also to Van Leersum's gold bracelet with a fastening, made in three variations (1968). Each bracelet is made up from a strip of gold with both ends cut diagonally so that they could be folded to form the bracelet. The fastening directed all the attention and became an ornament in itself (fig. 120). This ornamental aspect was completely rejected at the time. When describing her practice, Van Leersum spoke in terms of a process of rational decisions: 'The particular characteristics of gold, such as its hardness and especially its resilience, are exclusive to this material. So here it is obvious that gold is used for the sake of its material peculiarities and not for the sake of "glamour".'[7]

> 120

It is clear, and for obvious reasons, why Van Leersum and her colleagues did not talk about ornament in those days. It was a period saturated by the 'form follows function' movement in design and architecture; one could not escape from it. Van Leersum discovered the liberating force of restricting the creative process to a rational set of, in Van Leersum's own words, 'applications, ideas and actions' based on geometric shapes. Under such conditions ornament was associated as something redundant. Yet nobody can deny the aesthetic effects of the interventions of Van Leersum on the materials she chose, they certainly had a beautifying effect. In the words of James Trilling, writing not about jewellers but about the pioneers of the modern movement: '[They] created a new ornamental style which they could pretend was a rejection of ornament.'[8]

The history of the reception of jewellery in the 1970s and 1980s, especially in northwest Europe, shows an alarming neglect with respect to pieces that had an expression and appearance other than the rational abstract one. Ornament was one of those tricky things in jewellery, suffering under a general disapproval, just like the use of gold and precious stones. A firm and resolute break with Modernism in the Netherlands was made by Robert Smit, who was never in favour of the sober Dutch jewellery school anyway and who stood aloof from the jewellery scene for quite a long time working as visual artist. In the Netherlands, one of the cradles of Modernism and blessed with a strong Calvinist attitude, people were taken by surprise when, in 1985, Robert Smit exhibited his pure gold ornaments under the title of *Ornamentum Humanum* at Galerie Ra in Amsterdam. By naming the collection thus, he deliberately provoked the prevailing tame, calm and neutral Dutch jewellery scene. Everything atrocious was there: the word 'ornament' for jewellery, the gold, the spontaneous painterly treatment of the gold and the absence of a concept. It led to a public discussion in a Dutch art magazine between the protagonists of two opposing attitudes, Robert Smit and Gijs Bakker, in which the latter blamed Smit for restoring the old idea of jewellery as old-fashioned '*Schmuck*' – bearing in mind that by using the German word it was meant as an insult as Dutch jewellers found themselves far superior to their German neighbours.[9] The crux of the discussion was the incompatibility of what was observed to be 'good' jewellery, in which concept comes first and material follows, and 'bad' jewellery, which was according to Gijs Bakker sentimental, expressive, artistic, individual, without meaning (no concept) and smart because of the use of gold. In the discussion, Gijs Bakker expressed his fear that contemporary jewellery would become merely decorative. It showed how much he was indebted to Modernism – under its spell the ornament had gained a bad reputation as mere decoration. What drove European jewellers such as Bakker was the wish to make work that had the same intent and effect as fine art – it was worn on the body, yes, but in their eyes it was a self-referential entity, not a decoration. Their dilemma was the supposed subordinate character of jewellery.

The first serious critique of the ornament was formulated within the parameters of early twentieth-century architecture, crafts, industry and society by the Viennese architect Adolf Loos. Loos's famous public lecture *Ornament und Verbrechen* (*Ornament and Crime,* Vienna 1908) contributed a lot to the misinterpretation of the function of the ornament and gave way to the Modernist redemption of ornament and the maxim 'less is more'. Loos's condemnation of the ornament, as a primitive human need to decorate everything from his face to his belongings, must be valued within the context of his time, when newly 'discovered' people in other continents were still described as primitive, exotic and savage. The complete and omnipresent super-ornamentation of nineteenth-century craft objects and architecture, which showed no connection at all with his time, was the inspiration for his rejection of the ornament: 'Ornament is no longer the expression of our culture', he contended.[10] Loos put forward a serious economic and social complaint against the ornament. In his view, the workers who were making ornaments were like slaves to their skill; this craft work was too labour intensive and they had to work too many hours in order to earn a decent living while modern factory workers who worked in a rationalised industry had a much healthier job. He saw them as victims of economic and social developments: 'Even greater is the damage done by ornament to the nation that produces it. Since ornament is no longer a natural product of our culture, so that it is a phenomenon either of backwardness or degeneration, the work of the ornamentor is no longer adequately remunerated. The earnings of a wood-carver and a turner, the criminally low wages paid to the embroideress and the lacemaker are well known. The ornamentor has to work twenty hours to achieve the income of a modern worker earned by a modern worker in eight'.[11] In his view, ornament was wasted labour, wasted health, wasted material and wasted capital. To Loos, the banishment of ornament was a matter of progress of culture.[12] His pamphlet was a sincere charge against social and economic abuse in craft and industry, but it was misread by others as a moral statement: ornament = crime. Conceived this way it became one of the most referred to sources for the twentieth-century curse on ornament in crafts, design and architecture. As a matter of fact, Loos as an architect did not abandon ornament completely. James Trilling points out that his use of green marble coverings and pillars in the facade of his famous 'Looshaus' on the Michaelerplatz in Vienna (1909–11) was actually in line with his thinking. In Trilling's view this was the first building with ornament in a new sense: 'Loos did not just offer an ornament without motifs, artifice, or history, he offered an ornament without anachronism or unnecessary labor.'[13]

In etymology the Greek word *kosmos* and the Latin word *ornamentum* are equivalent: *kosmos* means 'order' as well as 'ornament' in the sense of equipment and embellishment. This gives an interesting clue to the concept of ornament, namely that there is a connection between the whole and the detail and that this has to do with a sense of universal order. As Rumanian theorist Mihaela Criticos shows, medieval philosophical tracts take God as an architect who created the world, which was subsequently adorned by him with birds, animals and men: *Est ornatus mundi quidquid in singulis videtur elementis, ut stellae in coelo, aves in aere, pisces in aqua, hominess in terra* [The order of the world is all that appears in each of its elements, such as the stars in the sky, the birds in the air, the fish in the water, the men on the earth].[14]

Inspired by *De Architectura*, the treatise of Roman architect Vitruvius, Renaissance architects described the five different column orders, their parts, proportions and ornaments and expressed the classification of a building according to a hierarchical scheme: the Doric, being the most humble and reserved for military buildings, then the Ionic and Tuscan order for profane buildings, and at the top the Corinthian and Composite orders which were the most elaborate, rich and appropriate for sacred buildings. In the fifteenth century, Leon Battista Alberti wrote extensively about ornament in his *De Re Aedificatoria*. Alberti is very clear about the fact that ornament and beauty are connected. In this book he writes 'that any shortcomings an object may have in its ornament will detract equally from its grace and from its dignity.'[15] His view on ornament is, however, broad. He describes the adapted landscape along a military Roman road as an ornament to the road: 'All along these military roads there are examples to be seen of rocks pierced, mountains cropped, hills excavated, and valleys levelled – works of incredible expense and extraordinary labor; clearly each provides not only for utility but also for ornament.'[16]

Thanks to industrialisation and the decoration of machine-made products, the nineteenth century brought new discussions about ornament. The English writer and art critic John Ruskin, a lover of French and English High Gothic architecture, declares himself an advocate of ornament 'so long as the notion of use is not altogether lost'.[17] Ruskin thinks good ornaments are worked on with joy: 'Its true delightfulness depends on our discovering in it the record of thoughts, and intents, and trials, and heartbreakings – of recoveries and joyfulnesses of success […] and in that is the worth of the thing, just as much as the worth of anything else we call precious.'[18] Ruskin's moral view on labour and craftsmanship seems like a prelude to Adolf Loos's condemnation of the ornament, for instance when Ruskin writes about the production of glass beads by manufacturers in Venice. He describes the work of the labourers as lacking 'the use of any single human faculty', their only task to chop the glass rods and round them in the furnace – drudgery under the most horrible hot circumstances. 'And every young lady, therefore,' he continues 'who buys glass beads is engaged in the slave-trade, and in a much more cruel one than that which we have so long been endeavouring to put down.'[19]

At this point, we still do not know what an ornament exactly is; we can only feel the steady (moral) disapproval of using ornaments during the course of the nineteenth century. In her analysis of ornament, Criticos distinguishes four different functions of the ornament that are closely related: symbolic or representational, qualifying or adjectival, ordering and decorative. Here, I will discuss Criticos's theory at length, although not with the aim to apply it directly to jewellery. However, her analysis does show how ornament works and does teach us about jewellery as an ornament.

In Criticos's view, the *symbolic function* of ornament is very important because humans cannot live without symbols. In architecture, for instance, ornament appears exactly at those places where structural needs are fulfilled: at the frames of windows, doors or portals, on the bottom and tops of pillars or on vaults or bridges where large openings or spans are covered. Ornament in a way completes and emphasises the load-bearing object by embellishing its functional and constructional parts, thus giving them a metaphysical content. In Criticos's view, ornament was not only created for aesthetic reasons but it also acted as an 'indispensable accessory to public and private rituals or ceremonies, and became the sense-giving detail of the things, beings and places involved in the symbolic scenography of human existence.'[20]

The *qualifying function* of ornament connects the object with its peculiarities, and therefore is in fact interrelated with the symbolic function. Through ornament, different objects within a class are individualised. Criticos gives the example of 'the Italian palazzi of the Renaissance and Baroque period that, though sharing the same pattern [...], differ from one another and exhibit well-defined identities due to a great variety of decorative systems.'[21] This function is connected to identification or expressing identity. The *ordering function* tells us about how a signifying detail relates to the whole in a hierarchical system. In the Renaissance, ideas about a cosmic harmony were applied in a broader sense: there should not only be a connection between ornament and the load-bearing structure but also between the structure and its environment. The hierarchical system was very important in this period: 'Classical theory further develops the concept of *decorum* as *bienséance* or *convenance*, mainly focusing upon the legitimacy of any assigned ornament and condemning its excess and vulgarisation.'[22] Criticos shows that the ordering function still plays a role in twentieth-century architecture, for instance in the detailing and spatial organisation in Carlo Scarpa's and Frank Lloyd Wright's work, albeit now in a slightly different way. What is important in architecture and art, she explains, is the coherence between the different elements in a composition, or on a smaller scale, the coherence between a pattern and an ornament: 'The more regular and striking the scheme, the more "decorative" becomes the work, even in the figural arts.'[23] The *decorative function* connects ornament with man on a hedonistic level. Ornaments appeal to the senses, they give us joy and they contribute to our feeling of well-being. The decorative function of ornament is the satisfaction of purely aesthetic needs. When we talk now about the decorative beauty of something, we are talking about pure form. Criticos disputes the idea of decoration as a moral imperative. In her view, the fact that ornament has survived, despite it having been so rigorously wiped out during the age of Modernism, proves that it is fundamental to human beings, an opinion that is also subscribed to by theorist James Trilling, whose idea that ornament is intended to give pleasure is actually the basis of his writing. Ornament, he writes 'transforms the inessential into a theatre for passion and beauty, invention and bravura.'[24]

In her meticulous analysis, Mihaela Criticos 'debones' the function of ornament, as it were, in four different stages. By working like this she is able to address in detail all differences in the function and working of ornament. Looking at jewellery, her definitions seem less obvious but are applicable to some extent. Following Criticos's thoughts and applying these to jewellery we can postulate that a piece of jewellery should be observed in the first place as an ornament with a symbolic and a qualifying function as it is an object for representation. At the same time, its decorative function is part of a jewel's *raison d'être*, providing joy and enchantment to the maker, the wearer and the viewer. Within its decorative potency, in this microcosm of motives and patterns, we can discern ordering, qualifying and symbolising functions. Yet there is a world of difference between an architectural ornament and a piece of jewellery, not only in size but also in the way we perceive it.

Architecture, with its fixed structural elements, bases, walls, facades, doors, windows, roofs and all its adaptations and sublimations, is more 'readable' or understandable than a piece of jewellery, which has no fixed structural rules besides the fact that it needs (though not always) a fastening and a lock. Furthermore, architectural ornament is a supplement to a permanent structure, while a piece of jewellery, while also being supplemental, is attached to moving and living people, never carried in the same way or by the same person or on the same clothing. Therefore art jewellers have a different relationship to ornament than architects. While being aware that a piece of jewellery is supplemental, it is their main subject of research and artistic expression, and within the confines of this subject they can choose manifold ornamental approaches. They can debunk ornament or they can embrace it, they can make use of its properties to wrong-foot the viewer or to entice him. The rest of this chapter will focus on some jewellers, who in my opinion are key players consciously using the main functions of ornament in their work.

ORNAMENT AS A STATEMENT

Artists today can have many different reasons to get entangled in ornament. For a designer such as Gijs Bakker, who started his career during the heydays of Modernism and Minimalism in the Netherlands, ornament has always been an issue of controversy and comment. In the 1970s it had already become clear to him that the rationalist way of designing jewellery was not what concerned him the most. Bakker's monograph claims that he 'had become trapped in the very geometric forms that had once been so liberating.'[25] In 1970, Bakker had become a teacher at the Academy of Fine Arts in Arnhem, where he transformed the former jewellery department into a department for industrial design. He became a successful industrial designer of furniture and lamps. Although some people thought Bakker was lost from the jewellery scene, he began simultaneously to experiment with new types of jewellery, such as the 5 *Meter Necklace* (1973), which demonstrated an interest in the meaning of jewellery and questioned the value of gold and adornment. In 1982, he used the rose as universal token of love and beauty to create the large necklace *Dew Drop* (fig. 121). Bakker disapproves of such symbols and of people's need to adorn > 121 themselves, but he could not fight it: 'I used a cheap [...] poster. The title was deliberately in English because it conveys the sentimentality so much better. The idea came from an almost fatalistic sense of "what am I getting so worked up about?" People just want something pretty to look at, something to charm them – sometimes for opportunistic reasons. So I decided to throw all that bullshit back in their faces. A gallery owner in Krefeld was furious that I had produced something so degrading. She called it a violation and she was basically right.'[26] Some of his pieces of jewellery, such as the *Dahlia* (1984) and *Gerbera* (1985) neckpieces, were created as beautiful spirals, the petals ordered according to size. With their emphasis on floral motifs, order and stylisation these necklaces are pure ornaments that fit into the theory of ornament as formulated by Mihaela Criticos and James Trilling. Within the patterns of the *Torn Paper* necklaces (1985), the influence from the Memphis group and Postmodernism becomes most clear.

But Gijs Bakker was reluctant in admitting any decorative association or objective. In an interview I had with him in October 1984, during the period when he was engaged in making these necklaces, he stated several times how the decorative function of jewellery didn't interest him at all: 'For me the medium jewellery is a vehicle to express my ideas about people, myself and others [...] but the decorative aspect of a piece of jewellery doesn't interest me at all. In lectures I always say that I enjoy my profession because jewellery is the most insignificant product. A piece of jewellery is so vacuous.'[27] Around the same time he made the *Pforzheim 1780* necklace and *The Tongue*, which, both in their own way, mocked jewellery's love for diamond ornamentation. A remarkable aspect of the former's PVC collars is their size and stiffness. Instead of fitting the body or emphasising the corporeality – a subject that initially interested Gijs Bakker a lot – they separate the head from the body, creating a dramatic and beautifying effect. It may not have been his intention but these necklaces have a symbolic ornamental function.

Bakker's politics of irony and irritation inspired him to make jewellery that was always ahead of general tendencies in jewellery. From 1985 onwards gold, pearls and precious stones became central to his designs. In 1989, he presented a collection of five *Bouquet Brooches*. Again, using a banal object, a picture of a kitschy bunch of colourful flowers cut out from a postcard, he now added expensive gems (sapphires, diamonds and tourmalines) mounted proudly in gold settings, way beyond the banality of the brooch. The statement he made with these brooches was heavy; it was like cursing in the church. How could a designer like him, the pioneer of Modernism in jewellery, make this work, how could he suddenly rejoice in an abundance of carats, exclusivity, luxury, in the superfluousness he always dismissed? Discussions at that time were about the irony of combining banality with the utmost example of elevation: a postcard with a precious gem. Today these choices don't seem that important anymore for we've seen lots more of that over the years. Around 1990, no attention was paid to the fact that these brooches were obviously ornamental as well. Besides being a statement, they addressed our hedonistic side and were the satisfaction of an aesthetic need for colour and artistic freedom without any moral boundaries (we should not forget that up until that period in Dutch art jewellery history there was still a lot of dos and don'ts). In that sense this work is a kind of 'art for art sake' statement – wrapped in an ornament.

From then on Gijs Bakker's jewellery became more decorative than he would presumably ever admit. As Criticos and Trilling already showed, an ornament is not just a mere decoration; it can be a statement as well – a statement of the artist and of the wearer who identifies themself with the ideas of the maker. By wearing an ornament such as *Sports Figures* (1985–89, fig. 122), *Holysport* (1998), a brooch from the series *I Don't Wear Jewels, I Drive Them* (2001, fig. 123) or a brooch from the *REAL* series (2004–08) the wearer qualifies themself explicitly as being different from all other people wearing precious jewellery. These jewels are in fact, as Glenn Adamson writes, 'a brilliant exercise in the supplemental'; and isn't the supplemental exactly what ornament is about?[28] It is this change of emphasis in observing 'jewellery as something superfluous' to 'jewellery as something supplemental' that is essential to the present day perception of art jewellery.

The first of Gijs Bakker's *REAL* Series (2004–06) originated from the most loathed kind of jewellery: glass and metal costume jewellery made to imitate the sparkle, glitter and shine of fine jewellery. These works are completed with exact handmade miniature replicas in real materials: real gold, diamonds, sapphires, emeralds and tourmalines – executed by a professional goldsmith. These brooches can be described as ornamented ornaments, or, to quote Glenn Adamson, 'the pieces in the "Real" Series implicitly ask what is ornamenting what …'[29] This play of mimicry is performed with masterliness, resulting in a highly decorative collection of jewellery with a conceptual content – only recognisable by connoisseurs. Whether recognised as a conceptual piece of jewellery (by the wearer) or identified as a sparkling supplement (by the unaware viewer), these brooches are ornaments with a highly symbolic and qualifying character. In our 'Post-postmodernist times' a concept can be wrapped in a glamorous shelter, can become an ornament and can cost a small fortune.

> 122

> 123

In the wearing of them, however, these pieces can become merely ornamental; a fact that no doubt crosses the mind of the maker's mind.

While Gijs Bakker prefers a reluctant position with regard to the ornamental character of (his) jewellery, American designer Emiko Oye addresses the subject openly in her work. As a recycling artist she strives to transform the identity of everyday objects and materials, such as discarded toys and industrial scrap. Her *My First Royal Jewels Jewellery Collection*, created in LEGO, involves reconstructions of early twentieth-century fine jewellery by famous jewellery houses (fig. 124). The collection was exhibited in 2008–09 in > 124 the Museum of Craft and Design in San Francisco, together with images of the historic examples and informational texts about these pieces, which once belonged to the European and American elite. The installation invited people to try on the necklaces and take digital images as they were wearing the jewellery. The obliged use of white gloves stressed the idea that these pieces of jewellery, no matter how mundane their material, should be handled with care as artworks in a museum context. By recapturing fine jewellery in this way and making the stories behind these jewels explicit, Oye created a platform for reflection and discussion on jewellery as valuable and as ornament.

Other artists discovered that there is no need to comment or to educate when you like to work with ornament unabashed. Helen Britton is a good example of a jeweller who creates highly decorative, festive ornaments (fig. 125), set with shells, diamonds, plastic, > 125 emeralds and glass ornaments. Her joy in ornamentation results in colourful constructions that depict floral, architectural, industrial and urban motifs. Britton has a keen eye and a camera. Photography became a way to come to terms with life in Europe, which proved to be difficult for an Australian girl: 'Living in Europe can be hell. Homesickness knows no mercy. I have always spent a lot of time in the bush […]. Dealing with Europe is also about dealing with the fantasy that I grew up with about Europe, the mystery, the romance.'[30] Europe brought her new insights, inspirations and materials as seen in her Bohemian glass adaptions (fig. 126). It is impossible to determine how Australian or European (German) > 126 her work is, but perhaps we can better conclude that her jewels are the result of a process of experiencing, observing and absorbing. Most of her brooches and a selection of necklaces have a special radiancy: they are spontaneous, positive, alive and cheerful. On the body these ornaments are statements; not only do they enhance the wearer, they also infect the viewer.

ORNAMENTS DEPICTED

At the end of the twentieth and beginning of the twenty-first centuries, gemstones – those centrepieces of luxurious jewellery and, as such, historical ornament – offer a rich source of inspiration for reflections, depictions and contemporary interpretations. Jewellers of today are interested in the history of jewellery, in its tales, myths and legendary stories. Generations of art jewellers from the 1960s to the 1980s, in line with general issues of the time, had to deal with a deep-felt resistance against anything declared luxurious, expensive, upper class, elitist and historically inspired. Jewellers of the twenty-first century feel free to plunge into history. They consider the history of jewellery a rich source of information about how people behaved, dressed, thought and connected to each other in different periods of time and also how jewellers worked and were appreciated. They research phenomena such as beauty, luxury and preciousness and try to reinterpret historical ornament in contemporary techniques and materials. They don't mock or condemn but instead study their subject passionately.

The inconvenience of the jewellery, finery and frills of sixteenth-century Queen Elizabeth I of England, who was portrayed in many paintings bejewelled from top to toe, inspired Uli Rapp to make contemporary ornaments that reflected the grandness of this courtly Renaissance style in a much more convenient, casual way. What interested Rapp especially about Queen Elisabeth was her use of clothing and jewellery as a means of communication. The Queen is famous for having ordered exclusive *reticella* lace from Italy for her lavishly elaborate dresses and then introducing luxury laws which determined who was allowed to wear lace in order to guard its exclusivity. These themes of identity and exclusivity inspired Rapp to concentrate on the T-shirt, a democratised mass product, with the idea of converting it into something exclusive and unique to be worn as a contemporary means to express these values. Interested in textile techniques since her education at the Sandberg Institute in Amsterdam, Rapp knows how to apply advanced textile-printing techniques. The *Maiden's Blush* T-shirt collection (2002–04) presents images of ornaments

> 127

printed on garments (fig. 127). The ornamented T-shirt with its decorations of lace and jewels is a contemporary and democratised but equally lush variation on the royal look of the Renaissance period. The designs, made in limited editions, follow the original Renaissance patterns quite faithfully. Some designs with lace ornaments are made with a technique called *devoré*, which etches away the pile of the fabric, producing beautiful, open,

> 128

lace details that lie against the skin. Uli Rapp's *Facettes and Stones* collection (2010, fig. 128) involved a variety of necklaces made from two layers of silk-screen printed textile, which were filled with a layer of rubber and then the patterns on which cut out by hand. As easy to wear, fashionable ornaments they are produced in series. These shiny and attractive depictions of gemstones and other luxurious jewels on opposing and cheap materials also appeal to other – much younger – audiences than that of the regular jewellery gallery. The function of these appealing ornaments for the wearer is not only decorative and pleasing; as ornaments they are also 'the sense-giving detail' that distinguishes the wearer.

American artist Anya Kivarkis has an interest in Baroque and Victorian ornament, especially in the way we perceive it. Her jewellery is aimed at directing our ways of perception. Kivarkis works with renderings of historic jewellery in drawings and paintings, incorporating distortions and elements that are hidden in the clothing. By doing this she makes pastiches of antique gem jewellery in gold or silver, neutralised by a thick layer of white enamel, denying and concealing its historical forms or questioning it by way of including strange oblong 'blind spots' as if part of the jewel has been taken out. The piece has a secret

> 129

history which we cannot detect (fig. 129). The blind spots are suggestive of the way archaeologists reconstruct antique broken vases or sculptures. Reality – or how we see reality – how we think in order to see what we see and how we are used to finishing images in our mind, appropriating them to what we know and have seen before, is Kivarkis's main theme. Her jewellery pieces are the result of a multilayered rendering of reading jewellery. Kate Wagle writes about the elusive character of Kivarkis's work: 'The pieces hover in a perceptual space between drawing and "thing", past and present. They are constructed renderings of historical records, filtered through an informed contemporary sensibility. Not the real thing, but an analytically driven interpretation of the interpretive that determines its own fresh reality. Kivarkis is interested in how she will misread the original, how she will reconstruct it, even when she is not aware of doing so.'[31] Kivarkis's *Red Carpet Jewelry* (2008) is based on paparazzi photos of famous movie stars at the Academy Awards and similar events. In these images the jewellery is only partially seen or seen from a distorted perspective. The *Rebecca Miller Academy Awards* (2008) double brooch consists of two parts: a slightly distorted, big round diamond brooch and a half bow – both pieces are made from silver and lacquered with black paint, and both draw directly from an image in a magazine. In its abstract, estranged rendering, isolated from the heat of the flashlights, it holds the magnifying power that is part of the original piece. This art jewellery is the embodiment of man's fascination for precious jewels.

THE USE OF ORNAMENT AS A SYMBOL AND SIGNIFIER

For Dutch jeweller Ruudt Peters, classical ornament became a catalyst in finding a way to make jewellery again. Peters studied jewellery at the Gerrit Rietveld Academy in Amsterdam during the heydays of Modernism, the years of the great taboo in jewellery in the Netherlands. For anyone who worked more intuitively, or preferred to use gold and silver, these were ungenerous years. After graduating in 1974, Ruudt Peters started to make sculptures and became quite successful. In this period he discovered (neo-)classical architecture and ornament. Peters's discovery of the work of the eighteenth-century Italian graphic artist Giovanna Battista Piranesi made him more confident about the use of decoration. One etching in particular, of a column heavily ornamented in a baroque style on one side while completely bare on the other, opened his eyes. In an interview, Peters once told: 'It was Piranesi's theory that the mass of ornament on the one side is as empty as the naked sculpture behind it. Both incite the same image. This made it possible for me to think again about decoration and to apply it in my work. Ornaments without function are empty.'[32]

In 1983, a design for a Formica bracelet with the image of an architectural capital seen from above reflected Peters's interpretation of Renaissance theory and architecture. The Formica *Capital* bracelet embraces the arm – as a capital – that the arm becomes a column. By taking the capital, Peters introduced the ultimate ornament in jewellery. With this work, and the simultaneous *Column* brooch, Peters became one of the first Postmodernist jewellers in the Netherlands, not only because of the use of ornament but also because of its material. Yet Peters did not continue on this path.

His historical, spiritual and religious interests led him to symbols and their applications. In the *Symbol* bracelets (1986), plain symbols (for example, a fish or comet) were made wearable. His dialogue with ancient history also made him think about the meaning of objects and its direct connection to people. The *Dedicated To* series (1989), consisting of objects and connected brooches based on the form of the discus, dealt with the act of offering a gift to another person. They were dedicated to friends and can be observed as vehicles for memories and emotions. The double vessels, quite heavy and solid, were decorated with single ornaments or a pattern of repeated forms. In this series Peters discovered the power of the sign, for example, the Christian symbol for rock, the spiral, the zigzag hieroglyph for water, or the sun, when applied in a prominent position on top of each object.

In most of the subsequent *Interno* brooches (1991), which represented architectural domes of existing churches, ornamental patterns and signs were secretly hidden inside, as if Peters still felt hesitant about it, which was not surprising in view of the Dutch jewellery scene at that time. The *Interno* brooches, characterised by a rather closed formality, are in marked contrast with his next series of *Passio* pendants (1992), which were exuberant and voluptuous in their rich use of materials, forms, ornaments, mesh and chains. Combinations of symbols representing different religions and cultures became obvious in these pendants, which looked like Roman Catholic censers yet had an inarticulate sensuous expression as well. Some were completely covered with symbols and other ornaments: *Isis* was covered with a pattern of half moons, *Alexis* with an irregular pattern of handwritten male names, *Ludwig* with baroque palmette motives and *Machiavelli* with all sorts of individualised signs, sawn from a plate of silver and attached with red threads to the globular round body of the pendant, and adorned with a Christian cross (fig. 130).

From here on Peters seems to have reconciled himself with the ornamental character of his work. Based on his symbolic language in *Passio*, Peters, commissioned by a housing corporation (1992), made a balcony for a social housing project in the Czaar Peterstraat in an immigrant neighbourhood in Amsterdam. He applied symbols, each from a variety of cultures and religions, in a regular sequence onto different transparent layers of a third-floor balcony fence. As passers-by cycle or walk past the facade, they can see how these symbols merge into new signs. The symbols referred to the multicultural background of the inhabitants and showed the positive perspective of a new symbolic identity within a new urban context, a merging of different cultures, religions and identities. With this work Ruudt Peters proved that jewellers are perfectly capable of handling ornament. In the architectural setting of an urban neighbourhood this was exactly the kind of ornament architecture was in need of: beautifying, qualifying and signifying.

Some years later Peters had another public ornamental architectonic assignment. This commission, shortly after the presentation of his *Lapis* collection (1997), was about ornament without added signifiers; that is, signs or symbols. This time the ornament itself had become a symbol, as was the case with his earlier *Ouroboros* (1995) and *Lapis* jewellery. With the *Vinkhoek* project (1997) in the Amsterdam's Kinkerstraat, Peters provided a plain red brick facade of a social housing project with ornaments that had meaning not only in themselves but also added meaning to the architecture.

The *Lapis* jewellery collection was about the alchemist's search for gold and the philosopher's stone; Peters ground minerals to powder, mixed the powder with liquid resin and poured it into moulds of several different minerals. In doing this, he created his own stones, strange colourful hybrids with a crystallised structure reminiscent of nature but purely man-made, tourmaline in the body of a garnet, jade in the body of an agate. They were radical pieces because of the uncompromising and 'disrespectful' treatment of 'eternal' materials.

The architectonic ornaments for *Vinkhoek* are positioned in horizontal rows under the windows of each floor: three rows of 20 crystalline amethyst stones are set in alternating materials of iron, copper, lead, tin, silver and gold – according to the sequence of metals. The sequences of plated non-precious and precious metals are joined by an invisible gutter that drains off the rainwater through a system of short copper tubes which lay under the roof exactly above the stones. 'Philosophical water' will drip from stone to stone and end up in a stone gutter at street level, where alchemist signs mark the holes that collect the water. The alchemic meaning of this artwork may remain out of reach for the residents of the building and passers-by but the ornamental function of this work is rich. This is the result of the rhythmic sequence and the beautifying and signifying meaning of the work. In the regular repetition and sequence, people may notice a resemblance with the occurrence of architectural ornaments on the nineteenth-century facades of other houses in the same street. Residents can even indicate their window with reference to the colour of the stone underneath it. Peters's use of ornament and symbol in jewellery or architecture turns out to be quite functional, as it signifies, beautifies and enhances the underlying structure or body.

Otto Künzli has also been investigating the ornamental and symbolic qualities of jewellery. In 1984 he took picture frames, in all different sizes and forms, and hung them around the neck of beautiful models. They were the subjects in a series of Cibachrome pictures called *Schönheitsgalerie* [Beauty Gallery]. Künzli used the picture frame, an ornament meant to protect and glorify the importance and beauty of the thing being framed, in order to comment on the ornamental role of jewellery. It is as if he says: look, we can have all kinds of ideas and ideals about jewellery but its main function is to be an ornament to man. In 1992 Künzli had his first solo museum exhibition in the United States. The title *Oh, Say!*, the opening words of the American national anthem, can also be read as an expression of amazement. Künzli was fascinated by the American culture that he had only recently become acquainted with, and the new work he had created for the show concerned itself completely with American symbols and emblems. *The Big American Neckpiece* (1986) is the epitome of his fascination with America, formed by a steel wire with thirteen symbols attached to it, among them the Liberty Bell, the Christian cross, the dollar sign, the swastika and a star. *The New Flag* (1992) was a polyester wallpiece showing one central ornament consisting of a Christian cross merging with a heart with Mickey Mouse ears and a Ku Klux Klan hat. A golden brooch in the form of this newly created symbol was the title piece of the exhibition (fig. 131). In their work, both Peters and Künzli demonstrate ＞ 131 how sign, symbol and ornament are related and how they gain even more power when applied in the medium of jewellery.

THE CELEBRATION OF ORNAMENT AS AN OBJECT OF VIRTUOSITY AND DESIRE

While some jewellers may have a love-hate relationship with the ornamental aspect of jewellery, other artists rejoice in it. Daniel Kruger is one of those jewellers who celebrate ornament with absolutely no restraint. In his work, time, culture and style seem to evaporate. Kruger knows no hierarchies: a pebble or a diamond, a shard of glass or a refined, elaborate ornament, textile or gold, baroque or tribal all merge into a rich and ornamental contemporary language. The seven shards of glass pointing through the little links of a gold chain, and the three big pebbles hidden in a shining, dazzling yellow-gold wrapping, both part of the *Ornamenta* exhibition (1989) in the Schmuckmuseum Pforzheim, were statements of a jeweller with no inhibitions. But these pieces were more than just statements, they had an ornamental character, too: symmetrical, harmonious and beautifully in balance, raw yet stylised and expressing the joy in the finding, combining and creating of the maker. In the hands of Daniel Kruger the equal treatment of opposite materials, pebbles versus gold, becomes a loving and consoling act (fig. 132). He loves them both ＞ 132 and finds beauty in the common and the precious. Kruger doesn't seem to suffer from any of the moral imperatives that were so characteristic of that time, especially in the Netherlands – a country where Kruger has been exhibiting his work on a regular base at Galerie Ra in Amsterdam since 1984. Kruger has neither the need to convince nor the anger to provoke, which is so characteristic of Gijs Bakker's jewellery. Where Bakker punches, Kruger teases, where Bakker uses the banal, Kruger uses the common, when Bakker uses precious materials they proclaim a message, when Kruger uses precious materials he celebrates their beauty. There is an unmistakable urge and speed in Kruger's making; his output comes in a steady stream and ideas seem to tumble over each other. Over the years Kruger's jewellery became bolder, more colourful and eclectic (fig. 133). There was a ＞ 133 period of sturdy architectonic forms, a period of curly baroque bows, a period of colour and a period of hollow perforated silver bodies. Although it may look as if different people made these works, there is a typical 'Daniel Kruger touch' with an emphasis on patterns, symmetry, rhythms, spheres, dots and colour that makes his jewellery pieces highly ornamental.

Daniel Kruger claims not to prefer a raw uncut stone to a faceted stone: 'It is a question of what I can afford. I have worked with expensive cut stones with great interest and pleasure when a client has made them available to me. Raw uncut stone represent the natural, un-worked, the original, which holds potential in them. I often do something to these raw stones, cutting or polishing an area to show an interference – Art/Artifice and Nature. In other instances, crystals are used as they are because of their natural facets.'[33] The colours of Kruger's jewels are mostly fierce, yet the forms can be raw and harmonious at the same time. Their ornamental character is solid and elegant, and their inventiveness is appealing. All of Kruger's jewels show his lust for colour and form. As Daniel Kruger contended at different occasions, he does not know what jewellery can be other than ornament for the body.

Although ornament has become an object of investigation, there is still a lot of mis-understanding and mistrust accompanying its rediscovery. Ornament is still under the suspicion of artifice, and there are only a few who take ornament as the core of their work. German artist Vera Siemund turns to those long despised days of the decorative arts in the eighteenth and nineteenth century to find inspiration for her jewellery. Intricacy and ambi-guity, two major properties of ornament according to James Trilling, are the essence of her work.

Her pieces are made from industrial sheet iron, or other sheet metals such as copper, silver and gold, and are combined with industrial enamels. Patterns are sawn out or pressed into the metal sheet, juxtaposing the cheapness of the technique with the elabor-
> 134
ateness of the making and the opulence and elegance of the ornament (fig. 134). A golden necklace from 1999 is treated this way. It is made from six equal pieces of very thin gold sheet, which are stamped with a repeated flower motif. The pieces are then joined to form a circle with an undulating contour. The contours of the necklace are intensified by the undulating impressions on the surface made by stamping and mounting. Yet the entire impression of the piece is rather confusing, reminiscent of the paper napkins underneath a cake, completely out of tune with the fragility of the material. Over the course of time Siemund's forms became more intricate, showing combinations of sawn-out classical orna-ments (mythological figures, elaborate crosses, exotic and rococo floral motifs and gar-lands) in silhouette. These overlapping rich forms aimed to give an overall impression of opulence and luxury and are very hard to read in detail. Because of their depiction in sil-houettes, these ornaments become abstract variations of historical examples. It is not mimicry but a present day reflection on a vocabulary we are all familiar with, a vocabulary that is, in a way, etched in our communal memory. But far from merely copying this vocabulary, Siemund transforms it by introducing a spatial ambiguity to it.

More recently Vera Siemund has tried to distance herself from classical motifs and nineteenth-century ornament. She has become increasingly interested in female portraits, which she enamels on the circular links that form a necklace or on the round parts of her brooches. Not only is the nineteenth-century melancholic female beauty depicted but also, in Siemund's own words: 'divas from the 1960s and 1970s with their cool expressions. The speckled effect of the portraits fascinated me too – the paring down to light and dark, with no shading, the aesthetic of the psychedelic. I am interested in the beauty of femmes fatales in all their iconic aloofness; the cliché and the effectiveness of these portraits.'[34] In the plainest pieces, portrait medallions are linked to form a necklace. The cool frontal portraits
> 135
which stare at the viewer are as confronting as Medusa and hardly bearable (fig. 135). In other pieces this effect is suppressed by introducing ornamental elements, such as flowers, plush cushions and lampshades, which form an extra layer. In these pieces Siemund uses

ornament to beautify and to emasculate, resulting in jewellery which 'continues the service of gracing and enhancing the wearer.'[35]

A delightful way of dealing with ornament is found in the narrative tableaux of Dutch
designer Iris Nieuwenburg. Inspired by the opulence and excess of eighteenth-century
French interiors in the heydays of the Rococo period, Nieuwenburg makes three-dimensional assemblages from interior fragments and other scenes. With this work she has positioned herself in the vanguard of young Dutch design, her work having also been selected
by Droog Design. The many layers, the multiplication and displacement of motifs and the
inclusion of refined details, such as miniature silver chandeliers with candles or miniature
porcelain services, enhance the opulence of these jewels. The different layers work like
pop-ups, another source of inspiration for Nieuwenburg. The brooches look like small
stages, furnished with miniature still lifes, precious carpets, wallpaper, furniture, cutlery
and chandeliers, always leaving the suggestion that something has happened there, as if
the actors have just left the scene. The basis of each brooch is a sumptuous interior photograph, full of ornaments and frills, mostly derived from books on eighteenth-century
French interiors, and Victorian illustrations (fig. 136). In order to protect and preserve the
fragile material, the photo paper is mounted on Formica and then treated with a top layer
of thick and translucent shiny resin coating developed by the artist herself. This material
also enables her to saw the image, to cut notches in it and to open it up as if it were lace.
All material experiments and interventions serve to create an atmosphere of fairy tales,
fantasy and dreams. In some cases fragments can be taken out and worn separately from
the framework, most of which also carry a small picture hook on the rear side. As a result
these objects celebrate ornament in different ways; as a fancy supplement to people and
as a decorative addition to the interior, paying tribute to this period in art history that Ernst
Gombrich in his *The Story of Art* so strikingly characterised as the 'aristocratic dreamworld'
and the 'happy-go-lucky tradition'.

> 136

Ornament adds aesthetical value to an object and is made with the intention to beautify,
or in the wording of James Trilling: 'Ornament with no aesthetic value of its own, however
subliminal, is a contradiction in terms'.[36] But ornament also has a signalising function,
directing our eye and giving us clues to what we are looking at while at the same time
holding symbolic messages. During the twentieth century, ornament was condemned to
the insignificant status of addition, a mere decoration. This had consequences for the way
people perceived jewellery. A piece of jewellery as a supplement became underestimated
and even looked at with contempt. Although Modernists also used some sort of ornament
it was never acknowledged as such. Towards the end of the twentieth century, as a result
of ongoing changes in art, architecture and society, ornament was discovered again as a
phenomenon that had never been completely lost. Finally, ornament was liberated from
its subordinate role; it is now agreed upon that decoration can produce meaning besides
being just a feast for the eye.

Jewellery is a different kind of ornament: it is not permanently attached to a load-
carrying structure, but, at the same time, it does carry ornament – ornament taken as
surface or three-dimensional decoration in the sense of motif, repetition, rhythm and
pattern. Since the 1980s, ornament has become part of an artistic policy for some while
being a playground for aesthetic and artistic research for others. Thus ornament in jewellery is used in different ways. These ways or attitudes can be categorised but only while
keeping in mind that there are no categories without exceptions and that categories never
exist in a pure form.

1. Ornament as a comment: Jewellery that involves ornament as a way of comment or pastiche on conventions, traditions and history, sometimes offering subtle criticism but also offering twenty-first-century alternatives to historical jewellery (Gijs Bakker, Emiko Oye).

2. Ornament as a reinterpretation: Jewellery inspired by historical or classical examples reworked in contemporary materials, modes and techniques (Ulli Rapp, Anya Kivarkis).

3. Ornament as a symbol: Jewellery involving symbols and signs that communicate generally recognisable ideas about our society, religion and human relationships (Ruudt Peters, Otto Künzli).

4. Ornament as a play: Jewellery that is made to embellish the wearer and which is characterised by the joy of elaborating materials and forms (Daniel Kruger, Vera Siemund, Iris Nieuwenburg).

1 James Trilling, 2003. *Ornament: A Modern Perspective*. Seattle: University of Washington Press, p. XIII. The author writes: 'Ornament is a specific word for a specific thing, yet it cuts across all the arts. It is the art we add to art: shapes and patterns worked into an object or building for the pleasure of the outline, color, or fantasy.' Yet Trilling also thinks that ornament as being that which we add to art is not a working definition. In his book he explains how design, decoration and ornament are intertwined, and how recognisable, narrative elements can be ornament.

2 Even today this idea is still alive. It is, for instance, one of the incentives for Gijs Bakker to start his brand 'Chi ha paura…?'. In the first press releases and catalogue of 'Chi ha paura..?' it reads: 'The "Chi ha paura…?" Foundation asks designers playing a prominent role in the international design world to design a piece of jewelry that is more than just decoration.' Catalogue *Chi ha paura…?*. Amsterdam: 'Chi ha paura…?' Foundation, 1996.

3 James Trilling, 2001. *The Language of Ornament*. London: Thames & Hudson, p. 6.

4 Robert Baines, associate professor at RMIT Melbourne, did his PhD on *The Reconstruction of Historical Jewellery and its Relevance as Contemporary Artefact* (2007). Baines researched historical jewellery in the Metropolitan Museum of Art in New York during stays in 1997, 2000 and 2003. While working there he used a scanning electron microscope (SEM) and an energy-dispersive X-ray fluorescence spectrometer (EDS).

5 See: Emmy van Leersum and Liesbeth Crommelin, 1979. *Emmy van Leersum*. Amsterdam: Stedelijk Museum.

6 The notion of 'the sense-giving detail of the things, beings and places involved in the symbolic scenography of human existence' is adopted from Mihaela Criticos, 2004. 'The Ornamental Dimension: Contributions to a Theory of Ornament', in *New Europe College Yearbook*, special edition, p. 193.

7 Emmy van Leersum (see note 5), unpaginated.

8 Trilling (see note 1), p. XV.

9 Godert van Colmjon, 1986. 'Een onpersoonlijk lijf tegenover de borst van Rob van Koningsbruggen: Godert van Colmjon in gesprek met Gijs Bakker en Robert Smit', in *Museumjournaal*, nos. 3&4, pp. 169–79.

10 Adolf Loos, 1971. 'Ornament and Crime', in Ulrich Conrads, 1971. *Programs and Manifestoes on 20th-Century Architecture*. Cambridge: MIT Press, p. 22.

11 Ibid.

12 Adolf Loos (1870–1933) lived and worked for three years in the United States, where he became influenced by American modern architecture, especially that of Louis Sullivan. Loos probably knew Sullivan's remark: 'It could only benefit us if for a time we were to abandon ornament and concentrate entirely on the erection of buildings that were finely shaped and charming in their sobriety.' (Conrads (see note 10), p. 19).

13 Trilling (see note 1), p. 218.

14 Criticos (see note 6), pp. 18, 215. The text comes from *Glosae super Platonem* by Guillaume de Conches. Guillaume de Conches was an important French philosopher, who lived in the first part of the twelfth century.

15 'Book Six, On Ornament', in Joseph Rykwert, Robert Tavernor and Neil Leach, 1991. *On the Art of Building in Ten Books. Translation of De Re Aedificatoria*. Cambridge: MIT Press, p. 155.

16 'Book Eight, On The Art of Building. Ornament to Public Secular Buildings', in Joseph Rykwert, Robert Tavernor and Neil Leach (see note 15), p. 244.

17 John Ruskin, 1982. *Val d'Arno*, ch. VI, § 146, in Kenneth Clark, 1982. *Ruskin Today*. Harmondsworth: Penguin, p. 257.

18 John Ruskin. The Seven Lamps of Architecture, ch. II, § 19, in Clark (see note 17), p. 235.

19 Joan Evans (ed.), 1980. *The Lamp of Beauty: Writings on Art by John Ruskin*. Oxford: Phaidon, p. 235.

20 Criticos (see note 6), p. 193.

21 Ibid. pp. 196–7.

22 Ibid. p. 199.

23 Ibid. p. 200.

24 Trilling (see note 1), p. 6.

25 Ida van Zijl, 2005. *Gijs Bakker and Jewelry*. Stuttgart: Arnoldsche, p. 31.

26 Ibid. p. 35.

27 From an unpublished text of a recorded and transcribed 38-page interview with Gijs Bakker on 25 Oct. 1984 as part of my thesis *Sieraadvormgeving en vrije kunst*, at the University of Amsterdam, June 1985, p. 34–5 (translation by LdB).

28 Glenn Adamson, 2008. *Gijs Bakker: Real?* Amsterdam.

29 Ibid.

30 Helen Britton, 2010. *Helen Britton: Jewellery Life.* [Munich], p. 7.

31 Exhibition *Anya Kivarkis: Blind Spot*, Sienna Gallery Lenox, MA, Aug.–Sept. 2007.

32 Ruudt Peters, interview with the author, Amsterdam, 23 Mar. 1994.

33 Email from Daniel Kruger, 15 Dec. 2009.

34 *Marzee Magazine*, no. 72, 2010, p. 16.

35 Daniel Kruger, 2006. 'Tradition and the Present', in Daniel Kruger and Vera Siemund, 2006. *Vera Siemund Schmuck: Work from 1999 to 2006*. Nijmegen: Galerie Marzee, p. 8.

36 James Trilling (see note 1), p. 46.

VIII. Jewellery and Tradition

On 24 September 2010, Belgian silversmith David Huycke defended his doctoral thesis *The Metamorphic Ornament: Re_Thinking Granulation* at the University of Hasselt in Belgium. The research involved a thesis and a collection of about forty pieces exhibited at Z33, the house for contemporary art in Hasselt. David Huycke is one of those skilled craftspeople that pair a love of traditional techniques and materials with a contemporary and artistic outlook. In his meticulous and methodological practice he is the kind of maker that has become rather uncommon in crafts nowadays. In the introduction to his thesis, he makes a stand against a popular present way of thinking about crafts, in which a surplus of technical skills are observed as something that would stand in the way of true expression and in which even the lack of apparent refined skills would point at the presence of some kind of intellectual concept. Huycke refers here to an article by Glenn Adamson who draws attention to a new trend: 'the sloppy craft movement', an outcome of the 'post-disciplinary art environment' and today's way of educating skills, 'blurring the line between hobbyism and professional endeavor'.[1] Huycke's research should be observed in the light of this discussion, for sloppiness and haphazardness have become the new standard in contemporary crafts. Although David Huycke is a silversmith not a goldsmith, I would like to present him here as an example of a relatively young generation of craftspeople who are interested in how they can bring traditional techniques and materials further as a serious contemporary means of artistic expression.

The fact that Huycke took an age-old goldsmith's technique as the theme for his doctoral research can be observed as a case against its falling into oblivion. The outcome of his research shows that old techniques have a contemporary relevance indeed and can still be used in an innovative way. Huycke investigated whether granulation can also be used for constructive purposes in silversmithing. One of his discoveries was that in jewellery granulation is mostly used as a decoration applied to plate materials. Huycke claims to be the first in 2,500 years to rejuvenate granulation by using minuscule metal balls as a constructive material, like building stones. The granules were first examined for their constructive qualities through the process of making sculptural objects, mostly bowls, out of them. In Huycke's thesis: 'They form the structure as well as an artistic impression. If one would compare them to a painting, then the granules would be at the same time the canvas, the paint and the image on it.'[2] During the course of his research, the granule became the subject matter of his sculptural work, leading to a group of works that points at other properties of the granule, especially with respect to ideas about order and chaos. Although some of them are made of painted stainless steel, polyurethane and aluminium instead of silver, this whole body of work is characterised by a strong aesthetic cohesion.

The skilled and detailed work of David Huycke is far remote from twenty-first century author jewellery although both belong to the domain once known as metalsmithing (known in Dutch as *edelsmeedkunst*, the art of forging precious metals). Both are still taught in conjunction with one another at certain schools and academies, for example in

Belgium, Sweden and Australia, and both are presented in the same galleries. While silversmithing suffers a rather outdated image and goldsmithing has been transferred to the periphery, jewellery has transformed into a fashionable discipline that requires no complicated skills or knowledge. Jewellery makers invent their own techniques and technical applications, they apply composite materials, or they re-use materials, prefering stone and glass over gems, copper and brass over silver and gold, and glue and tape over solder. In how far this tendency is connected with the fact that most academic courses are limited to only three years is a matter that falls beyond the confines of this chapter.

With the best will in the world we cannot call today's author jewellery the work of goldsmiths. But what happened to the goldsmith? How do contemporary goldsmiths, who work with traditional techniques and precious materials, find new ways for artistic expression? And how is it appreciated? Is there an equivalent for David Huycke in the world of goldsmithing? There are certainly goldsmiths who are looking for innovative applications for traditional techniques and costly materials. Giovanni Corvaja and Robert Baines are examples of jewellers who take filigree and granulation to another level of conceptual and artistic expression. There are also artists who try to overcome the conventional notions of enamelling by pushing its boundaries and challenging the material properties, such as Bettina Dittlmann (fig. 137), Christiane Förster, Silvia Weidenbach (fig. 139), Annamaria Zanella, Kirsten Haydon, Elizabeth Turrell, Philip Sajet and Ralph Bakker. Furthermore, there are skilled goldsmiths such as Peter Bauhuis and David Bielander (fig. 140) who both expand the perception of what goldsmithing is.

> 137

> 139

> 140

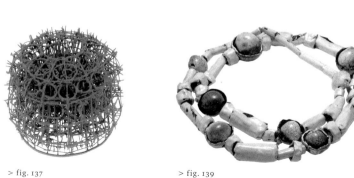

> fig. 137   > fig. 139

There are only a few schools in Europe that have managed to keep an element of the goldsmith's tradition, such as the Istituto statale d'arte 'Pietro Selvatico' in Padua, Italy, also known as the Padua School, and the Burg Giebichenstein University of Art and Design in Halle, Germany under Dorothea Prühl. These schools are not merely schools in the meaning of a building with a teacher, although their teachers are important, for instance Francesco Pavan and Giampaolo Babetto in Padua and Dorothea Prühl in Halle. The notion school also applies to a specific body of knowledge, dependent not only on individual teachers but also on factors such as a sense of place, history, tradition and availability of materials (and skills), intensified by isolation, whether geographically, politically or through language. This chapter is dedicated to those individual artists and schools who value the virtues of traditional skills while breaking unwritten rules in order to find deeper layers of knowledge and extended understanding of techniques. However, a chapter about a subject such as this can't be written without first an introduction about the appreciation and perception of gold and craftsmanship in recent times.

With the descent of the New Jewelry in the 1960s the nexus between the goldsmith and gold was severed, and for good reason. In 1963 Graham Hughes wrote: 'Artists' pieces made of iron or horn may be provocative, but as jewels they fail because they have too little material value [because] precious stones really are desirable, and add to the jewellery mystique.'[3] However, in the epilogue of his book, Hughes seems to have changed his mind to some extent, observing that modern jewellery has a 'ridiculously low artistic status'. This was triggered by the fact that for the first time in the auctioneer house Christie's history a modern jewel by Georges Fouquet had been sold for a price that was more than ten times its melting value.[4]

The melting value is exactly what has been hindering jewellery for decades, not only physically – innumerable amounts of fine jewellery have been lost because of their inherent material value, prompting Hughes to call jewellery 'the most impermanent of the arts today' – but also mentally: it became a barrier for real artistic exploration. Gold had always been handled with respect precisely because of its value and incorruptibility, and it took a cultural turnover, another way of thinking inspired by the industrial and scientific efforts and the social changes of the time, to break this barrier.

Less than ten years after Hughes's book, Ralph Turner published his famous anthology of contemporary jewellery, which for many interested people at that time and the years to come was like a bible because it brought together from all around the world all the new tendencies in artistic jewellery research. Turner paid particular attention to those artists who worked with synthetic and industrial materials because according to him this was the area of experimentation. Turner is, however, also interested in gold, and although he thinks 'jewelry in gold tends to be of a conventional nature',[5] he did manage to find examples of non-conventional uses of it, for instance in the early corporeal work of Bruno Martinazzi. Traces of a new attitude are also readable in the work of artists in different countries across Europe: Reinhold Reiling, who as early as 1967 combined gold and gems with new photo-etching techniques, Fritz Maierhofer, Claus Bury, Rüdiger Lorenzen and Robert Smit, who around the year 1970 started to combine gold and silver with industrial materials such as acrylic and steel. In Britain a new generation of goldsmiths, such as David Watkins, Gunilla Treen, Susanna Heron and Roger Morris, combined acrylic with silver and gold in partly figurative and partly decorative jewellery. Further traces are found in Gijs Bakker's *Shadow Jewellery* – nothing more than an organic imprint of jewellery on the body – and Van Leersum's translucent acrylic bracelet, both of which not only presented a radical annihilation of jewellery and material but could also be considered echoes of the dematerialisation of art. This was a concept introduced in 1968 by Lucy Lippard and John Chandler in an article in *Art International* considering the new trend in art to move away from the object and materialisation in favour of the concept and idea.[6] Robert Smit's contribution to the 'Artists' Statements' section of the book was also radical. The young Dutch goldsmith, who had received profound technical and artistic training in Pforzheim in Germany, changed his practice during this time to drawing and provocatively stated: 'In short, it all happened on a beautiful warm day in May, Ralph, a really *great* day with a superfabulous happening: the day I sold my goldsmith's equipment for 2000 guilders.'[7] In the north-west of Europe, particularly in the Netherlands, the first serious cracks in the bastion of skills, intrinsic values and conventional thinking had begun to form.

Why was the Dutch movement so radical? Why did it turn so fiercely against precious materials, traditional techniques and the old craft? Anyone born in a country in the north-west of Europe probably knows the rather complicated attitude that we have towards the wearing of gold and precious stones. In this part of the world we somehow seem to miss a

75

76

77

78

75 Atelier Ted Noten, installation detail *Mima Project / Art Rehab*, 2011, various dimensions. /// **76** Atelier Ted Noten, *Mima Project / Art Rehab*, 2011. /// **77** Dinie Besems, participation event *Moet hij dan geen broek aan?* (Shouldn't He Wear Pants?), Salon Dinie Besems, 2010, various paper garments, prints. /// **78** Dinie Besems, *Mannen sieraden* (Jewellery for Men), 1996, various objects and jewellery, mixed media. SM's – Stedelijk Museum 's-Hertogenbosch, Centraal Museum Utrecht and MMK Arnhem.

79

80

81

79 Dinie Besems, necklace *Nooit meer naakt* (Never Naked Again), 1997, silver, floorplan of Dinie Besems' house 1:1. SM's – Stedelijk Museum 's-Hertogenbosch. /// **80** Ted Noten, project *Chew Your Own Brooch*, contest in the Museum Boijmans Van Beuningen, Rotterdam, with 600 children participating, 1999. /// **81** Ted Noten, brooches, series: *Chew Your Own Brooch*, 1998, gold plated 925 silver, various dimensions.

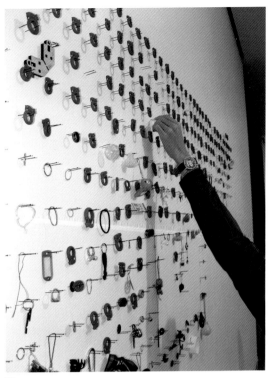

82

83

82 Atelier Ted Noten, installation detail *Wanna Swap Your Ring?*, Museum of Contemporary Art, Tokyo, 2010, rings, 3D printed glass filled nylon, various materials, various dimensions. /// 83 Atelier Ted Noten, project *Red Light Design, Be Nice to a Girl, Buy Her a Ring*, red-light district, Amsterdam, 2008, red sprayed metal rings, vending machine.

84

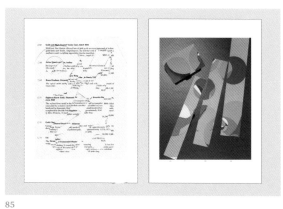

85

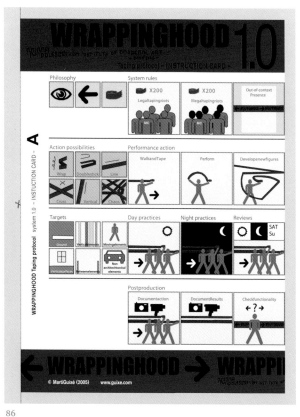

86

84 Suska Mackert, *Addenda & Errata – Sentimental Jewellery*, 2005/06, paper, 15 × 21 cm. The Stedelijk Museum, Amsterdam. /// **85** Suska Mackert, *The Andy Warhol Project*, 2008/09, paper, 27 × 21 cm. /// **86** Martí Guixé, project *Wrappinghood Tape*, 2005, tape actions in Middlesbrough for the exhibition *Wrappinghood* in 2005, tape, 5 × 400 cm. Photo: Valentina Seidel.

spring/summer 05 | **›Miniskirts‹**

Seidel & Pietzsch / WRAPPINGHOOD at Middlesbrough Institute of Modern Art / 12 May – 26 June 2005

87

87   Susan Pietzsch/Valentina Seidel, project *Spring/Summer 05 Miniskirts*, 2005, poster in advertising hoardings, print on semi-gloss paper, 100 × 150 cm. Photo: Valentina Seidel.

88

89

90

88 Yuka Oyama, *Schmuck Quickie:* Naoko Kanezuka ('I would like to have a piece like a pet that you can carry and walk around with'), SQ Daikanyama, Japan, 2003, various recycled materials. Photo: Becky Yee. /// **89** Yuka Oyama, public participation project *Schmuck Quickies*, various locations, 2003–2007. /// **90** Yuka Oyama, *Berlin Flowers*, Schwedenhaus north front, Hansaviertel, Berlin, 2007, social gathering and production processes and installation involving 500 participants, recycled materials.

91

92

93

91   Mah Rana, public participation event *Meanings and Attachments*, ongoing project since 2001, Lisbon, 2005.   ///   92   Mah Rana, brooch *First Class Ticket to Worthing*, 2005, 22 ct gold, oil paint, glass, ø 6 cm. Self portrait.   ///   93   Mah Rana, poster *First Class Ticket to Worthing*, 2005, paper, 59.4 × 42 cm (edition of 1000).

94

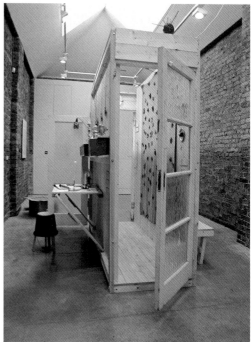

95

94   Naomi Filmer, object *Ball in the Small of My Back* for Alexander McQueen's show *El baile del toro retorsido* (spring/summer 2002), 2001, glass, silver plated copper (electroformed), 28 × 28 cm.   ///   95   Hans Stofer, installation *Walk the Line*, Gallery SO, London, March 2010.

96   Hans Stofer, *Off My Trolley*, 2009, ART applied objects, mixed media, objects ranging from jewellery to water jugs to disused shoes, 107 × 115 × 60 cm.

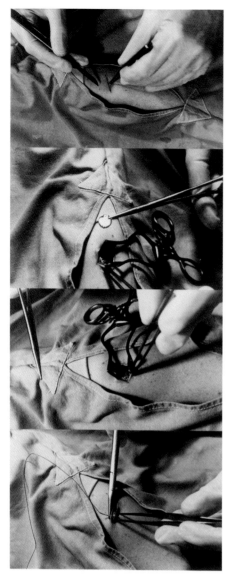
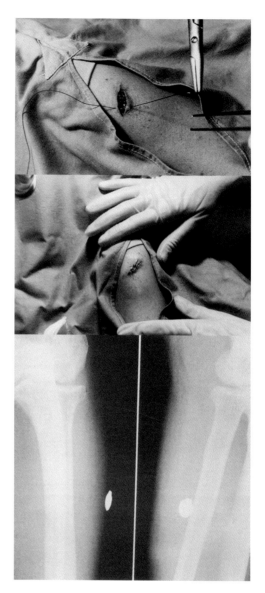

97

97 Peter Skubic, *Schmuck unter der Haut* (Jewellery under the Skin), 1975.

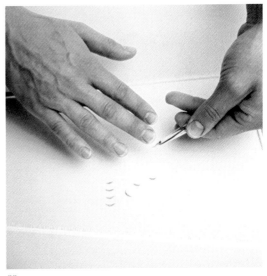

99

100

98 LAM de Wolf, body piece *Wearable Object 1982*, 1982, wood, painted textile, 140 × 60 cm. The Audax Textile Museum, Tilburg. /// **99** Gerd Rothmann, *Gold unter meinen Fingernägeln* (Gold under My Fingernails), 1983, mould in ten pieces, 18 ct gold. /// **100** Hans Appenzeller, ear jewellery, 1969, anodised aluminium, 11 × 11 × 2 cm.

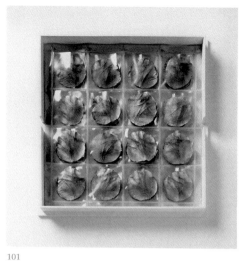

101

102

103

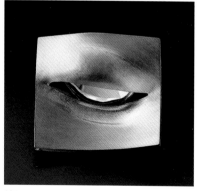

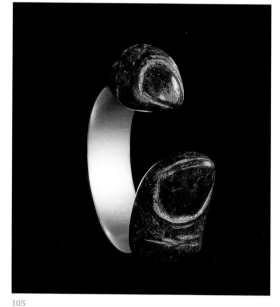

104

105

101 Gerd Rothmann, *Sammlung: 107 Handflächen von Freunden und Bekannten* (Collection: 107 Palms of Friends and Aquaintances), 1982, moulds, pewter, each mould 0.6–0.7 cm. /// **102** Gerd Rothmann, necklace *The Balls: Von ihm für seine Freundin Rosetta* (The Balls: From Him for His Girlfriend Rosetta), 1986, gold plated silver, 0.83 × 0.5 × 0.22 cm. /// **103** Bruno Martinazzi, brooch *Backside*, 1968, 925 silver, 3.1 × 3.8 × 1 cm. Private collection. /// **104** Bruno Martinazzi, brooch *Occhio*, 1968, 20 ct gold, 18 ct white gold, 4 × 4.5 × 1 cm. Private collection. /// **105** Bruno Martinazzi, bracelet *Tempo*, 1976, marmo rosso Levanto (red marble), 18 ct white gold, 6.7 × 6.3 × 2.5 cm. Collection of the artist.

106

107

106   Marjorie Schick, sculpture for the neck *A Plane of Sticks*, 1986, painted wood, riveted and painted, 68.58 × 91.44 × 15.24 cm.   ///   **107**   Pierre Degen, wearable object *Square Frame*, 1982, wood, string, paper, cotton, ca 135 × 135 cm.

108

109

110

108   Christoph Zellweger, *Body Pieces N10, N11*, 1996, expanded polystyrene, chrome plated silver, steel, 5 × 12 cm. /// 109   Christoph Zellweger, wall object *26 Stitches*, 2010, leather.   ///   110   Iris Eichenberg, necklace *R*, 2009, copper, enamel, pink plastic, rose gold, ribbon, 30 × 13 × 6 cm. Private collection.

111   Nanna Melland, necklace *687 Years*, 2006 – 08, IUDs iron, copper, 71 × 17 cm. The National Museum of Decorative Arts, Trondheim.

112

113

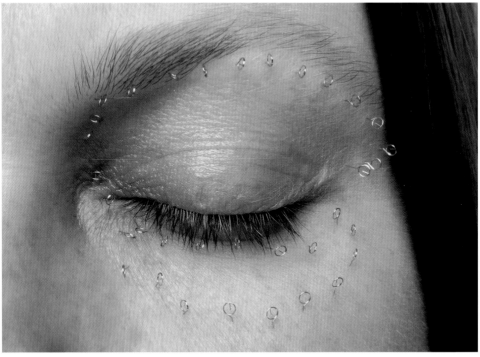

114

112   Frédéric Braham, *Inner Beauty*, 2005, ingestible homeopathic dilution of ruby, ruby, glass flask, nickel silver, copper, polyester thermolac, silicone, polyester thermolac coated 925 silver, 13 cm.   ///   113   Selina Woulfe, skin brooch *Silvergraft*, 2010, sterling silver, surgical steel pin, 5 × 4 × 2.3 cm (variable).   ///   114   Tiffany Parbs, photographic documentation of *Cosmetic*, 2006, stainless steel pins, digital print, 33 × 47 × 35 cm.

115

116

115 Stefan Heuser, necklace *The Egg*, 2009, mother milk, gold. /// 116 Lauren Kalman, *Lip Adornment*, 2006, inkjet print.

117

118

117   Aud Charlotte Ho Sook Sinding, *Animal Brooches*, 2004, hand painted silicon, linoleum, gold plated brass, ca
25 × 20 × 12 cm.   ///   **118**   Aud Charlotte Ho Sook Sinding, brooch *I Beg Your Pardon…*, 2001, latex, acryl plaster.

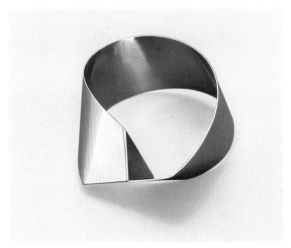

119 Evert Nijland, necklace *Rococo*, 2009, porcelain, hand woven linen, Ø 15 cm. Private Collection. /// 120 Emmy van Leersum, bracelet with fastening, 1968, 14 ct gold, Ø 7 × 3 × 0.5 cm. SM-'s – Stedelijk Museum 's-Hertogenbosch.

121

122

123

121   Gijs Bakker, necklace *Dew Drop*, 1982, photograph, PVC, 55 × 49 × 0.1 cm. Numbered edition.   ///   122   Gijs Bakker, brooch *De Boer*, series: *Sport Figures*, 1989, 14 ct white gold, spinel, newspaper, PVC, 12,7 × 11.8 × 1.5 cm. ///   123   Gijs Bakker, brooch *Ferrari Dino 206 SP 1966*, series: *I Don't Wear Jewels, I Drive Them*, 2001, 925 silver, fire opal, colour photo, acrylic, 5.9 × 7.5 cm.

124

125

126

124   Emiko Oye, necklace *The Duchess 2*, 2008, LEGO, rubber cord, 925 silver, paint, 61 × 34.3 × 7.6 cm.   ///
125   Helen Britton, brooch *Big White*, 2009, silver, paint, glass, plastics, 10 × 7 × 6 cm. Private collection.   ///
126   Helen Britton, brooch *Bird*, 2007, silver, glass, diamonds, 4 × 3 × 1.5 cm. Private collection.

127

128

129

130

127   Uli Rapp, T-shirt *Maiden's Blush Majesty*, 2004, T-shirt, cotton lycra, textile screenprinting, etching techniques.   ///   **128**   Uli Rapp, necklace *Facettes and Stones*, 2010, cotton, screenprint, metal foil, silicone rubber, 44 × 20 × 0.5 cm.   ///   **129**   Anya Kivarkis, bracelet *Winona Ryder, Lost Jewels 2008*, 2009, 925 silver.   ///   **130**   Ruudt Peters, necklace *Machiavelli*, series: *Passio*, 1992, silver, silk, 7 × 7 × 11 cm.

131

132

133

131 Otto Künzli, brooch *Oh Say!*, 1991, gold, 9 × 9 × 0.6 cm. /// **132** Daniel Kruger, necklace, 2006, enamel on copper, silk, gold, silver, ca 18 × 18 × 3 cm. /// **133** Daniel Kruger, necklace, 2008, silver filigree, jade, pigment, 11 × 7 cm, 3.5 × 3.5 cm.

134

135

136

134 Vera Siemund, necklace, 2004, stamped and enamelled copper, silver, 33 × 20 × 1.5 cm, centre piece 8 × 7 cm. /// **135** Vera Siemund, necklace, 2009, copper, silver, enamel, 18 × 32 × 5 cm. /// **136** Iris Nieuwenburg, brooch *Golden Couple*, series: *Gilded Frames from Paris*, 2010, silver, veneer, photograph, lacquer, dismantled parts from an ancient cuckoo clock, elements of a doll's house and scale models gold plated 18 ct, plastic, 32 × 26 × 6.5 cm. The Susan C. Beech Collection, USA.

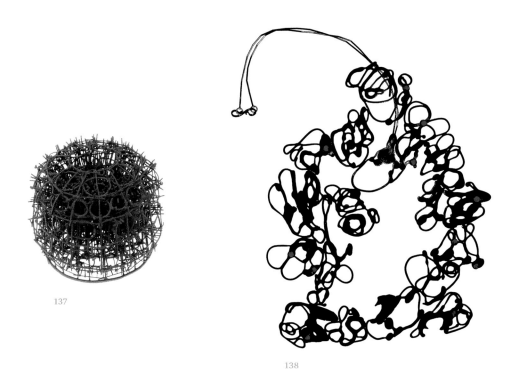

137

138

139

140

137 Bettina Dittlmann, brooch *Untitled (Red Brooch)*, 2007–08, iron wire, enamel, 7 × 7 × 7 cm. Victoria & Albert Museum, London. /// 138 Robert Smit, neck ornament *Schets voor Sleeping Beauty III* (Sketch for Sleeping Beauty III), 1991, gold, 18 × 14 cm. SM's – Stedelijk Museum 's-Hertogenbosch. /// 139 Silvia Weidenbach, necklace, 2009, enamel, copper, silk, l. 100 cm. /// 140 David Bielander, brooch *Enzian* (Gentian), 2011, titanium, 10 × 6 × 6 cm.

141

142

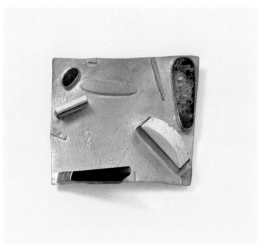

143

141 Marc Monzó, pendant *Sun*, 2009, 18 ct gold, 6.5 × 4 cm. /// **142** Otto Künzli, pendant *Traces of Movements VIII*, 2007, gold, 8.2 × 5.3 cm. /// **143** Hermann Jünger, brooch, 1993, gold, chrysoprase, haematite, lapis lazuli, raw ruby, lemon chrysoprase, ca 5 × 4.5 cm. Private collection.

144   Hermann Jünger, necklace, 1996, palladium, gold, pendant: ca 12 × 3 cm. Private collection.

145

146

147

148

145 Dorothea Prühl, Collier (neckpiece) *Tiere* (Animals), 1999, titanium, 35 cm. Galerie Marzee, Nijmegen. /// **146** Dorothea Prühl, Collier (neckpiece) *Fische* (Fish), 2008, cherry wood, length of one shape 10 cm. /// **147** Stefano Marchetti, ring, 2007, gold, silver, niello, 4.5 × 4 × 4 cm. /// **148** Annamaria Zanella, brooch *Water*, 1995, silver, iron, argentan, niello, acrylic enamels, 13 × 9 × 1.5 cm. Private collection.

149

150

151

152

149   Giovanni Corvaja, bracelet *The Golden Fleece: Commitment*, 2008, gold wire, platinum granules.   ///
150   Robert Baines, bracelet *Java-la-Grande*, 2005, gold, iron, plastic, 7.5 × 5 × 6.5 cm.   ///   151   Philip Sajet,
necklace *Feestslinger* (Garland), 1996, silver, gold, enamel, 2 × 16 × 13 cm. Collection: Nina Sajet.   ///   152   Ralph
Bakker, ring *A.L.E.X.*, 2008, gold, silver, enamel, 5 × 4.5 × 4.5 cm. Private collection.

153

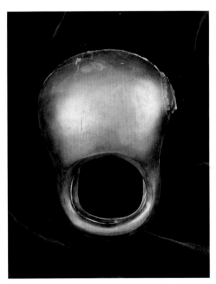

154

155

153 *Der Galliumhort von Obertraun* (The Gallium Treasure of Obertraun), rings, bangles and torques, gallium, various dimensions. Presented by Peter Bauhuis, 2011. /// 154 *Der Galliumhort von Obertraun* (The Gallium Treasure of Obertraun), bracelet *Schädelarmring*, gallium, ca 17 × 10 × 11 cm. Presented by Peter Bauhuis, 2011. /// 155 Stanley Lechtzin, *Brooch 63-B*, 1966, silver, tourmaline crystal, pearl, 7 × 8.9 × 1.3 cm. The Museum of Fine Arts, Houston; Helen Williams Drutt Collection, gift of the Morgan Foundation in honour of Catherine Asher Morgan.

156

157

158

159

156 Liesbet Bussche, *Stedelijke sieraden* (Urban Jewellery), 2009, plastic, closure: 4.5 × 19 × 16.5 cm, bucket: 10 × 23 × 23 cm. The Françoise van den Bosch Foundation/The Stedelijk Museum, Amsterdam. /// **157** Liesbet Bussche, *Stedelijke sieraden* (Urban Jewellery), 2009. The Françoise van den Bosch Foundation/The Stedelijk Museum, Amsterdam. /// **158** Claus Bury, ring, 1970, gold, acrylic, 2.2 × 3.8 × 3.8 cm. The Museum of Fine Arts, Houston; Helen Williams Drutt Collection, museum purchase with funds provided by the Mary Kathryn Lynch Kurtz Charitable Lead Trust. /// **159** Peter Skubic, *Spiegelbrosche* (Mirror Brooch), 2001, stainless steel, lacquer; sculpture *Idol*, 1989, iron, steel. Model: Karl Bollmann.

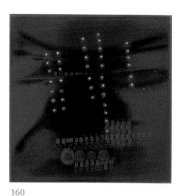

160

161

162

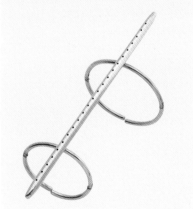

163

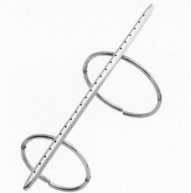

164

160 Robert Smit, brooch, 1970, 18 ct gold, acrylic, 7 × 7 cm. Private collection. /// **161** Tanel Veenre, brooch *Judith*, 2001, seahorse, coral, photo, resin, silver, gold. The Helena and Lasse Pahlman Collection, Helsinki. /// **162** Kadri Mälk, brooch *Nölv* (Declivity), 2000, cibatool (carved and painted), silver, almandine, onyx, 4.7 × 4.9 × 0.9 cm. The Helena and Lasse Pahlman Collection, Helsinki. /// **163** Nel Linssen, bracelet, 1987, paper, Ø 6 × 9 cm. The Marjan and Gerard Unger Collection, Rijksmuseum Amsterdam. /// **164** Lucio Fontana, bracelet *Concetto Spaziale*, 1967, gold, 7 × 20 cm. Limited numbered edition 3/30. SM's – Stedelijk Museum 's-Hertogenbosch.

natural bond with gold and gems. Although we do know about showing off (to a point), Dutch jewellery in general has been characterised by modesty, especially in daily life (the Dutch are noted for their thrift). It is not known if thrift is also the reason why the Dutch royal crown, a rather ponderous object made in 1840 by the Amsterdam jeweller Bonebakker, is not made of gold, rubies, sapphires and emeralds but rather of gilded silver and glass cut to look like real stones. However, it is clear that the new king, Willem II, didn't want to outdo his father, King Willem I, who had a crown made of gilded copper and fancy stones.[8] Apparently the Dutch didn't see much harm in presenting an imitation as real. In several nineteenth-century official accounts of the coronation of Willem II and even in twentieth century writings about Queen Juliana's coronation in 1948, the crown is credibly described, praising the costly and precious materials it was supposedly made of. Only in 1967 when the Bonebakker house published a book to celebrate its 175-year jubilee did the truth about the crown come to light. We may wonder if such deception would have been possible in other countries. In Britain, King George V, for instance, was prepared to wear the heaviest of the Crown Jewels, the official imperial crown of India, during a three-and-a-half-hour ceremony even though it weighed almost one kilo. The crown, made in 1911 at the cost of £ 60,000, is set with real emeralds, rubies, sapphires and 6,100 diamonds. This king physically experienced the splendour of power that weighs heavily.

In contrast to the pomp and circumstance, Dutch culture has often been denominated egalitarian because of its modesty. Yet this modesty is perhaps more the result of casualness than of egalitarianism. Egalitarianism also contradicts the culture of traditional jewellery worn in the countryside, which was meant to determine and signalise social structures. People could read the inherent sociological codes of the elaborate golden filigree female head adornment, the big silver or golden plates on the men's trousers, decorated with engraved bible scenes. As with everywhere else, jewellery and accessories were used to classify people.

Neither egalitarianism nor casualness can explain why some Dutch jewellers made such radical steps in the 1960s. References have been made to Calvinism, De Stijl and the Dutch history of design. Perhaps if your forefathers for many centuries had succeeded in fighting the water, conquering it and creating new land, there would be no need to consider a given as a fact; every given can be questioned, every fact can be transformed. The 1960s was a very fruitful period in the Netherlands; those were the years of the emancipation of different social groups, the liberation of sexual and moral standards and a belief in a 'makeable society'. There was a growing sense of one's professional position and attitude and of questioning traditional customs. 'Amsterdam was then known as Europe's "Magic Centre", the crux of a utopian dream where people believed anything could happen', or so the story goes.[9] It is this loose atmosphere and this culture of a belief in change that set the tone for the upheaval in contemporary jewellery. The younger generation felt drawn to new movements in the fine arts, such as Kinetic Art, Constructivism, ZERO and Fluxus. An important exhibition, an eye-opener to many young jewellers, was the big international jewellery exhibition in Museum Boijmans Van Beuningen in Rotterdam in 1965. The exhibition was organised by the Hessisches Landesmuseum Darmstadt and extended with a collection of contemporary Dutch jewellery. The original exhibition involved a section of jewellery by fine artists such as Georges Braque, Jean Arp, Jean Lurçat, Alicia Penalba, the Pomodoro brothers and Alexander Calder. Although Gerhard Bott, curator of the exhibition, wrote in his introduction to the catalogue that it was up to the viewer to decide about the artistic quality of the exhibited jewellery, the exhibition was meant to bring jewellery to a higher level: that of jewellery as art. Writing about the fact that people need courage to wear this jewellery, Bott states that during the opening of *documenta III*, in the summer of 1964 in Kassel, which was the renowned platform for international avant-garde art at that time, one could indeed see this kind of jewellery: 'There was a kind of distinguishing mark of this minority that wanted to free itself from the equalizing force of society'. With the aim of convincing the viewer that they have to 'classify these forged valuables in gold and silver in the range of art products of our time,'[10] Bott brought jewellery by goldsmiths and jewellery as a minor practice of major artists together in one exhibition.

The reception of this exhibition in the Netherlands is interesting. In one of the Dutch newspapers a critic concludes that Dutch jewellery is 'dignified and calm, not voluptuous',[11] an attribute he apparently applies to international jewellery. 'Voluptuous' seems like a rather odd qualification for jewellery, but it might be that the expressionist language of the international work and the excessive use of yellow gold was the reason for this description. The young Dutch jewellers who visited the show had mixed feelings. They were puzzled by the enormous amount of skill involved in making the exhibits, knowing that they did not want to work like this.[12] Under the spell of ZERO, introduced to them by teacher Henk Peeters – himself a member of the Dutch movement – at the Art Academy in Arnhem, they were more inspired by avant-garde contemporary art than by the glittering and decorative jewels on show. Klaas van Beek recalls: 'Banalities were used to create a new language. We were aware of what was going on in the visual arts. It made you think. Gold and silver were treated with such respect, whereas macaroni, cotton wool and beer crates aroused fierce opposition. That made you feel a kind of commitment to a way of life, and you justified that by expressing yourself in a corresponding way. At that exhibition in the Boijmans Van Beuningen I found all that craftsmanship repellent. The things by Braque and Dali were so labour intensive: there was so much craftsmanship involved that I thought, Oh, God [...] the discipline, ten years to learn all that, no thanks. So I just took a plate and started bending it. I just picked it up and tried to make it something special. I knew that they did the same thing at the Bauhaus and in Constructivism – I found support in history, impulses from the past.'[13] Emmy van Leersum and Gijs Bakker observed craft as something distastefully romantic, outdated and hindering the free exploration of form, construction and idea. They were quite radical in their rejection of the craft. This mentality was in line with a general tendency in Dutch society to reject anything considered conventional and traditional.

Soon after the first manifestations of contemporary jewellery, a new tone was set in the Netherlands. Goldsmith-jewellers became aware of their profession and how they wanted to work. They soon dropped the word *edelsmid* (goldsmith) and instead called themselves 'jewellery designers'. Inspired by the visual art movements of their time, they decided that they wanted to work like designers, striving for serial production and cheap industrial materials. In 1970, Gijs Bakker was appointed by the Art Academy in Arnhem in order to change the crafts department of goldsmithing into a department for product design, which was to be called the Department for Design in Metal and Plastics. At that time Bakker was of the opinion that students should not be concerned with learning any craft skills.[14] The change was radical, even the equipment was abandoned. It meant the complete loss of one of the three full-time goldsmith's courses at an academic level in the Netherlands.

In Germany, the neighbouring centre of jewellery renewal, the atmosphere was completely different. In 1974 Karl Schollmayer published *Neuer Schmuck: Ornamentum Humanum* as another attempt to define jewellery as art. The preciousness of jewellery remained the standard – even the pages dividing the different artists' sections were executed in luxurious, textured gold paper. The book comprises four generations of central and north-west European jewellers. Respect is the quintessential difference with the radical atmosphere in the Netherlands at that time. In Schollmayer's view, the young generation of goldsmiths, while dealing with serial jewellery, jewellery design, new materials or the autonomous creation and the 'jewellery object' is not doing so 'without paying respect towards the big efforts of the older generations'.[15] The most radical statement in the book is by the only Dutch artist in the book, Robert Smit, who at that time had just made a move from gold, abstract expressionist jewellery to steel and Plexiglas objects and rings set with rows of little holes or ciphers. He says: '[I] couldn't make jewellery for a bourgeois society anymore. I just can't make jewellery that is seen as "beautiful" in this domain. I also don't want to get in a situation having to make that kind of jewellery. All this is connected with my understanding of my position in today's society and with my mentality.'[16]

Therefore the attitudes in Germany and the Netherlands in the early 1970s were quite different: an overall respectful German attitude versus the general anti-bourgeois, anti-establishment and anti-tradition tendency in the Netherlands. The Dutch focus on serial and experimental jewellery was very much stimulated by a series of exhibitions on serial, conceptual and body jewellery organised by the Dutch Arts Foundation – some of which travelled nationally, others internationally, for several years. This active governmental art policy proved instrumental in stimulating an awakening new art form. In the catalogue *Sieraad 1975*, Marion Herbst, then chairwoman of VES, the society of Dutch jewellers and jewellery designers, states: 'From way back the function of jewellery has been to decorate people. It has a tradition of craftsmanship, connected with value and status (precious metals, gems). As a goldsmith you are a victim of heredity. You try to escape by dismantling jewellery and giving it an autonomous artistic function in return.'[17] Such was the atmosphere in the Netherlands in the first half of the 1970s.

THE NEW GOLD

Robert Smit's jewellery made during and shortly after his study years in Pforzheim (1963–66) was very much the product of the German school of jewellery, influenced by his teacher Klaus Ulrich. It was abstract and sculptural work, which showed a love for the textured, eroded surface, and had relief-like, engraved, punched or applied gold bars in geometric patterns, made from yellow gold and small precious stones. Back in the Netherlands around 1970, he began combining gold with lacquer and coloured Perspex dotted with little holes and numerical codes, influenced by the visual art of Jan Wagemaker, Jan Schoonhoven, Lucio Fontana and ZERO. His work also became bigger: in an interview in 1970, he mentions working on big stainless-steel reliefs with thousands of little holes.[18]

The work he came up with after his retreat from jewellery in 1985 was due to a new kind of goldsmithing. The gold was used as sheet material and folded, wrinkled, pleated, painted and embossed as if it were paper. In her book about Dutch jewellery in the twentieth century, Marjan Unger characterised the material qualities of Smit's work as 'rather casual'.[19] In contrast to his Germany and post-Germany years, he then began working directly on the material with rollers, hammers, punches and piercers. Making his own alloys he knew the material so well that he was able to use it as a painter would, achieving very special colourations. In later collections he completely covered the gold with paint and lead (1989) or applied blue-painted pearls (1992, fig. 138).

> 138

In 2007 Smit made an innovative move by printing gold sheets with ink with the aid of an Epson digital printer. It took him quite some time to research the problem of the adhesive layer but finally he invented his very own recipe – no one had ever done this before, after all. The resulting *Madonna delle Dolomiti* collection of necklaces, brooches, adapted photographs and computer drawings (2008) shows again that Robert Smit is an advanced goldsmith who has gone far beyond his craft. The vibrant colours and the compositions with scattered dots of colour, line and mounted pieces of gold and silver are more about the artistic process – rendered by computer – than about making jewellery. One may ask why you should use gold as a canvas for artistic expression – what does the gold add? The answer is pure love. After so many years, Smit knows the properties of the material to the core, he knows its history, myths and mysteries, he can manipulate it to his own wish even though he still feels challenged by it, and he knows the allusive and economic powers of gold. Above all he is taken by the cleanliness and the colour of the material so much that he has admitted he will be occupied with gold for the rest of his life. Yet, acquainted as he is with the temptations of gold, he wants to avoid any mystification.

> fig. 138

> fig. 141

To many young jewellers yellow gold seems far less alluring or challenging. Spanish jeweller Marc Monzó is known for his reduced form vocabulary and his preference for everyday materials. Plastic items, such as small hoops, sticks, rings or balls found on the beach, are electroformed and transformed into matt silver pieces of jewellery; plastic sticks are chained to form a necklace and simple flat silver forms are painted with coloured lacquer. The fundamental and reduced forms of most of these brooches make them look like signs. *The Half Ring* (1998) is a semi-circular object made out of 18 ct gold. It is an intriguing and stunning form: imperfection represented in a perfect material.[20] Monzó uses gold and silver, sometimes spray-painted with colour, on a regular basis. The material is hardly touched, so it seems. By sawing and bending gold sheet and thread he creates simple yellow-gold rings and brooches. Some parts may be soldered, but the overall impression is one of simple combination. There is no sign of the typical goldsmith's craftsmanship. In 2005, Monzó made a golden brooch by drawing with a permanent marker on a plain round golden form. He covered the form with a roughly sketched mountain landscape under a blue sky with two white clouds. Here Monzó was hiding the gold with colour and imagery – comparable to Robert Smit's approach – in an attempt to express something about the material by denying it completely. As is illustrated in this work, most of his jewellery made in the years 1998–2009 shows an abstention from handwork.

> Although it is clear that Monzó is a reductionist who pairs an economical way of working with sparse design, in 2009 he made a range of golden pieces that resisted this movement. The *Sun* pendants and *Fire* brooch were made of extremely thin (0.08 mm) sheets of 18 ct gold and were as radiating and alluring as gold can be (fig. 141). The pendants were folded to achieve the effect of radiation while through this folding technique the material

> 141

gained enough rigidity to make them stable and wearable. Monzó used simple, everyday things as tools, such as scissors, a compass and a ruler. He liked the directness of this work: 'Cutting metal with regular scissors, using a simple compass or ruler to mark out its area and imprint its surface really made me feel like a jeweller.'[21] In the same text he writes: 'I have wanted to make a series of gold pieces which would address their own materiality for a long time. "Sun" is an attempt to synthesize all the characteristics of gold which have seduced me. The technique I applied combines an expression of its physical qualities and a strong visual representation of what gold means to me.' This very direct hands-on 'cold working' method, without using heat or the traditional goldsmith's tools, reveals the properties of the material in an essential and powerful way.

Gold, so it seems, evokes contradictory feelings of rapture and awe. Otto Künzli has always been subject to this very special attraction of gold. Some of the works he made during his long career are explicitly about this, for example the *Gold Makes You Blind* bracelet, made for the first time in 1980. The bracelet was his way of dealing with all considerations a thinking goldsmith should have. It has to do with an awareness of the nature of gold, how in this pure material somehow everything that is considered either eternal and divine or mysterious and bad comes together. Being a goldsmith means dealing with this legendary status of the material. In Otto Künzli's words, 'with the decline of traditional craft forms and pursuits did gold jewellery become empty of content, interchangeable, arbitrary.' His black rubber bracelet with the hidden golden ball visible as a bump in the rubber bangle is a temporary finality in gold to 'achieve detachment in the hope that, after a period of abstinence, I would be able to re-appraise gold'.[22] The bracelet used a Modernist vocabulary to talk about the magic of gold – a subject that was certainly not examined at that time.

Indeed, he addressed gold again in his later work, for instance in his collection of pendants *Cozticteocuitlatl 1995–1998 B.M.*, which intertwined Latin American, European and American legends, and in his *Traces of Movement* and *Apokalypse* pendants (2009, fig. 142). The latter pieces of jewellery were part of his exhibition *Pi* at Galerie Wittenbrink in Munich. The exhibition had a rather absolute and definite character, a summing up of sorts. The title of the exhibition already pointed to that. Künzli's gold pendants relate to Marc Monzó's *Sun* pendants and *Fire* brooches as they stem from a kindred desire to master the gold through simple means. Yet there is also a distinctive difference: Monzó folded the gold, touching it, caressing it, falling in love with it. Künzli gouged the gold with a knife, in such a way that it actually hurt. The gouging, however, was not merely an act of hurting; the movements of the knife in the gold represented universal movements, such as a comet's rain or the traces of birds or airplanes in the sky – both apocalyptic and everyday. It is clear that Künzli made these pieces of jewellery himself: 'I have a certain idea about perfection, therefore I can better make it myself. But there is not a philosophy of the making behind it, such as with Hermann Jünger or Dorothea Prühl.'[23]

> 142

HERMANN JÜNGER AND DOROTHEA PRÜHL

It was because of Hermann Jünger, professor at the Munich Academy of Fine Arts from 1972 to 1990, that Munich became a centre for jewellery. His goldsmith's class had such a reputation it attracted many young students from abroad, who often stayed in Munich after their studies and consequently contributed to the city's jewellery culture.

There are not many books written by artists/makers that can be read in terms of a state of mind. Jünger's *Über den Schmuck und das Machen* (1996) is a rare example of such a book, and due to the author's influence as a goldsmith and teacher it demands closer investigation. The book considered the relationship of hand and head, and the joy of making and thinking through the process. Jünger observed that in recent times the notion of the maker had become a rather negative one and referred to the *Duden* German dictionary, which added the adjective 'intuitive' to the definition of the word 'maker'. Jünger finds this addition 'irritating' because 'it can no longer be taken for granted that the outcome of 'Making' is the equivalent of a complete activity in itself – it has lost its innocence. We must realise that 'Making' without any responsibility for the result is worthless. Ignore that, and it becomes a mindless, pointless exercise.'[24] In Jünger's view there is no separation between thinking and making. Jünger sees himself in an age-old tradition of jewellery making, yet despite being born in 1928 in the city of Hanau, home of the Staatliche Zeichenakademie Hanau founded in 1772 to improve the quality of the products of the local silver- and goldsmiths, he was not predestined to follow in this trade. However, having grown up in a city that was named 'Town of Noble Jewellery' by the Nazi's must have had its effects. Jünger describes how in his youth every event or art exhibition was connected with the Deutsches Goldschmiedehaus [German Goldsmiths' House]. According to Jünger's perception 'a goldsmith was one, who above all draws or sculpts; goldsmithing was another word for 'art'. It did not dawn on me that this activity starts first of all with craft, or at any rate, it appeared to me to be of minor importance.'[25]

In 1947 he enrolled at the Staatliche Zeichenakademie, which was in a deplorable post-war condition. The city had been heavily bombed, and there was no equipment. His education as a goldsmith started with drawing and painting which met his deepest desires and expectations about a proper goldsmith's training. By the end of his studies in Hanau in 1949, when technical skills had become more important, he had the feeling that he'd failed. Only some years later when studying at the Academy in Munich (1953–56) did he gain a good understanding of what making was, thanks to his teacher Franz Rickert. Jünger stresses the importance of Rickert's open-minded and intellectual approach to the craft which stimulated him to experiment on his own. In 1973, the Munich Academy of Fine Arts published an internal statement about the aim of the goldsmith's course, written by Jünger, who had been appointed as the professor of the goldsmith's class the year before. The text ended with the recommendation that every student should develop his or her own criteria for artistic quality and that 'the formal preciousness is not necessarily dependent on the use of expensive materials'.[26]

Jünger's own jewellery is characterised by a strong graphic and painterly quality, expressed with the use of enamel and colourful stones, yet as a child of his time, Jünger has also had to fight traditional conceptions about the value and use of materials. He is aware that when using gems the palette is limited because the colours cannot be mixed, but by combining extremely diverse stones he is able to achieve colourful compositions 'provided one does not allow their commercial value to hinder an uninhibited choice of these materials' (fig. 143).[27] When he began exhibiting his work in the early 1960s his jewellery caused serious critique because of his 'haphazard' way of working of leaving the metal roughly finished and using stones in an unconventional way. During the heydays of the New Jewelry movement drawing, sketching and painting remained important elements in Jünger's work, and his predominant interest remained in the unity of head and hand (fig. 144). This may have been looked upon as rather old-fashioned in other countries, yet Jünger believed in providing space for, and showing interest in, the more conceptual approach of his pupils.

The influence of Jünger as a teacher is invaluable but unfortunately has still not been fully assessed. Without defining the exact contours of his artistic legacy, we might say,

> 143

> 144

however, that it is to be found in the sensitive, intelligent and sometimes colourful handling of precious metals and in the artistic discourse with traditional goldsmith's materials and techniques. This attitude is visible in the work of other jewellers, such as Erico Nagai, Manfred Bischoff, Therese Hilbert, Alexandra Bahlmann, Daniel Kruger, Caroline von Steinau-Steinrück and Ulo Florack.

The world learnt about Dorothea Prühl in 1996, who at that time was almost sixty years old. 'Discovered' by Marie-José van den Hout, the owner of Galerie Marzee in Nijmegen in the Netherlands, Prühl was at first reluctant to show her jewellery abroad. Raised in the former German Democratic Republic of East Germany, she had until then lived and worked in the lee of the political circumstances in quiet isolation.

Although Prühl is only nine years younger than Hermann Jünger and both were professors of jewellery, their work is completely different: the painterly against the sculptural understanding of jewellery. Comparable though are their excellent educations, their dedication to teaching and their approach of jewellery as an artistic medium. Dorothea Prühl received her training as a goldsmith at the Burg Giebichenstein University of Art and Design (later School of industrial Design) in Halle an der Saale. Although the jewellery class only became an independent department in 1969, jewellery design and making was a subject from the outset. From 1957 to 1962, Prühl studied here in the metalworking class of sculptor Karl Müller. Afterwards, she worked for some years as a jewellery designer in the industry. In 1965 she was appointed as an assistant back at the University and in 1972 as a teacher, reinvigorating the jewellery class together with Renate Heintze. In 1991 she succeeded Heintze as head of the department and in 1994 was appointed professor for jewellery design.

Dorothea Prühl is inspired by nature and the cosmos. Her necklace *Animals* (1999, fig. 145) is characterised by restraint while still being sculptural. This sculptural austerity may give just a hint of a figurative motif. She prefers a simple cord for the strings of her necklaces while the chained elements may be meticulously formed in various metals and wood. Whether left bare or slightly oxidised, the materials speak for themselves.

> 145

Prühl's first exhibition abroad at Galerie Marzee presented her own choice of jewellery she had made over the years: twenty-five pieces forming the essence of what she wanted to express. In an interview during the exhibition, she declared: '[What is important is] reducing the thing to the essence of what it means to you. Reduction, reduction, reduction – that's what it is all about. Perhaps, when I become very old, I will once manage to make something that is nothing more than itself.' In her hands, economy becomes an artistic motive: 'There are too many things in the world. There is too much rubbish, waste, mess. My fundamental attitude is that a piece of jewellery is only good if I am convinced that it is valuable. That it has all my power in all its intensity in it. That I can feel responsible for it. And that it makes sense as a piece of jewellery.'[28] (fig. 146) Prühl is strict, not only as a designer but also as a teacher, and very much aware of her responsibilities as an artist. In the above interview she mentions self-criticism as an important lesson for students while also talking about the possibility of dismissing pieces, throwing them away as an act of liberation.

> 146

Dorothea Prühl was head of the jewellery class for a relatively short period. However during this period (1991–2002) she managed to create an environment where students could work fully concentrated in an atmosphere of attention and time. According to Prühl, art education was all about developing one's own personality. It is proven by the successful work of her students, such as Andrea Wippermann, Vera Siemund, Kathleen Fink, Beate Klockmann, Antje Bräuer, Beate Eismann, Rudolf Kocéa, Christine Matthias, Silke Trekel and many others, that her teaching was successful. Most of these former 'Burg' students have a sculptural approach to jewellery. Their knowledge of materials and techniques is profound while their preference for non-precious metals and enamelling is noteworthy. In contrast to the fast assemblage trend in jewellery, jewellery from Halle is the result of a process of making. It is an emanation of the relative isolation of the Burg and its jewellery department. Many of the former students of Burg Giebichenstein stay in Halle after finishing school. They appear to appreciate the calm atmosphere of this remote little town in the middle of the east of Germany, knowing that the periphery can be as eloquent as the centre.

GOLD, WIRE AND FILIGREE

There is probably no other place in the world where the art of the goldsmith is valued as much than at the Istituto statale d'arte 'Pietro Selvatico' in Padua, Italy, whose history incidentally dates back to 1867. The 'founding father' of the Padua Art School is Mario Pinton who started teaching at the institute in 1944. Other notable appointments were Francesco Pavan in 1961 and Giampaolo Babetto in 1969; together they all put their stamp on the education of the goldsmiths at the school. One peculiarity about the Padua School is that most of the students were born in Padua or its direct surroundings, the Veneto region. Fritz Falk notes that 'the goldsmiths of the Padua School are not a closed society'.[29] But the fact that the school is situated in a small city in the north of Italy and attracts mainly Italian students who do not speak any language other than their own makes it a rather closed community. The school attracts students at a very young age. Giovanni Corvaja, for instance, began his studies at the institute as a pupil of Francesco Pavan at the early age of fourteen, acquiring his first diploma three years later and finished at the school with a Maturità d'Arte Applicata diploma at nineteen – quite a common way of studying goldsmithing in Padua. Technical skills are taught on a high level but equal attention is paid to theory, aesthetics and design. It is as if gold is in their veins and in their hearts, together with a rather severe, geometrical approach to design. The school has produced a strong and recognisable, artistically coherent output over many decades.

Over the last twenty years new approaches have come to light, for instance, in the work of Graziano Visintin, Annamaria Zanella, Giovanni Corvaja, and Stefano Marchetti. In her book on the Padua School of jewellery, Graziella Folchini explains how the jewellery of Francesco Pavan and Giampaolo Babetto is connected to fine art movements of that time. The kinetic art of the 1960s with its special Padovan 'branch' the ENNE group, which had close contacts with groups like GRAV in Paris and ZERO in Düsseldorf, influenced Francesco Pavan's intricate white gold kinetic earrings (1970). These earrings consisted of ten circles, loosely attached to each other by hinges that enabled the circles to move in all directions from a flat surface to a sphere. Pavan's choice of materials was concise; he used gold, niello and rock crystal for optical and compositional reasons. In his view, gems had the same abstract function as the precious metals.

Jewellery of the Padua School is characterised by geometry, a reduction of form and an exploration of the artistic possibilities of gold and colour. Of course, exceptions are to be found, such as in the work of Giampaolo Babetto who made an exceptional collection of figurative jewellery inspired by Pontormo's *Vertumnus and Pomona* frescoes (1519–21), between 1989 and 1995. The jewellery of the younger generation, especially that of Annamaria Zanella and Stefano Marchetti, are manifestations of a freer handling of form and materials. Their jewellery means no radical rift with their teachers, although their use of gold mixed with other metals into a 'worn out', decrepit material, bearing not only a layer of patina but totally composed of this affected material, is rebellious within the context of the Padua School (fig. 147). Annamaria Zanella maltreats the gold by oxidising it or combining it with rusty iron and steel. As a true alchemist she creates new materials by using plastic, enamel, lacquer, papier mâché, oxidation, acrylic, niello and resin and applying these to gold and silver (fig. 148).

Goldsmiths are used to working on a very small scale, but filigree and granulation form the most minuscule and detailed work that can be done by human hands. One of the Padovan goldsmiths, Giovanni Corvaja, should be highlighted here as he has pushed these techniques to the extreme through his work with fine wire. Through his long technical research into the properties of gold and of textile weaving, he invented a technique to make gold as soft and fine as fur but strong enough to make jewellery. His stunning *Golden Fleece* collection, first presented in Munich in March 2009, proves that Corvaja is a virtuoso, a hyper craftsman (fig. 149). Corvaja, born in the city of Padua, has been fascinated – some may call it obsessed – by gold since his early childhood.

In the early 1990s he found a method to make gold thread, the thickness of which was one fifth of a human hair. It was his dream to make pieces of extremely fine, almost invisible gold thread that would be as soft as fur. The whole undertaking took him twelve years, starting with the search for a system that would draw a wire as refined as a silk thread, followed by the composition of a special alloy of gold that would be extremely ductile and have the right glowing yellow colour to finally the study of weaving techniques and the creation of several looms to weave the gold thread. In one of the many articles written about this astounding research, the artist is quoted: 'I made six different looms myself, one out of 22,000 different parts […] none of which did work.'[30] An ancient Japanese weaving technique, a cross between weaving and braiding, finally made it possible to use the gold thread as if it were fibre and enable the creation of an absolutely soft, furry surface. The appearance of the four pieces made with this technique, the headpiece, necklace, bracelet and ring, can only be described in terms such as soft, light or airy. On his website visitors can see pictures of the most stunning of these pieces – the headpiece – being made on an intricate loom. At its presentation at the TEFAF art fair in Maastricht in 2010, the *Golden Fleece Bracelet* was presented in an international magazine for collectors. Its price: some € 200,000. Its technical specifications describe it as being 'made from over 1.2 million single gold wires – some 28 km of wire in total – and has taken 1,250 hours to confect.'[31] The accumulation of numbers, of thousands of hours of work, of trial and error, and the making and applying of hundreds of kilometres of gold wire, can only be explained by a firm belief in your abilities, eagerness and unlimited ambition. Of course, Corvaja wanted to realise his dream but as he stressed in interviews, the process was just as important as the final results. It goes without saying that Giovanni Corvaja is a master at his skill, comparable to the Belgian silversmith David Huycke. And like Huycke, Corvaja believes that the mastering of techniques and craftsmanship foster creativity.

Filigree, or filigrain, and granulation (Lat. *filum* meaning metal thread and *granum* meaning grain) are very old techniques, dating back into antiquity. In European countries as far away as Norway, Portugal and the Netherlands, they were often used to create jewellery for traditional costumes. The advantage of these techniques is that you can make beautiful, shiny gold pieces which are relatively light and cheap. A Portuguese exhibition catalogue mentions certain regions where women, on festive occasions, were covered with filigree gold jewels around their necks and shoulders – they radiated proof of the economic success of the family. Today there are few centres of filigree left in Europe, namely in Valle,

Norway, Póvoa de Lanhoso, Portugal, and in the uplands of Berne in Switzerland: regions where traditional costume is still cherished on special days.[32]

These traditional and folkloristic connotations, however, do not add to the appeal of filigree in art jewellery. You would have to come from a culture without these age-old traditions to be able to bend this rather stuffy procedure to your will. Robert Baines, associate professor and head of the gold and silversmithing department at the Royal Melbourne Institute of Technology, succeeded in injecting new life into the technique. In 2006 he carried out his PhD on *The Reconstruction of Historical Jewellery and its Relevance as Contemporary Artefact*, undertaking his technical research in the Metropolitan Museum of Art in New York. For some years he studied ancient Greek, Etruscan and Roman filigree jewellery with the help of a scanning electron microscope (SEM). Thanks to his research he could identify stylistic configurations and was able to connect different pieces on the basis of chemical and individual characteristics of making. Besides this, Baines made laboratory reconstructions with the help of ancient technology: a charcoal fire, a pair of bellows and a blowpipe. It meant that he could put himself in the position of a maker in ancient times. He used this knowledge for his own artistic interpretations: a play with history and fiction.

In 2004, Baines bought a silver filigree brooch in a bric-a-brac shop on the Estonian island of Saaremaa. In a catalogue text, Baines meticulously describes the 'excavation site', the way it was displayed, priced and wrapped, equating it with the archaeological finds he used to work with: 'The wire brooch once relocated in my studio in Melbourne was available for examination. Not having the facility of an electron microscope or even a stereomicroscope, measurements were recorded and the piece photographed and drawn. The reference document now understood awaited copying, replication and interpretation. The birthing of a new jewellery group from Saaremaa.'[33] The piece was copied by Baines and reproduced in silver and gold. It was turned into a bracelet or left as a brooch and was adorned with car lights and miniature plastic and metal cars, always with reference to the historical piece. Earlier, in the period between 1994 and 2001, Baines made elaborate jewellery and objects from colourful powder-coated silver wire. Although this work referred to filigree he carefully avoided the F-word, as he called it. He preferred to call these 'wire constructions' instead to exclude any historicism – apparently he needed a secure scientific basis before he could freely play with such ideas. The *Java-la-Grande* bracelet, made in 2005 for the Ars Ornata Europeana symposium in Lisbon in Portugal, is a masterpiece of craftsmanship and humour (fig. 150). The rosettes of the bracelet made from turned gold wire and gold granules are copies of rosettes from a sixteenth-century Portuguese chest in the National Museum in Lisbon. Cleverly mixing historical evidence and fiction, this masterpiece turns out to be the 'missing link' in the genesis of Australia.

> 150

ENAMEL

Just like granulation and filigree, enamel is a traditional technique which is time consuming, difficult to learn and taught only at a few schools around the world.[34] Some artists, however, manage to master it without having had a proper education. This happened, for instance, in the Netherlands, where students could only learn basic enamelling skills at a vocational level. Vitreous enamel has always been used for decorative, embellishing purposes; sometimes it was applied as a cheap substitute for precious gems. Because of this supplemental nature, innovation in this field is not very apparent.

British jeweller and researcher Jessica Turrell, however, is engaged in the practice-led research project 'Innovation in Vitreous Enamel Surfaces for Jewellery' at the University of the West of England; she is, as far as I know, the only person who is investigating enamel jewellery on a theoretical, academic level. Her published results are therefore very useful when writing about enamel. Turrell investigated the work of 175 international jewellers in order to be able to categorise enamel work into three groups: skilled (fine), new and innovative. Skilled enamel has a commercial and mainstream character while new enamel jewellery 'engages with contemporary ideas', but the technique is used simply and without taking any risks. With innovative enamel the artist combines skilfulness with 'a desire to use enamel to explore contemporary aesthetics and concerns.'[35] The last category, innovative jewellery, denotes experimental enamelling techniques, yet what is 'new' and what is innovative? In Turrell's view, the new enamel is confined to aesthetics, the paint-like qualities, while the technique is used in an 'extremely rudimentary' way. The form, the feel, may be contemporary but nothing is done to bring the technique any further than the '"sift and fire" approach in which a single colour of enamel is dry sifted over the surface of a piece and then fired.'[36] Turrell thinks that this rather reserved way of using enamel is caused by a certain fear to show too much craftsmanship.

Turrell's view that renewal is not possible when using the old-fashioned 'sift and fire' technique can be countered by several examples of contemporary enamel work, for instance that of the Dutch jewellers Philip Sajet and Ralph Bakker. In the work of both artists enamel is used as a layer of colour on top of metal forms, but both artists make intelligent work that has nothing to do with reduction or fear of skill. Both artists use the material skilfully and with understanding and, at the same time, are not interested in being observed as a virtuoso. Their work is neither hyper-making nor rudimentary because it is not about the making as such. Sajet and Bakker have stayed faithful to the old skills of the goldsmith, indicating a strong commitment to the Dutch culture which has been so opposed to the decorative and the supplemental. For both artists, technique is a way to get somewhere. Philip Sajet uses different goldsmith's techniques and a wide range of materials to make pieces of jewellery that combine attractiveness and wearability with content and comment. Ralph Bakker, on the other hand, has dedicated his life to enamel, making flexible structures built from small elements that have been enamelled on both sides. Sajet uses enamel to speak about colour, as illustrated as his *Palette* necklace (1998). In the ring series *Unique Replicas* (1999/2000) with its copies of twelve famous multi-carat diamonds, the colour of the enamel supports the colour of the rock crystal copy. And many of the miniatures in the collection of the twenty-three pieces of birthday jewellery he made for his daughter Nina between 1988 and 2011 are enamelled in festive colours (fig. 151). > 151 However, over the years the pieces for his daughter became bigger and less colourful, becoming more in line with the work he normally makes and is known for.

Ralph Bakker meanwhile makes intricate constructions while playing with our expectations and tactile sensations. Although Bakker is an excellent enameller, his jewellery can have a sense of incompleteness that a traditional goldsmith would not allow and might actually see as a shortcoming, for example open chain links or evidence of soldering (fig. 152). > 152 These 'imperfections' are a conscious choice and a direct result of his working methods. The polishing and camouflaging that take place as standard procedure in the art of a goldsmith horrify him. He prefers to search for more radical solutions, such as an element that would catch your eye because of its unusual presence and that would offer an extra rhythm to the composition. In contrast with Turrell's assumption that the new enamel is confined to aesthetics, the work of the two Dutchmen shows that sloppiness can be an act of conscious and skilled goldsmithing and that concept and content can go hand in hand with skilfulness. Turrell finds an innovative attitude in the work of jewellers such as Bettina Dittlmann, Christine Graf and Annamaria Zanella because they challenge the material which leads to a certain grittiness. According to Turrell the work of these artists shows 'that the tacit and material knowledge they have obtained through time dedicated to the mastery of their chosen material allows them the freedom to experiment and push the material to its limits in the pursuit of aesthetic and conceptual goals.'[37]

It is confusing that Turrell is making such a strong distinction between skills and ideas, the hand and the head. Although she is an advocate of 'an acceptance that innovation can only really exist in a place where skill and concept are not seen as mutually exclusive', she unfortunately gives evidence of a contradictory mindset by using the categorisations 'skill without ideas (fine)' and 'ideas without skill (new)'.[38] The innovation of a technique is not merely found in the wish to explore the technical possibilities to its extreme. The desire to push the medium forward, as Turrell calls it, can result in work that is done only for experiment's sake while 'traditional' enamel can be applied in a non-traditional way in pursuit of a deeper story that can only be told in this way.

We are living the days of 'post-disciplinary art education' according to Glenn Adamson, and of the 'post-studio model, forced upon students that do not have that classic education' as Bruce Metcalf sees it.[39] Both denominations describe the situation at this moment in time but from a different perspective. Adamson sees no harm in a deskilled crafts education. In his view DIY, or learning techniques only at the moment you need them and to a certain calculated level, is typical for today's open-source culture. In the end it is the concept that counts, and amateurism can match the idea perfectly. Bruce Metcalf, on the other hand, is sincerely concerned about the maintaining of higher crafts education. He raises the question: 'To what extent is higher education responsible for cultural preservation?' and is furthermore concerned about the 'half empty artistic toolkit' of students after graduating.[40]

Metcalf's plea for saving specialised crafts programmes is so passionate because reality is already pretty much deskilled. The status quo in art and crafts education is the result of an ongoing movement that started about forty or fifty years ago. It questioned the value of skills over ideas and that of the melting value over material expressiveness. This questioning resulted in a deeper understanding of techniques and materials and their uses. Gold became an important issue: Why do you use gold as a goldsmith? What are the inherent messages of this material? The gold issue was extremely prevalent in the Netherlands, resulting in a taboo on the use of gold for almost two decades. In Germany the gold issue was more of a philosophical one as a reaction to the Modernist policy of stripping all meaning from its use. In Italy, fear and respect could not break the love for gold while in other countries gold has been gradually appreciated once more over the past decades. Individual artists now support this reappreciation of 'traditional' materials and goldsmith's techniques in contemporary jewellery. Their goal is not to become hyper-skilled but they do need their skills to make expressive work. Knowledge of materials and techniques can result in work that combines both materiality and craftsmanship with an intriguing conceptuality and temporality, as is the case with the collection of semi-antique jewellery cast in gallium, a metal with an extremely low melting temperature. *Der Galliumhort von Obertraun (ca. 600 v. Chr.)* consisting of arm, finger and neck rings was brought into the public eye by the Institut für neuere Archäologie [Institute for New Archaeology] and Peter Bauhuis in 2011 (figs. 153, 154). The myth of this treasure was enhanced by its presentation in the Bavarian State Archaeological Museum in Munich.[41] Although made with age-old

> 153, 154

melting techniques, resembling antiquities, physically unwearable (they will melt at the body temperature) and shown in a museum, this collection has reached the summit of what is current in contemporary jewellery.

1   Glenn Adamson, 2008. 'When Craft gets sloppy', in *Crafts,* no. 211, March/April, pp. 36–41.

2   David Huycke, 2010. 'The Metamorphic Ornament: Re_Thinking Granulation', PhD thesis. Hasselt University, p. 15 (translation by LdB). The thesis is published on David Huycke's website *www.davidhuycke.com*. Accessed 21 Jan. 2011.

3   Graham Hughes, 1968. *Modern Jewellery: An International Survey, 1890–1967*. Revised edition, London: Studio Vista, p. 8.

4   Ibid. p. 217. Hughes meticulously mentions date (23 July 1963), place (Christie's, Kings Street, St. James, London) and price (selling price £ 420, melting value approx. £ 30) as facts in a historical event.

5   Ralph Turner, 1976. *Contemporary Jewelry: A Critical Assessment, 1945–1975*. London: Studio Vista, p. 48.

6   L. R. Lippard and J. Chandler, 1968. 'The Dematerialization of Art', in *Art International,* vol. XII, no. 2, pp. 31–6.

7   Ralph Turner (see note 5), p. 172.

8   See: M. G. Emeis jr., 1967. *Bonebakker 1792–1967*. Amsterdam, p. 56, and René Brus, 1996. *De juwelen van het Huis Oranje-Nassau*. Haarlem. Schuyt, p. 133.

9   Neal Bedford and Simon Sellars, 2007. *The Netherlands*. Footscray, Victoria/London: Lonely Planet.

10 Gerhard Bott, 1964. *Schmuck, Jewellery, Bijoux*. Darmstadt: Hessisches Landesmuseum (translation by LdB).

11 Dolf Welling, 1965. ,Nederlandse sieraad, waardig en koel, niet wulps', in: *Rotterdamsch* Nieuwsblad, 27.3.1965.

12 This is how they reflect on the exhibition twenty years later in a group interview, involving (Nicolaas) Klaas van Beek, Gijs Bakker, Lous Martin, Jerven Ober and Bernard Laméris. See: *Images: Sieraden – Schmuck – Jewellery*. Amsterdam: VES, 1986, p.100–01.

13 Ibid. p. 100.

14 Jeroen van den Eynde, 1994. *Symfonie voor Solisten – Ontwerponderwijs aan de afdeling Vormgeving in Metaal & Kunststoffen van de Academie voor Beeldende Kunsten te Arnhem tijdens het docentschap van Gijs Bakker 1970–1978*. Wageningen: Veenman, p. 34. In Gert Staal, 1989. *Gijs Bakker. Vormgever: Solo voor een Solist*.'s-Gravenhage: SDU, on p. 11, Bakker admits that this was not for the good of his students after all.

15 Karl Schollmayer, 1974. *Neuer Schmuck: Ornamentum Humanum*. Tübingen: Wasmuth, introduction, n. p. (translation by LdB).

16 Ibid. p. 171 (translation by LdB).

17 *Sieraad 1975: 4e Manifestatie van Nederlandse edelsmeden en sieraadontwerpers in Amersfoort*, Amersfoort 1975.

18 Martin Uitvlugt, 1970. 'Robert Smit: het sieraad moet een gebruiksgoed worden', in: *AKT, Kunsttijdschrift,* vol. 18, no. 3, pp. 85–90.

19 Marjan Unger, 2004. *Het Nederlandse sieraad in de 20ste eeuw*. Bussum: Thoth, p. 436.

20 Monzó's book from 2008 *Marc Monzó Jeweler*. Barcelona: Klimt02 begins with an image of this object.

21 Quotation taken from an unpublished text written by Marc Monzó during his exhibition at Galerie Wittenbrink FUENFHOEFE in Munich, 2009.

22 Otto Künzli, 1991. *Das dritte Auge, The Third Eye, Het derde oog*. Amsterdam: Stedelijk Museum, p. 20.

23 Otto Künzli, interview with the author, Munich, 15 Mar. 2009.

24 Hermann Jünger, 1996. *Über den Schmuck und das Machen*. Frankfurt/Main: Anabas, p. 126.

25 Ibid. p. 125.

26 Hermann Jünger, 1993. 'Das Studienziel der Klasse für Goldschmiedekunst an der Akademie der Bildenden Künste in München', in: Helmut Bauer (ed.), 1993. *Münchner Goldschmiede: Schmuck und Gerät der Gegenwart*. Munich: Klinkhardt und Biermann, p. 26–7 (translation by LdB).

27 Hermann Jünger (see note 23), p. 137.

28 *Marzee Documentatie 5/96* (translation by LdB).

29 Fritz Falk, 2005. 'The Padua School', in Graziella Folchini Grassetto, 2005. *Contemporary Jewellery: The Padua School*. Stuttgart: Arnoldsche, p. 10.

30 Emma Critchton-Miller, 2009. 'Obsession With Golden Fleece Alive in Collection' in *The New York Times*, 10 Dec. 2009.

31 Susan Moore, 2010. 'Maastricht Beckons', in *Apollo, The International Magazine for Collectors,* March, p. 54.

32 There are some schools that have recently organised filigree projects. In 2004, ESAD (Escola Superior de Artes e Design) in Porto, Portugal organised the exhibition *Lightness, Reviving the Filigree* which travelled to different venues throughout Portugal. In 2006, Setesdal Vidaregående Skule in Valle, Norway, organised a filigree project for Dutch and Finish students at vocational schools. There is a private vocational institute in Athens that teaches filigree and there are some traditional Asian crafts centres in Malaysia and India where the technique is passed on.

206   33 Robert Baines, 2004. *Partyline*. Melbourne: RMIT University Press, p. 19.

      34 Independent enamel departments on a BA or MA level are highly endangered species. In 2010, the Cleveland
          Institute of Art was considering merging the enamel and jewellery and metals programmes. In 2011, the
          University of the West of England in Bristol was intending to close the Enamel Research Unit, highly acknow-
          ledged throughout the world due to the work of Elizabeth Turrell, while many more enamel programmes
          have already been closed.

      35 Jessica Turrell, 2010. 'Surface and substance: A call for the fusion of skill and ideas in contemporary jewellery'
          in *Craft Research*, vol. 1, no. 1, September, pp. 85–100.

      36 Ibid. p. 92, 93.

      37 Ibid. p. 97.

      38 Ibid. p. 98/99.

      39 Bruce Metcalf, *Saving enameling @ CIA or trying to*, letter to the president of the Cleveland Institute of Art,
          dated 6 Jan. 2010, published on his weblog CraftGadfly at *www.brucemetcalf.com/blog*. Accessed 10 Jan.
          2011.

      40 Ibid.

      41 *Der Galliumhort von Obertraun, Geschichte einer Wiederentdeckung*, Archäologische Staatssammlung
          München, 16.3–8.5.2011.

IX. Collecting Jewellery

Wallis Simpson, the Duchess of Windsor, was famous for her jewellery collection. In April 1987, these legendary jewels were sold at auction by Sotheby's in Geneva. The collection was offered in 305 lots and sold for approximately $ 50 million – the amounts change according to the source consulted, adding mystery to the iconic status of the collection. Many items sold for up to ten times their estimated price.

Edward, the former future king of England, showered his mistress Wallis with jewels even when she was still married to her second husband Ernest Simpson.[1] In return, Wallis gave Edward jewels or jewelled objects, all made for special occasions, often with engravings of a personal nature on them. In 1935, she gave him an 18 ct gold Cartier cigarette case engraved with a map of Europe and North Africa mapping the routes of their holidays together which were highlighted with enamel and thirty-seven gemstones marking their premarital sojourns. The story goes that Edward spent many hours with designers, discussing his own ideas and suggestions for the custom-made pieces. The designs, however, were completely subordinate to the quality of the stones. The reputation and history of the the rubies, diamonds, emeralds and sapphires, which were easily remounted in new pieces when fashion dictated, added much to the reputation of a piece of jewellery – and Wallis was very much aware of this. When she found out that an emerald and diamond necklace, created by Harry Winston in 1957, consisted of emeralds that used to be part of the anklets of the Indian Maharani of Baroda, she was not at all amused and refused to wear it again. Stones of such a humble and ethnological origin, how beautiful they may be, were an affront for people like the Windsors who were noted for their racist tendencies. A couple of years later she exchanged the necklace for another one containing an emerald that once belonged to King Alfonso XIII of Spain.

But what made this collection so valuable? Was it the superb craftsmanship of the pieces, the masterly and exceptional designs, the costly materials and the unique gems, the historical and sentimental element or the special concern, knowledge and taste of the collectors that made this jewellery collection so special? And how should we valuate this jewellery collection? Is it comparable to an art collection?

The Windsor collection had character indeed and was the outcome of the shared passion for jewels and the taste of two individuals. In choosing mainly Cartier and Van Cleef & Arpels, the couple favoured daring designs, such as the wildlife and spectacular India-style jewels created by Cartier in the 1940s (note that 'India style' is explicitly different from 'of Indian origin'). Their taste was for big colourful gemstones and yellow gold. Madame Jeanne Toussaint was one of the designers behind the Windsor jewels who worked with Cartier from 1915 and created the 'great cat menagerie', of which the Windsors acquired different examples. Other designers of note in the collection are Harry Winston and David Webb.

With regard to the question of whether or not this jewellery collection is an art collection, the answer is given in one of the many essays written about it, which says that it would have been good if the collection had been donated to a museum of natural history.

From the viewpoint of a gemmologist and the big jewellery houses this is true. A Cartier necklace is never looked upon as an artwork as such. Its main function is to display one or more beautiful and exceptional gems. Many jewels from the famous jewellery houses, especially the custom made ones, contradict the eternal status ascribed to them – in reality this status only applies to the gemstones. Gold and silver can easily be melted and reused again, but exquisite gems will forever be remounted – they are literally as solid as a rock. The designs of the jewels are secondary to fashion and taste, changing according to an elusive set of prescriptions in the fashion magazines, so that jewels of this kind are more likely to be the subject of valuation than of reflection.

Another intriguing aspect of jewellery that is unveiled by the Duchess of Windsor's collection is that the Duke and Duchess owned the jewellery in every aspect. The names of designers and jewellers and the history of certain gems and historical pieces were all subordinate to their love story – besides money, their jewellery represented sentiment. It was the Duke's wish that in the event of his wife's death, all gems were to be removed from their settings and stored away. He couldn't bear the thought that anyone else would wear them. But he died before her and so could not prevent socialites such as Elizabeth Taylor and Kelly Klein wearing his wife's jewellery.

For the Duke, the economical and distinguishing value of jewels was just as important as their sentimental value. Jewels meant money that he could have invisibly invested in the financial world, yet he preferred visible investments in the spectacular pieces of jewellery that suited his wife so well and that fit perfectly in a busy society life. Although the Duke of Windsor apparently appreciated the work of the designers at Cartier and Van Cleef & Arpels, he didn't value their creative output, as was quite common in this area of jewellery. At the top end of the jewellery market the name of the (former) owner adds far more extra value to a piece than the name of the maker.

Over the years, the great jewellery houses also became aware of notions such as art and design, and tried to recognise these values in retrospective exhibitions. Van Cleef & Arpels (established Paris 1906, New York 1939), for instance, was noted for its innovative methods of jewellery making. Their most famous technical innovation is the Serti Mystérieux, the mystery setting (1933), which made it possible to set stones without any visible evidence whereby the prongs were concealed beneath the gems they held. By doing this, Van Cleef & Arpels jewels are made in sculptural forms set with closed surfaces of rubies, emeralds and diamonds, which give way to a certain abstraction in the design. The exhibition *Set in Style: The Jewelry of Van Cleef & Arpels* (2011), sponsored by the same company, in New York's Smithsonian Cooper-Hewitt National Design Museum aimed at stimulating a new understanding and appreciation of this kind of jewellery.

In 1984, the Cartier firm started the Fondation Cartier for contemporary arts in Paris, which was explicitly not intended for jewellery. In the same year the firm started the Cartier Collection, a collection of historical pieces selected for their 'style, inspiration, materials, craftsmanship and, for certain pieces, their historical dimension.'[2] In the past, exceptional pieces were taken apart for remounting without scruples, such as those made for the *Exposition of Modern Industrial and Decorative Arts* in Paris in 1925. As Judy Rudoe writes in her book on Cartier, the exhibition 'was a matter of intense national pride. Other countries were naturally invited to participate, and the pressure on French exhibitors to excel was enormous.'[3] However, none of the exhibited, allegedly exceptional pieces survived the common practice of dismounting and resetting. Nowadays the Cartier Collection and the Fondation Cartier both demonstrate a policy aimed at gaining art status. The jewel collection has been widely exhibited in the best international museums, such as the

Hermitage Museum in St. Petersburg, the Metropolitan Museum of Art in New York and the British Museum in London.

In art jewellery, ideas such as the Duke of Windsor's or Cartier's are inconceivable, and it was exactly because of such practices that contemporary jewellers wanted to radically change course. Jewellery created by authors, that is, artists, has a different rationale. While fine jewellery is dependent on contemporary taste, fashion and the market, author jewellery wants to express artistic ideas and concepts that still pay respect to taste, fashion or society, albeit on its own conditions. This kind of jewellery bears a signature; it is characterised by a special handwriting and more general meaning that is different from a private, a ritual or a social meaning.

The difference between the two categories can be put down to the idea of ownership. Fine jewellery is traditional due to the amount of carats used but also because it is very much specific to the buyer or owner. Designs are subject to the whims of time, taste and fashion, and so dismantling is an accepted option whenever a piece is no longer *en vogue*. Extraordinary and exclusive pieces that do survive the whimsicalities of time and taste become secondary to their famous owner; it is their name that bestows a piece of jewellery with history, class and magic.

In contrast, author jewellery complies with the existing 'laws' of art. In essence, this type of jewellery, which is created under completely different circumstances in small individual studios, liberated jewellery from its private sentiments. Author jewellery distinguishes itself from any other jewellery category by setting its own rules. The urge to make this jewellery is driven by the need for artistic expression; it is not made for a certain market other than the art jewellery gallery. Using the modifier 'art' is not meant as a qualifying tool but rather an identifying one. It is not used with the intention to claim that this kind of jewellery is art as such, and it is not used to suggest a kind of hierarchy within jewellery that places art jewellery at the top. But by using this notion we are able to identify its *raison d'être*, an artistic and autonomous one, free of consideration for marketability, investment or fashion.

In 1968, the Dutch jewellery designers Gijs Bakker and Emmy van Leersum, who were known for their radical statements, argued in the American magazine *Sculpture International* that 'status symbols [...] and safe-seeming investment in conservative jewellery have until now hindered the freedom of form in jewellery design. Through experimentation we are striving to break through the constricting bonds so common in this branch of art. The diverse properties inherent in the materials we use have led us to an absolute form – a form which excludes all decorative elements. Out of this theory has resulted a fusing of the human body, of metal forms and of clothes design into a single aesthetic unity.'[4] In interviews they criticised the fact that conventional jewellery had nothing to do with its time and that its forms and styles were derived from historical examples. They were eager to claim a connection with the arts, lifestyle and politics of their time. In sources from this founding period, we can read frequently how Bakker and Van Leersum state: 'Form is just the covering of an idea', and in press articles, their shoulder pieces were referred to as 'anti gala necklaces'. But their main idea was that the jewel was as a single aesthetic unity, not incriminated by any other reason (financial, status, fashion, taste, for example) than that of the work itself – it became the hallmark and motto of many generations of art jewellers to come. In the early days, German designer Claus Bury also took a clear position: 'To me jewelry is first and foremost an intellectual confrontation with the environment, and identification with the artistic statement expressed is a prerequisite to the correct understanding and using – that is wearing – of my jewelry'.[5] While Austrian designer Fritz Maierhofer, who at the beginning of the 1970s created wall ornaments with detachable wearable pieces of jewellery, declared: 'It was important to me to achieve an active, spatial relationship between the wearer of the jewellery and my work; in other words, to create a confrontation between me and the wearer.'[6]

By putting it this way, the artist had moved to the centre of his creation, thus jewellery became unassailable and inviolable in regard to those 'recycling' practices that had up until now been so usual in jewellery for so long. But it took courage to make one's own path: many 'new jewellers' ended up as sculptors, either because breaking with the gold standard meant breaking with the small scale or because they were confronted with the assumption that it was impossible to make a living from this kind of jewellery. British jeweller Gunila Treen concisely put the latter dilemma into words in 1975: 'The main problem with working in essentially non-precious materials for jewellery is that people do not regard it as an investment!'[7]

However, the melting value was soon successfully abandoned as a standard in art jewellery. A gold bracelet by Van Leersum is now worth much more than its intrinsic gold value. A Bernhard Schobinger laser-light drilled, raw diamond will never be alienated from its archaic setting to be cut in the conventional way, because the raw diamond has gained an extra 'art' value through the intervention of the artist. To dismantle a Schobinger ring or to melt a gold Van Leersum bracelet would be seen as an unacceptable destruction of artworks – no matter how small they are – and the annihilation of ideas that have been vital to our times. Furthermore, jewellers even go so far nowadays as to destroy (semi-)precious materials and then reuse them in their work, for example Karl Fritsch, who drills holes through gems or Ruudt Peters, who grounds gems into powder. Their acts demonstrate and present what is most valued: the artist or the material. Thus, in contrast to fine jewellery, author jewellery is more about artistic rather than intrinsic value, more about content than about investment, more about the maker than about the buyer. However, these young jewellery designers cannot do without buyers.

Ever since author jewellery manifested itself as a strong and new branch of artistic expression, there have been people who have recognised its potency and power and started collecting it. For many collectors of contemporary jewellery the idea of wearing is appealing. In many cases, they understood just how they could be part of a certain cultural elite by wearing such provocative pieces on their body. Art jewellery can express strong artistic ideas and raise questions about the reason for its existence. They are perfect conversation pieces: An electroformed silver brooch by Stanley Lechtzin was one of the first acquisitions of the American collector Helen Drutt (fig. 155). In the 2007 publication about her collection of jewellery she remembers how people who saw her wearing it in 1969 during the heydays of space travel and just after the first moon landing thought it was a landing ship from Mars.[8] And on the other side of the Atlantic, the wearing of reduced, predominantly conceptual jewellery designed and made by Gijs Bakker and Emmy van Leersum was, for a short time, a sign of belonging to a circle of avant-garde artists and connoisseurs in Amsterdam.

> 155

Although the wearing of jewellery can be important to many (though not all) jewellery collectors, they are equally interested in the artists and their artistic development. A collector of jewellery will buy more pieces than he or she could ever wear and even knows that certain pieces will never be worn, either because of their vulnerability or because it simply does not fit with the ideas of the collector as a wearer – it may be too big, too outspoken, too extravagant. In the words of Helen Drutt: 'There's only one thing to look for, and that's quality – that's it: quality and a singular creative vision by the artist. The same you use in any other work of art: Does it have an innovative creative sensibility? Is there a uniqueness that identifies it with an individual?'⁹ Jewellery collectors can also have the ambition of completion, striving to 'fill a void in the history of that artist or in the history of ideas…' as Helen Drutt continues.¹⁰ Some collections represent a certain period in time and a certain approach in jewellery making. American collector Donna Schneier owns one such example, which spans the 1980s, an interesting period of Postmodernist New Jewelry in Europe and America focusing on rather bold neck pieces made from non-precious materials. She hung her pieces on her office walls in New York City. Schneier's view on collecting is that of a typical Maecenas; in her collector's statement in the catalogue *Zero Karat* on presenting her collection as a gift to the American Craft Museum in New York, she explained: 'It has always been my understanding that artists make their work for posterity. For however long we as individuals are caretakers of their work it is but a brief time in the history of art. Art is meant to be shared. The most I can do as an appreciator of art is to help this process along. Art has been good to me. It is now my turn to be good to art.'¹¹

> fig. 155

Collecting mostly starts with love at first sight, a confrontation with a piece that hits you right in the heart. Friendships, studio visits and fruitful exchanges of ideas often are catalysts in acquiring work from an artist. Donna Schneier recalls a trip to London, organised by the American Craft Museum in 1985, where she was introduced to art jewellery. She came home with eleven pieces of jewellery – the start of her collection. The passion can become infectious; collecting is often a passion shared within a couple but it can even be that of an entire family. The members of the Italian Mignucci family are famous within the European jewellery community for being very active art jewellery collectors in Europe. Mother Fiorenza, sons Aldo and Andrea and daughter-in-law Maria are passionate people who attend every fair and exhibition and who seem to be permanently engaged with their collection.

Collecting affects one's way of living; it can even be a way of living. It involves travelling, meeting artists, dealers and fellow collectors and, foremost, being curious and prepared to look good, over and over again, being a visionary and taking risks. Most collections do have some kind of system, but this may be very subjective and incomprehensible for a person outside of this world because the system is based on passion rather than on rationale. To many, the advantage of the small scale and wearability of jewellery add to its appeal. The fact that art jewellery pieces are normally one-offs and that materials in jewellery are mostly used as a carrier of meaning are direct connections with fine arts. And all of these characteristics of author jewellery contribute to its attractiveness as an object of collecting.

The presence of private and institutional collectors would indicate that there is a market for author jewellery. However, profits in clever deals or good prospects with regard to the increase of market value have not entered the domain of author jewellery yet. If we take the 1960s as its starting point, the phenomenon of art jewellery is relatively young. The earliest collectors of it began around 1970, and the first private donations of art jewellery to museums date from the 1990s. Most museums that hold collections of art jewellery began collecting at the end of the 1960s and in the 1970s, with a few earlier exceptions, such as the Schmuckmuseum in Pforzheim and the Deutsches Goldschmiedehaus in Hanau. The very first private collectors from this period have now aged, and their collections must find a home somewhere. Some will go to museums, many will be sold.

The field is waiting for a real market to emerge, hoping that with the rise of auctions for contemporary author jewellery some kind of market will finally develop. Yet up until now, modern and contemporary jewellery has been mainly sold as a small, relatively minor, part of general design auctions.[12] Considering the auction results from the last five years, it is remarkable that there is still a gap between the market value of jewellery known as 'Modernist' and that of art or author jewellery. One of the reasons might be in the naming and identifying of the field. Modernist jewellery is a clearly recognisable subcategory of Modernist design, a class of objects that can be listed as modern vintage and popular among collectors. While the class of jewellery objects created in the late 1960s has not been able to be clearly identified until now. Furthermore, contemporary jewellery still has to fight the prejudice of the importance of the inherent material value when it is traded. In the jewellery market it is hard, if not impossible, to break through this barrier. Some exceptions have occurred though, such as the sales of early Minimalist jewellery by Emmy van Leersum and Gijs Bakker. A price of € 1,000 for a two-coloured nylon Emmy van Leersum bracelet and necklace set (1982–84), produced in limited series, may seem like a good amount of money but the price still contrasts sharply with the £ 15,000 paid for a Wim Delvoye Cloaca machine-made *Faeces*, a vacuum-packed edition in Plexiglas. North American Modernist jewellery sells far better: prices up to $ 28,000 are paid for an Art Smith *Lava Cuf* brass bracelet. In an Internet article, Art Smith is characterised as 'one of the only African American mid-century designers with an established market and whose work is collected by US museums, according to design experts.'[13] Other Modernists who have made good prices for copper, brass, glass and silver jewellery in the art market include Harry Bertoia ($ 4,688), Ed Wiener, Sam Kramer ($ 5,313) and Claire Falkenstein ($ 21,250).[14] These prices equal those of the Hermès Bags sold at the Branded Luxury Auction organised by the auction house Wright on 25 April 2006, which fetched prices of up to $ 19,000. Alexander Calder's jewellery, also made from cheap materials, sells for even higher prices, however, his standing as a famous sculptor and a fine artist explains his market value. His unique jewellery was sign of an extraordinary artistic vision, but this cannot be said for the majority of jewellery designed and fabricated – and often produced in numbered and signed series – by other fine artists, such as Pablo Picasso, Georges Braque, Jean Arp, André Derain, among others. When these are auctioned, even though they are minor works of major artists, the atmosphere at the auction becomes excited and prices go up. Again, it is the name of the artist that bestows a piece of jewellery with history, class and magic; the fact that most of these objects are made in gold also helps.[15]

The fact that a good, unique piece of author jewellery is not valued for its artistic significance and a branded leather handbag is valued higher than a genuine and limited edition one-off piece of art jewellery indicates that there is still something wrong with jewellery's reception. The question is how can this situation be changed? Probably a combination of more research, more supply in the form of collections of art jewellery being auctioned, and more well-thought-out donations of jewellery collections to museums will be needed to help stimulate the demand.

Over the years private jewellery collections have become the basis of some museum collections or have given them a boost in the study and presentation of author jewellery. There are even signs of a private collectors' policy. The Austrian jeweller Peter Skubic, who in 1993 donated his collection of contemporary jewellery to Die Neue Sammlung – The International Design Museum Munich, made one such important step. According to Florian Hufnagl, the museum's director: 'This was done […] under the essential condition that the one-off jewellery would find an active forum in the future in the Neue Sammlung.'[16] Because of this, the museum was able to acquire other collections, such as that of Galerie Spektrum in Munich. The Danner Rotunda for jewellery in the Pinakothek der Moderne in Munich was built with financial support from the private Danner Foundation, who also sponsored the interior design and furniture. Built under the central hall of the museum, it was part of an agreement which involved the long-term loan of the foundation's collection of author jewellery (about 450 pieces dating from 1945 onwards) by the Munich museum. The Rotunda opened in March 2004; Hermann Jünger and Otto Künzli curated the first permanent presentation. In March 2010 the second permanent presentation was opened, curated by Karl Fritsch who introduced a revolutionary new kind of display. In each showcase he used pieces from the collection along with borrowed work from artists as elements in a composition. In these tableaux, each individual piece of jewellery relates to the others, not through chronology, provenance or material but rather on an artistic level.

The Françoise van den Bosch Foundation, established in the Netherlands in 1980 as a private initiative, aims to stimulate contemporary author jewellery. There are no similarities between the Danner and the Françoise van den Bosch Foundation apart from the fact that they are both privately run organisations. The major differences between them is the amount of capital involved and that the Danner Foundation, established in 1920 in Munich by Therese Danner in memory of her husband Benno, is sixty years older.

Françoise van den Bosch was one of the pioneers of Dutch jewellery at the end of the 1960s and 1970s, around the same time as when she started her jewellery collection. A graduate of the jewellery department at the Academy of Fine Arts in Arnhem in 1968, she was the youngest participant in the exhibition *Objects to Wear by Five Dutch Jewelry Designers*, which travelled in the USA between 1968 and 1973. As a twenty-two-year-old, she exhibited her academy pieces alongside famous works of the already renowned artists Gijs Bakker and Emmy van Leersum. Her works held their own within the context of this show because of their inner force and strong formal unity. Shortly after, she must have begun swapping jewellery with colleagues. When she died unexpectedly at only thirty-three years old, she left a small collection of some twenty works of jewellery, small objects and ceramics. When her father and friends started the Françoise van den Bosch Foundation in 1980, these pieces and some inherited pieces by Françoise, such as trials and unfinished pieces, were bequeathed to the foundation. Since then the collection has grown with gifts from her family, comprising mostly jewellery and objects by Françoise and with acquisitions made by the foundation's board. The policy of the foundation is to buy one or more pieces from every recipient of the biannual Françoise van den Bosch Award and to buy work from up-and-coming, young talented artists. The collection comprises around 150 pieces of jewellery, photographs and objects. What makes the collection interesting is that it is not obstructed by reasons of practicality or wearability. The foundation sees no problem in buying work that goes beyond the borders of what is accepted as jewellery. Therefore, every now and then work is acquired that has a materiality other than that typically found in jewellery, such as the photographic work by Japanese designer Yuka Oyama and the photography, poster and object piece made by Belgian artist Liesbet Bussche (figs. 156, 157). The foundation's collection is on loan to the Stedelijk Museum in Amsterdam where it forms a substantial part of the collection of contemporary jewellery within in the crafts and design department.[17]

> 156
> 157

PRIVATE COLLECTIONS

The United States has a number of highly interesting private collections of art jewellery, some of which have become museum collections. Donna Schneier decided to spread her private collection over three different museums, the American Craft Museum (now known as the Museum of Arts & Design) in New York, the Metropolitan Museum of Art in New York and the Racine Art Museum in Wisconsin. As a result of this strategic decision her collection will be shown to a broader public and in many different contexts. Also renowned is the American studio jewellery collection from 1940 to 1960, acquired by the Montreal Museum of Decorative Arts from the private collection of three partners in the Fifty50 Gallery in New York. In 2007, a selection of 150 pieces of jewellery from Daphne Farago's collection was presented in the Museum of Fine Arts in Boston (MFA) under the title *Jewelry by Artists: The Daphne Farago Collection*. The exhibition was organised to celebrate the recent gift of the collection of 650 pieces of twentieth-century studio jewellery created by American and European artists, which could be added to the collection of jewellery that the museum already held. In July 2011, a new gallery opened, housing jewels, gems and treasures from the ancient to the modern. In rotating exhibitions, different selections from the 10,000 ornaments in the museum's collection are displayed, among them pieces from the Farago Collection. A surprising result of the generous gift from Farago is the installation of a jewellery curatorship, sponsored by private funding.

These collection transfers from the private to the public sphere are often celebrated with an exhibition and a publication; for example, the Montreal Museum of Decorative Arts published a book on their Modernist jewellery while the American Craft Museum in New York released a book about the Donna Schneier Collection. To celebrate Helen Drutt's donation of her collection to the Museum of Fine Arts, Houston (MFAH) in 2007, a book of more than 500 pages entitled *Ornament as Art* was published. The museum acquired this excellent collection of avant-garde jewellery in 2002, partly as a gift and partly with the aid of a group of private benefactors. The Museum of Fine Arts, Houston is a general museum of arts, presenting works ranging from antique to contemporary, from American to Asian, Latin American, Pacific and European art. The acquisition of this jewellery collection meant not only an extension of the museum's interests but also a shift in their policy. The contemporary jewellery collection thus became part of the Decorative Arts and Design collection, which, although at the time did not comprise a specific body of jewellery, opened up a whole new world.

It is noteworthy that the Helen Williams Drutt Collection was procured with the help of many private persons, friends of the museum and private foundations. It took the curator of the museum, Cindi Strauss, many hours of talking with private benefactors in order to teach them about art jewellery in general and also specific pieces from the collection (fig. 158). This way the MFAH was able to introduce the Houston audience to a new field

> 158

of artistic expression. This 'bespoke' form of sponsorship is an interesting way of audience education and of ensuring the museum support within a local community. A donation like Helen Drutt's has profound consequences, not only in the educational and scientific effort but also for changing a museum's policy.

In 2007 the MFAH made a further step by acquiring a collection of 500 pieces of modern and contemporary ceramics assembled by the well-known scholars and art dealers from New York Garth Clark and Mark Del Vecchio. With both acquisitions the museum made a statement that could not be misunderstood: the museum takes applied art as seriously as visual art. In the foreword to the Helen Drutt Collection catalogue, Peter Marzio, the museum's director, elucidated the museum's stance: 'The Drutt collection attacks traditional academic, art-historical categories. This subversive challenge forces us to abandon certain conventional modes of thought and to redefine ideas of sculpture, painting, decorative arts, and so forth. How can a necklace be compared to a sculpture? It's heresy. That's the point.'[18] The MFAH put together an exhibition celebrating the Helen Williams Drutt Collection, which travelled from Houston to Washington DC, Charlotte, NC and finally to Tacoma in 2009. This touring exhibition was another way of attracting more visitors and finding new audiences for contemporary jewellery.

Germany, Austria and the Netherlands also have their own interesting private collectors of contemporary jewellery. In March 2011, the Neuer Schmuck Association organised an exhibition showing jewellery from six Munich collections. Karl and Heidi Bollmann from Vienna have also been engaged in collecting author jewellery (fig. 159) since the beginning of the 1970s. Their collection is rather large and requires a lot of time to manage its documentation and loans, among other things. They are true advocates of jewellery, both wearing remarkable pieces by Manfred Bischoff or Peter Skubic with apparent ease and dignity. Mr. Bollmann, a lawyer, has also written about art jewellery.

> 159

In the Netherlands, according to a small investigation done by collector Jurriaan van den Berg, there are about fifty to sixty serious collectors of contemporary jewellery – although it cannot be explained why there are so many collectors in this small country. The Dutch couple Ida and Rom Boelen, collectors of African and contemporary art, were among the pioneers of art jewellery collectors. When they visited an international jewellery exhibition in Darmstadt in Germany in 1964, they were 'so excited about the new ideas revealed in the work' that they began collecting jewellery – mainly from German, Austrian and Eastern European as well as some Dutch artists.[19] Their main interest was in lyrical and abstract expressionist work – quite the opposite of what became known as the Dutch Minimalist style that was so powerful at the time. Over a period of about ten years they built up a remarkable collection of top jewellery pieces. Their son, Roland, remembers that his mother sometimes furnished an artist with money in order for him to make a piece of jewellery for her in peace and freedom; some artists were supported for years. Yet the story of their collection had a sad ending. In 1975, it was divided up when the couple divorced, and part of it appeared to be lost when Rom Boelen later died. His wife survived him by many years and before she died in 2006, negotiations had started with the Stedelijk Museum in Amsterdam, though regrettably not leading to any concrete result. The collection is still kept in a bank safe – the worst place for jewellery. The collection contains jewellery by Reinhold Reiling, Hermann Jünger, Claus Ullrich, Claus Bury, Friedrich Becker, Mario Pinton, Anton Cepka, Robert Smit (fig. 160), Nicolaas van Beek, Alicia Penalba, Arnoldo Pomodoro and Pol Bury, among others. It is a wonderful legacy of the period of informel and material art, lyrical abstraction and kinetic art. As far as cultural heritage is concerned, it is a tragedy that this seminal collection of art jewellery is still

> 160

locked away and may finally move to a country other than the Netherlands or be split up and sold. With examples of gold, Perspex and enamelled sculptural 'German' jewellery, this collection unfortunately does not reflect the restrained aesthetics and Constructivist concept of Dutch jewellery of the same period. This kind of jewellery is not represented in any Dutch museum collection – apparently the Dutch still suffer from a rather odd taboo.

Helen Drutt and Ida Boelen were friends; they met through jewellery. They were also friends with the Viennese collector Inge Asenbaum, who established Galerie Am Graben in Vienna in 1972 where she showed gold- and silversmithing of the Wiener Werkstätte alongside contemporary and international jewellery. In the beginning of the 1970s Helen Drutt, Ida Boelen and Inge Asenbaum were the main protagonists of international art jewellery. Asenbaum, who first discovered Wiener Werkstätte jewellery in a period when it was not *en vogue*, developed an understanding for the jewellery of her time. Her collection contains, besides antique pieces by Dagobert Peche and Josef Hoffmann, jewellery by David Watkins, Gerd Rothmann, Hermann Jünger, Peter Skubic, Fritz Maierhofer, Manfred Nisslmüller and Otto Künzli, to name but a few. According to a verbal statement from her son Paul Asenbaum, the collection is locked in a safe without any prospect of an Austrian museum acquiring it.[20]

Helen Drutt, Inge Asenbaum and others started collecting because, apart from their passion, they felt a certain responsibility. Helen Drutt, a teacher and gallery owner herself, noticed how exhibitions came and went and were not properly documented. Feeling that there was something in the air, she started collecting art jewellery 'realizing that acquiring to hold history was becoming essential'.[21] The same applies to Lasse and Helena Pahlman from Helsinki, who realised nobody else was interested in contemporary jewellery in Finland.

The Pahlman couple started buying art jewellery in 1975, which they encountered in their engagement with the visual arts and crafts. There were no galleries or museums that exhibited this kind of jewellery in Finland at the time, but they soon made their own net-
> 161 work and became friends with many artists in Finland and Estonia (fig. 161). As a result they were invited to join jewellery seminars at which they met international artists, whose work they began acquiring in the 1980s. They also commissioned Finnish painters, sculptors and designers to create pieces of jewellery. They now own an impressive collection of
> 162 more than 1,000 pieces from Finnish, northern European and international artists (fig. 162). To this present day they are the only people who collect author jewellery in Finland, and to their amazement they even belong to the very few in Scandinavia. Like most collectors, the Pahlman couple seriously document and archive all of their art and jewellery acquisitions, and like many collectors they hope these pieces can stay together in the future. In 2009, their collection was the starting point for a comprehensive exhibition about Finnish jewellery from 1600 to 2009, organised by the Design Museum in Helsinki. Unfortunately though, like the Boelen and the Asenbaum collections, the Pahlman collection is also without a clear future.

Strategic choices are important in the field of donating collections to museums. You should not wait too long, you have to choose the right museum and you have to find a good balance between your own conditions and ambitions and those of the museum. The donation of Marjan and Gerard Unger's collection of twentieth-century Dutch jewellery to the Rijksmuseum in Amsterdam, the National Museum of Art and History, was a surprising one. Nobody had ever thought about the possibility of placing jewellery by Gijs Bakker, Robert
> 163 Smit, Ted Noten and Nel Linssen (fig. 163) in close vicinity to Rembrandt, Vermeer and Paulus Potter. Marjan Unger did, and in 2010 she bequeathed the couple's jewellery collec-

tion, comprising some 500 pieces of Dutch jewellery. The Rijksmuseum already had a small 'sleeping' collection of jewellery mainly from the Renaissance and Art Nouveau periods, yet it made sense to house this new collection, as the Unger collection not only spans one hundred years of jewellery making – the whole of the twentieth century – but also contains fashion and popular jewellery alongside early twentieth-century crafted jewellery, production jewellery and avant-garde jewellery. For decades Unger has combed markets, auctions and antique shops to discover unknown jewellery by Dutch craftspeople from the period 1930 to 1970 – a period of jewellery design that is not represented in any other Dutch museum – and her research resulted in a comprehensive publication about Dutch twentieth-century jewellery.[22] According to the precious and non-precious metals curator Dirk Jan Biemond, the Unger collection fits well in the museum policy which takes jewellery 'as an art form in its own right within the precious metals collection'. Furthermore, jewellery is collected there for historical reasons, either as part of Dutch fashion within the costume collection or 'as symbols for historical subjects' as part of the Dutch History Department.[23] In the future, when the renovated building is reopened, a permanent display of jewellery will be shown from the museum's collection (including that of the Ungers) spanning the period of the eighth century, Middle Ages and Renaissance up to the present day.

Some collectors concentrate on a certain theme in jewellery, such as only rings or only necklaces or jewellery made from non-precious materials. In 2001, Dutch collector and former gallery owner Threes Moolhuysen-Coenders compiled a richly illustrated book on this subject, documenting her collection.[24] The book tells how she began combing flea and antique markets in London in the 1950s, searching for historical jewellery made from non-precious materials dating back to the mid nineteenth century. At first this was because she didn't have much money, but soon she recognised the very special quality of these *bijoux* items made from Bakelite and imitation ivory, coral, onyx, jade, amber, and so forth. Her interesting collection of experimental non-precious art jewellery from 1970 onwards is a logical extension to her historical pieces.

We may conclude that private collectors are invaluable cultural ambassadors of contemporary jewellery and initiators of historical research. Their purchases, be it at markets or in galleries, hold history.

MUSEUMS IN EUROPE

The Schmuckmuseum in Pforzheim is the only museum in the world that is fully devoted to jewellery, possessing thousands of pieces spanning six millennia. In the eighteenth century, the city of Pforzheim became a centre for jewellery and watch making. The beginnings of the jewellery collection go back to the last quarter of the nineteenth century. Historical pieces were collected to serve as examples of the jewellery industry, which produced historicising pieces at that time. In 1877 the school for handicrafts and the society for the fine arts and handicrafts were founded. Both institutions collected pieces of jewellery and in 1938 the collections were merged, resulting in the Städtisches Schmuckmuseum Pforzheim [the Municipal Jewellery Museum] in 1939. During World War II it had to be closed, and the collection was carried to safety in the nearby Black Forest. By doing this, it survived the complete destruction of Pforzheim through allied bombings in February 1945. When the city was rebuilt after the war, a new jewellery museum was built between 1957 and 1961. In the new Reuchlinhaus, a fine example of Modernist design in the form of a glass cube by architect Manfred Lehmbruck, the museum shared premises with the public library, municipal archives, an archaeological collection and an exhibition space of the Kunstverein [Arts Society]. Since 2002, the Reuchlinhaus has been home to the Schmuckmuseum, each year organising several temporary exhibitions on both historical and contemporary subjects.

Many other museums worldwide collect and exhibit jewellery as part of a general collection of modern art and design or as part of a design museum or general art history museum.[25] The Victoria & Albert Museum in London and the Musée des Arts Décoratifs in Paris both have excellent collections of jewellery dating from ancient to modern times as well as contemporary work. In the Netherlands, there are four museums, namely in Amsterdam, Arnhem, Apeldoorn and 's-Hertogenbosch, which collect author jewellery from Dutch and international artists on a serious scale. The Stedelijk Museum in 's-Hertogenbosch is the only museum in the world collecting jewellery made by visual artists of the twentieth century. The collection, put together by former museum director Yvònne Joris over a period of twenty years, comprises pieces of precious jewellery by renowned artists such as Arman, Jean Arp, Georges Braque, Pablo Picasso, André Derain, Max Ernst

> 164

and César. It also houses excellent pieces by Alexander Calder, Lucio Fontana (fig. 164), Man Ray, Louise Bourgeois, Rob Scholte, Carel Visser and remakes of designs by Meret Oppenheim. Most pieces are made in limited editions (up to 100 or 200 pieces) but the collection also contains one-offs by Calder, César, Man Ray and a series of design sketches by Meret Oppenheim. The collection of 150 pieces was exhibited and represented in a publication on the occasion of Joris's departure from the museum in November 2009. In the publication, she gives an account of the underlying reason for this collection. She sees artists' jewellery as 'a modest yet fascinating histoire des mentalités, reflecting the great art-historical movements of the 20th century.'[26] Unfortunately no effort was made to truly research the history, meaning and artistic value of these pieces, many of them the result of commercial commissions.

If we have a look at the list of museums that hold collections of jewellery, it might appear that jewellery is quite well covered in many different countries. Yet the list does not tell of the difficulties jewellery is facing as a historical category within the context of fine art and design. In many museums, jewellery is not permanently on display; if it is, it is only a very small selection. However, it is clearly harmful that jewellery is even subject to the whimsicalities of directors and curators, who store it away with no intention of putting it on show again. As has unfortunately happened in the Netherlands and also in Spain, the fashion, crafts and jewellery departments often are the first victims of new museum policies.[27]

Collectors are important protagonists of contemporary jewellery. By collecting it, they stimulate artists and recognise this relatively new field of artistic expression. In the United States, where private art collectors are held in high esteem, the popularity of collecting as an advantageous and adventurous activity is demonstrated by the associations established for collectors in different fields. In 1997, the Art Jewelry Forum was founded, initiated by Susan Cummins, a former gallery owner and a collector of contemporary jewellery. The idea was to bring together a group of people who could benefit from each other's knowledge and enthusiasm. Today the forum has hundreds of members. Trips are organised to exhibitions, studios, fairs, private collections and lectures, while the members donate an amount of money (anywhere from $ 50 up to $ 1,000) towards different funds, such as the emerging artist award (a cash award of $ 5,000) and a grant programme. A blog is maintained, involving contributions by international writers and critics.

Today the art of collecting has changed: in the 1960s when Inge Asenbaum, Ida Boelen-van Gelder and Helen Drutt started collecting there were hardly any jewellery galleries. In fact they started their own in Vienna, Amsterdam and Philadelphia respectively. These women travelled a lot; they visited artists from all around the world and also invited many artists to come and visit them. They supported jewellery in many different ways. In 1977, for instance, Ida Boelen set up the International Society of Friends of the Schmuckmuseum Pforzheim, an organisation with international members aimed to support the museum 'both spiritually and materially'.[28] Today the amount of jewellery galleries is still growing and so is the amount of collectors. The jewellery world has become more professional than it was in the 1970s and also more anonymous. Warm and year-long friendships between artists and collectors are less obvious today.

It is clear that museums can benefit tremendously from private collections, either through bequests, donations and sales, or through loans, exhibitions and publications. Private collections are sometimes dismissed as being a private passion, a subjective choice of an individual. Yet private collectors also save cultural heritage: they hold history. People who collect items such as art jewellery should also be praised for running the risk that their collection will never bring them a profit.

There is hardly any market for art jewellery at the moment, but nobody knows how this will be in ten or twenty years' time when the pioneers of the 1960s have finally become design icons. In fact many of the pieces of jewellery made since the end of the 1960s have the potential to become desirable aesthetic objects. However, they will never match the value of the trinkets of the Duchess of Windsor and similar customised jewellery made especially for very rich clients. After all, for the benefit of their artistic statement, the appealing safe investment is exactly what the pioneers of art jewellery wanted to get rid of.

1   All information about the Duke and Duchess of Windsor and their jewellery is based on Stefano Papi and Alexandra Rhodes, 1999. *Famous Jewelry Collectors*. London: Thames & Hudson, p. 114–29.

2   *www.cartier.com/tell-me/living-heritage.* Accessed 15 Oct. 2010.

3   Judy Rudoe, 1997. *Cartier 1900–1939*. New York: Abrams.

4   *Sculpture International,* vol. 2 (1968), no. 2, p. 16.

5   Ralph Turner, 1975. *Contemporary Jewelry: A Critical Assessment, 1945–1975*. London: Studio Vista, p. 138.

6   Ralph Turner, 1975. *Jewellery in Europe: An Exhibition of Progressive Work*. Edinburgh: Scottish Arts Council, p. 30.

7   Ibid. p. 50.

8   'Q & A with Helen Williams Drutt English Conducted by Cindi Strauss on February 9, 2005', in Cindi Strauss (ed.), 2007. *Ornament as Art: Avant-Garde Jewelry from the Helen Williams Drutt Collection.* Stuttgart: Arnoldsche in association with the Museum of Fine Arts, Houston, 2007, p. 48.

9   Ibid. p. 52.

10 Ibid. p. 54.

11 Donna Schneier, 2002. 'Collector's Statement', in Ursula Ilse-Neuman and David Revere McFadden, 2002. *Zero Karat: The Donna Schneier Gift to the American Craft Museum*. New York: American Craft Museum, p. 9.

12 Auction house Pierre Bergé in Brussels has recently started auctioning author jewellery twice a year. Each auction sells fine jewellery by renowned and lesser-known jewellery houses (predominantly antique), precious jewellery by fine artists and contemporary author jewellery. Christie's and Philips de Pury every now and then organise design auctions also comprising some loose items of art jewellery and the auction house Wright in Chicago specialises in modern and contemporary design. Up until now, jewellery has only been a relatively small part of the auctions on general design.

13 Lindsay Pollock. 'Sotheby's, Christie's Design Auctions include Art Jewelry', in *Art Market Views*, June 22, 2010. Accessed 12 Oct. 2010.

14 Prices mentioned are the auction results from *What Modern is: The Collection of Mark McDonalds*, Sotheby's New York, 10 Mar. 2011.

15 A Hans (Jean) Arp silver brooch-pendant with a pebble, marked 'Design by Arp' and numbered 25/100, was sold at Pierre Berge's Precious Design auction of 16 Dec. 2008 for € 9,000. A nice one-off pendant, *Tête de Vénus*, by Man Ray, made in bronze and iron gauze and created around the year 1937, fetched € 75,000 at the same auction. A gold Pol Bury bracelet, made in 1968, sold at Sotheby's Paris on 26 May 2010 for € 24,750.

16 Florian Hufnagl, 2011. *Peter Skubic: Radical Skubic Jewelry*. Nuremberg: Verlag für moderne Kunst, p. 11.

17 The history of the Stedelijk Museum jewellery collection dates back to the 1960s, when the museum started organising exhibitions of young jewellers. In 1967, Emmy van Leersum and Gijs Bakker were invited for the third exhibition in a row, together with Nicolaas van Beek, Franck Ligtelijn and Clara Schiavetto. On that occasion Van Leersum and Bakker organised a catwalk show in the museum – an absolute novelty. As a consequence the museum began collecting contemporary jewellery on a serious basis. In 1971, the museum earmarked a small budget for the set up of a collection of contemporary jewellery, as is mentioned in the introduction to the catalogue of Emmy van Leersum's exhibition in the Stedelijk Museum in 1979.

18 Cindi Strauss (see note 8), p. 7.

19 Ibid. p. 27.

20 In 2008, the Wien Museum on the occasion of the exhibition *Glanzstücke: Emilie Flöge und der Schmuck der Wiener Werkstätte* had an appendix in the form of a showcase with some jewellery from Inge Asenbaum's collection and documentation from the Galerie am Graben.

21 Cindi Strauss (see note 8), p. 8.

22 Marjan Unger, 2004. *Het Nederlandse sieraad in de 20ste eeuw*. Bussum: Thot. Her donation to the Rijksmuseum was officially announced when she received her doctorate with the thesis 'Sieraad in Context', Leiden University, Mar. 2010.

23 *The Rijksmuseum Bulletin,* vol. 58, no. 3, 2010, p. 26.

24 Threes Moolhuysen-Coenders, 2001. *Onedel, Non-precious*. Schiedam: Stichting Tekens en Ketens.

25 See the list of museums on p. 221–5.

26 Yvònne Joris, 2009. *Private Passion: Artists' Jewelry of the 20th Century*. Stuttgart: Arnoldsche in association with the Stedelijk Museum, 's-Hertogenbosch, p. 7.

27 Under the former director (2001–07), the Museum for Modern Art in Arnhem closed the permanent display of jewellery. Under the new managegment, the museum's policy turned in favour of contemporary jewellery and in 2008 the museum acquired a good part of Jurriaan van den Berg's collection, some 250 pieces of contemporary Dutch art jewellery from the 1960s onwards. However, there is no permanent display. At the end of the 1980s, the Costume Museum in The Hague, which housed an important collection including fashion jewellery, had to close its doors. The collection was handed over to the Gemeente Museum [Municipal Museum] in The Hague, where a new fashion gallery was designed in the basement of the premises which opened in 1996. In 2005, the permanent fashion display was closed due to the vulnerability of the material, according to the museum's website. Many people still remember though how the director at that time (2001–09) caused a row when he stated in interviews that he would be glad to be rid of the fashion collection. In Barcelona (Spain) the Museum of Decorative Arts holds an interesting collection of contemporary Catalan art jewellery from the period 1940 to 1990. The collection of 126 pieces by thirty-two artists was put together in 1997. Later Mònica Gaspar organised a travelling exhibition with a catalogue, documenting and reflecting on each item in the collection. Unfortunately the museum decided to publish the catalogue *El laboratory de la joieria 1940–1990* (2007) only in Catalan. The collection is now stored away and there are no plans to have it on display in the new premises of the Dissseny Hub Barcelona (which opens in 2012).

28 Cornelie Holzach and Tilman Schempp (eds.), 2006. *Schmuckmuseum Pforzheim: Museumführer*. Stuttgart: Arnoldsche, p. 143.

There is an estimable amount of museums world-wide that collect jewellery on a regular basis: national museums, modern art museums, design and applied arts museums and museums dedicated to specific materials, such as textiles or glass. Only museums that fulfil at least one of the following conditions are listed:

1. Contemporary art jewellery is acquired on a regular basis.
2. Contemporary art jewellery is displayed permanently (as part of a general display or separately) or in temporary exhibitions that take place on a semi-regular basis.
3. Contemporary art jewellery is one of the cornerstones in the museums' collection.
   Details are up to date at time of publishing.

AUSTRALIA

Art Gallery of South Australia, Adelaide
www.artgallery.sa.gov.au
COLLECTION: 170 pieces of historical and contemporary Australian jewellery. The collection is actively growing annually. The museum administers the Rhianon Vernon-Roberts Memorial Collection of Australian Contemporary Jewellery. Permanent display changes every four to six months. Temporary exhibitions, but not on a regular basis.

National Gallery of Australia, Canberra
www.nga.gov.au
COLLECTION: about 570 pieces of Australian jewellery and about 70 pieces of international jewellery, approximately 80 per cent of which is post-1960. A permanent display gallery dedicated to the Australian and international jewellery collection, comprising historical and contemporary jewellery from the mid-nineteenth century to the present, changing twice a year. Temporary exhibitions, but not on a regular basis.

National Gallery of Victoria, Melbourne
www.ngv.vic.gov.au
COLLECTION: about 90 pieces of contemporary jewellery, both Australian and international. The international twentieth-century design galleries feature a display of modern jewellery that changes every two years. Temporary exhibitions, but not on a regular basis.

Powerhouse Museum, Sydney
www.powerhousemuseum.com
COLLECTION: about 2,500 pieces of jewellery from antiquity (small dormant collection) and Australian colonial gold jewellery to the contemporary studio production. The current focus is on contemporary jewellery. Periodic long-term displays. Temporary exhibitions, but not on a regular basis.

BELGIUM

Diamantmuseum, Antwerp
www.diamantmuseum.be
COLLECTION: contemporary and historical jewellery with diamonds. Permanent display of contemporary jewellery and historical jewellery from different time periods, changing twice a year. Temporary exhibitions at least twice a year.

CANADA

Montreal Museum of Fine Arts, Montreal
www.mbam.qc.ca
COLLECTION: about 250 pieces of contemporary jewellery. There is no focus, but the museum has an important collection of American studio jewellery from 1945 to 1965 and several art jewellery pieces by artists such as Salvador Dalí, Pablo Picasso, Max Ernst, Arnaldo Pomodoro and Alexander Calder. Permanent installation of objects from the Renaissance to the present. About 54 pieces of jewellery from 1945 to the present are part of this exhibition.

DENMARK

Designmuseum Danmark, Copenhagen
www.designmuseum.dk
COLLECTION: several hundred pieces of contemporary and historical jewellery from Denmark and abroad. The museum also administers the collection of the State Arts Council, approximately 200 pieces of Danish jewellery from the past 30 years. These jewels can be borrowed for official occasions in Denmark, Western Europe, North America or Australia by official Danish representatives. Permanent display of around 50 pieces of contemporary art jewellery, Danish and international, classic designs (1950s–1960s) and historic pieces especially by the Danish silversmith Georg Jensen. Temporary exhibitions about once a year.

ESTONIA

Estonian Museum of Applied Arts and Design, Tallinn
www.etdm.ee
COLLECTION: over 2,250 pieces of jewellery, from nineteenth-century national jewellery to contemporary Estonian jewellery design. The nucleus of the collection is formed by jewellery from the 1950s to the 1980s. The museum collection also includes samples of serial production and artists' limited series of the Art Production Factory of the ESSR. Permanent exhibition of Estonian design, divided

into time and style periods. One to three exhibitions per year from Estonian as well as international designers.

FINLAND

Design Museum, Helsinki
www.designmuseum.fi
COLLECTION: around 600 pieces, mainly Finnish jewellery from the 1950s to the present, both art and design jewellery, plus a small collection of contemporary international jewellery. Jewellery is incorporated in the permanent and in temporary exhibitions.

FRANCE

Musée des Arts Décoratifs, Paris
www.lesartsdecoratifs.fr
COLLECTION: 1,200 jewellery items are on view in the museum. Permanent chronological display of decorative arts, including medieval to contemporary jewellery. In the permanent exhibition it is also possible to view the rest of the collection on computer. Temporary exhibitions, but not on a regular basis

Espace Solidor, Cagnes-sur-Mer
www.cagnes-sur-mer.fr/culture/espace_solidor.php
COLLECTION: a small but growing collection of about 100 pieces. The gallery has an active acquisition policy. The gallery's collection is on display once a year. Three temporary exhibitions of international art jewellery (in spring, summer and autumn).

GERMANY

Museum für Kunst und Gewerbe Hamburg
www.mkg-hamburg.de
COLLECTION: besides a collection of antique and Art Nouveau jewellery the museum owns a collection of 485 pieces of contemporary jewellery. The museum administers the Teunen & Teunen Collection (Jan and Mieke Teunen) including many early pieces of jewellery by Gijs Bakker and Emmy van Leersum.

Deutsches Goldschmiedehaus, Hanau
www.hanau.de/kultur/museen/dgh/
COLLECTION: about 780 pieces. The museum administers the collection of the Goldschmiedehaus, the Burgel Collection and the Ebbe Weiss-Weingart Collection. Mainly contemporary jewellery and holloware, from the 1950s onwards. The Goldschmiedehaus acquires jewellery with a focus on contemporary jewellery. Continually changing exhibitions every two to three months on jewellery artists, holloware and historical jewellery.

Museum für Angewandte Kunst Frankfurt, Frankfurt/Main
www.angewandtekunst-frankfurt.de
COLLECTION: about 500 pieces, from Egypt, Greek and Roman antiquity, the Middle Ages, the Renaissance, the Baroque era, the nineteenth century and Art Nouveau and Art Déco jewellery to contemporary (mainly German) jewellery. The acquisition policy is focused on art jewellery. A selection of the jewellery collection is on display for around four months per year, changing at least once a year. The museum has smaller temporary exhibitions that change two to four times a year called 'ShopStop'.

Grassi Museum of Applied Arts, Leipzig
www.grassimuseum.de
COLLECTION: about 200 pieces of art jewellery, including 80 pieces on loan by Ebbe Weiss-Weingart. Jewellery is integrated in the permanent exhibition of Art Nouveau to contemporary arts and crafts. Temporary exhibitions, but not on a regular basis.

Die Neue Sammlung – The International Design Museum Munich
www.die-neue-sammlung.de
COLLECTION: about 460 pieces. Since 2004, Die Neue Sammlung has been showcasing international contemporary art jewellery in the Pinakothek der Moderne. This means that for the first time one of the most varied contemporary forms of artistic expression has found a permanent home in a museum of this kind, alongside art, architecture, graphic art and design. These are the aspects upon which the international collection of the Danner-Stiftung (about 400 pieces) and its presentation in the Danner-Rotunda are concentrating. The 2004 opening exhibition was curated by Professor Hermann Jünger, who taught the jewellery class at the Munich Art Academy from 1972–1990, and Otto Künzli, who took over the chair in 1991. They are succeeded by Karl Fritsch as a representative of a younger generation. Temporally exhibitions are usually held in March because of the International Handicrafts Fair 'Schmuck' that takes place in Munich that month.
COOPERATION: The Danner Foundation, Munich and Die Neue Sammlung

Schmuckmuseum Pforzheim
www.schmuckmuseum-pforzheim.de
COLLECTION: jewellery from 300 ad to the present. The museum administers the Philip Weber Collection of pocket watches, the Eva and Peter Herion Collection of ethnographic jewellery and a collection of 1,200 rings. The museum also acquires contemporary jewellery. The permanent exhibition consists of three main galleries that show jewellery from antiquity to the nineteenth century, Jugendstil to the twenty-first-century and post-1950 jewellery. Four temporary exhibitions each year on varying themes.

NETHERLANDS

Rijksmuseum, Amsterdam
www.rijksmuseum.nl
COLLECTION: includes some major pieces from the nineteenth and early twentieth century as well as 16 works by Bert Nienhuis. The museum administers the collection of around 500 pieces of Dutch jewellery by Marjan and Gerard Unger which covers the period from 1905 to 2008. The emphasis of this collection is the period between 1930 to 1970.

Stedelijk Museum, Amsterdam
www.stedelijk.nl
COLLECTION: international contemporary jewellery, around 700 pieces in total. The museum administers the collection of the Françoise van den Bosch Foundation. Regular exhibitions on contemporary jewellery, including thematic, group and solo exhibitions, have always been part of the museum's policy.

CODA, Apeldoorn
www.coda-apeldoorn.nl
COLLECTION: around 3,900 pieces of contemporary international jewellery from the mid-1960s to the present. The museum administers the archives of Onno Boekhoudt, Chris Steenbergen and Nicolaas Thuys. Besides jewellery these archives contain texts, sketches, drawings, pictures, catalogues, etc. The jewellery collection is a vital part of the museum; therefore there is always jewellery on display. Temporary exhibitions on a regular basis.

Museum voor Moderne Kunst Arnhem
www.mmkarnhem.nl
COLLECTION: around 1,000 pieces of Dutch contemporary jewellery. In 2009, the museum received a private collection of 250 pieces of Dutch jewellery from c. 1968 to 2000. Temporary exhibitions about once a year.

SM's – Stedelijk Museum, 's-Hertogenbosch
www.sm-s.nl
COLLECTION: jewellery from 1945 to the present, around 1,500 pieces in total. Special focus on Dutch contemporary jewellery and American jewellery. The museum administers the archives of Marion Herbst, Emmy van Leersum and Gijs Bakker. The museum has a collection of about 150 pieces of jewellery by fine artists, among them Alexander Calder, Lucio Fontana, Pablo Picasso and Meret Oppenheim. Temporary exhibitions are organised once or twice a year.

AUDAX, Textielmuseum, Tilburg
www.textielmuseum.nl
COLLECTION: about 160 pieces of textile jewellery from the 1970s to the present made by designers from or based in the Netherlands. The main focus of the museum is on textiles, therefore the jewellery collection is rarely exhibited. Objects of the jewellery collection are sometimes integrated in other exhibitions.

Centraal Museum, Utrecht
www.centraalmuseum.nl
COLLECTION: about 200 pieces of contemporary jewellery from 1968 to the present. Temporary exhibitions on jewellery about every five years.

NEW ZEALAND

Auckland War Memorial Museum, Auckland
www.aucklandmuseum.com
COLLECTION: the collection involves 194 pieces, 179 of which are from New Zealand. The main focus of the collection is on contemporary jewellery from New Zealand. The museum has had two permanent contemporary exhibitions since 2006. One showcases New Zealand jewellery practice and the other international jewellery.

The Dowse Art Museum, Lower Hutt
www.dowse.org.nz
COLLECTION: collecting since 1980, the museum now has a collection of 200 pieces. Its aim is to develop a unique collection of work made in or in relation to Aotearoa (New Zealand), which reflects the cultural values of the community. There is an exhibition on jewellery about once a year. Jewellery is also often included in other exhibitions.

Museum of New Zealand Te Papa Tongarewa, Wellington
www.tepapa.govt.nz
COLLECTION: over 300 pieces of contemporary jewellery from New Zealand as well as international jewellery with a link to New Zealand or the museum's collection. The museum administers the Kobi Bosshard and the Bone Stone Shell collections. No permanent display, but pieces are included in other permanent exhibitions that change every five years.

NORWAY

Permanenten, West Norway Museum of Decorative Art, Bergen
www.kunstmuseene.no
COLLECTION: 100 pieces of contemporary Norwegian jewellery as part of the contemporary Norwegian crafts collection. There is no specific collection policy on jewellery. Permanent display of objects since 1998, in which jewellery is included. Temporary exhibitions, but not on a regular basis.

National Museum of Art, Architecture and Design, Oslo
www.nasjonalmuseet.no
COLLECTION: around 300 pieces of art jewellery and experimental jewellery. Pieces from the collection are incorporated in the permanent exhibition together with fashion and other crafts and design. Temporary exhibitions every three years.

Nordenfjeldske Kunstindustrimuseum, Trondheim
www.nkim.no
COLLECTION: around 500 pieces of contemporary jewellery mainly from Europe and the United States, but also from Australia, Japan and Korea. A small part of the collection is on show on a permanent basis. Temporary exhibitions around once or twice a year.

SWEDEN

Röhsska Museum, Gothenburg
www.designmuseum.se
COLLECTION: around 250 pieces of modern and contemporary international jewellery from the 1950s onwards, including fashion jewellery. Initially, jewellery was part of the silver collection. The museum has a good collection of Scandinavian Modernist jewellery. Jewellery is integrated in the permanent exhibition of crafts and design from 1851 to the present. Retrospective exhibitions of Swedish and Scandinavian jewellery artists have been organised by the museum. Also the Nordic Jewellery Triennials are shown in the museum.

Nationalmuseum, Stockholm
www.nationalmuseum.se
COLLECTION: around 300 pieces of contemporary jewellery. Contemporary jewellery is incorporated with other objects in permanent exhibitions. The museum holds temporary exhibitions on jewellery or exhibitions that also include jewellery.

SWITZERLAND

MUDAC, Musée de design et d'arts appliqués contemporains, Lausanne
www.mudac.ch
COLLECTION: 184 pieces of contemporary jewellery (including 110 pieces of the Contemporary Jewellery Collection of the Swiss Confederation). A permanent exhibition room for jewellery, planned to open in 2012, is in preparation. Since 2000, there has been a couple of curated thematic exhibitions. Jewellery is part of design exhibitions and often shown in the showcase at the entrance of the museum.

UNITED KINGDOM

National Museum of Scotland, Edinburgh
www.nms.ac.uk
COLLECTION: around 400 pieces of contemporary British jewellery and international art jewellery, a few pieces of artist's jewellery, twentieth-century costume jewellery and commercial jewellery. The department of World Cultures collects contemporary Japanese jewellery. Jewellery is incorporated in permanent exhibitions in various galleries. Temporary exhibitions, but not on a regular basis.

V&A – Victoria and Albert Museum, London
www.vam.ac.uk
COLLECTION: the collection consists of around 9,000 pieces predominantly of jewellery made in the Western tradition since about ad 1200. There are also collections of ancient Egypt, Greek and Roman jewellery as well as Asian jewellery. The museum mainly acquires jewellery made in Europe and in the Western tradition, including that from North America and Australasia. International contemporary jewellery is a central strand in its current work. The V&A administers the Patricia V. Goldstein Collection of twentieth-century jewels in which Tiffany and Cartier are well presented. The William and Judith Bollinger Gallery, redisplayed in 2008, shows about 3,500 jewels from Ancient Egypt to the present. New acquisitions, mainly contemporary jewellery, are added to the displays about twice a year. Temporary exhibitions which consist only of jewellery are occasional. Jewellery is frequently included in the large thematic exhibitions.

mima, Middlesbrough Institute of Modern Art, Middlesbrough
www.visitmima.com
COLLECTION: around 200 pieces of contemporary jewellery comprising work by international artists. No permanent display, but the collections are accessible via regular store tours and by appointment. The jewellery collection is regularly exhibited and can also be displayed incorporated with other objects as the museum makes no differentiation between fine art and craft. The exhibitions are changed every four months.

UNITED STATES OF AMERICA

Museum of Fine Arts, Boston MA
www.mfa.org
COLLECTION: 11,000 pieces of adornment from ancient to contemporary studio jewellery to costume/couture jewellery. The museum administers the Daphne Farago Collection (650 objects) which consists of studio jewellery. The Rita J. and Stanley H. Kaplan Family Foundation Gallery, a permanent jewellery gallery, rotates exhibitions every two years. Jewellery is on view throughout the museum.

Mint Museum, Charlotte NC
www.mintmuseum.org
COLLECTION: approximately 76 items of contemporary international jewellery. A permanent selection, about 20 to 25 pieces of the collection, is on view. Every two to three years the museum has an exhibition on jewellery or an exhibition that includes jewellery.

Fuller Craft Museum, Brockton MA
www.fullercraft.org
COLLECTION: a small collection of about 50 pieces of contemporary jewellery. Jewellery is incorporated in the permanent collection exhibition, rotating every nine to twelve months. Every year there are exhibitions on jewellery.

Corning Museum of Glass, Corning NY
www.cmog.org
COLLECTION: the museum collects glass from antiquity to present, including glass jewellery. For the contemporary section the museum is actively acquiring jewellery in glass and mixed media as well as handmade glass beads. Some jewellery is integrated in permanent exhibitions on, for example, Greek and African objects.

Museum of Fine Arts Houston, Houston TX
www.mfah.org
COLLECTION: over 800 pieces of contemporary jewellery. The majority comes in the form of the Helen Williams Drutt English Collection. The museum always has some contemporary jewellery on view in the museum in mixed media presentations. These exhibitions can last anywhere from three to six months. Since Ornament as Art: Contemporary Jewelry from the Helen Williams Drutt Collection (2007–08), the museum has not hosted a temporary exhibition devoted solely to jewellery.

Newark Museum, Newark NJ
www.newarkmuseum.org
COLLECTION: at least 500 items of ancient, ethnic and European/American jewellery. The European/American department focuses on all types of jewellery: production jewellery (commercial), art jewellery, contemporary studio jewellery. Newark, New Jersey, was the chief jewellery manufacturing centre in the United States for a long time, which is another aspect of the collection. There is a permanent small gallery known as the Lore Ross Jewelry Gallery. The museum also has a permanent Asian jewellery gallery.

MAD, Museum of Art and Design, New York
www.madmuseum.org
COLLECTION: ethnic silver jewellery, principally from Asia, the Middle East/North Africa and Mexico, with Native American jewellery and contemporary art jewellery by US and international artists. The ethnic collection contains 800 pieces and the art jewellery collection 600 items. About 50 works of contemporary art jewellery are permanently displayed in drawers which can be accessed by the visitors. Every three to six months this exhibition is changed. Every three to four months the museum has a temporary exhibition on jewellery, focusing on either specific themes or materials and/or techniques.

Racine Art Museum, Racine WI
www.ramart.org
COLLECTION: around 500 items from emerging and established artists. The museum administers the Donna Schneier Collection of 49 pieces of art jewellery, by both US and European artists. Exhibitions that feature only jewellery occur about two or more times a year and jewellery is often included in larger theme-oriented exhibitions.

Tacoma Art Museum, Tacoma WA
www.tacomaartmuseum.org
COLLECTION: 191 pieces by jewellery artists from the Pacific Northwest, representing the studio art jewellery movement from about 1945 until the present. Approximately 80 per cent of the collection is on view in 'open storage' cases. The museum organises a large temporary exhibition on jewellery approximately every three years. The museum also strives to include jewellery in all of its thematic exhibitions.

Smithsonian American Art Museum/Renwick Gallery, Washington DC
www.americanart.si.edu
COLLECTION: about 200 pieces of contemporary jewellery. Jewellery is integrated in the permanent art exhibition. These exhibitions are reinstalled twice a year. Temporary exhibitions, but not on a regular basis. Since 2000 the gallery also organises 'Renwick Invitational'. These exhibitions are part of a series meant to exhibit mid-career artists who should be better known. Jewellery artists are also included in this series.

Galleries

Alternatives Gallery, Rome (IT)
www.alternatives.it

Articula, Lisbon (PT)
www.teresamilheiro.com

ATTA Gallery, Bangkok (TH)
www.attagallery.com

Bærbart, Copenhagen (DK)
www.galeriemetal.dk

Beeld en Aambeeld, Enschede (NL)
www.beeldenaambeeld.nl

Galeria Bielak, Krakow (PL)
www.galeriabielak.pl

Galerie Biró, Munich (DE)
www.galerie-biro.de

Lesley Craze Gallery, London (UK)
www.lesleycrazegallery.co.uk

Gallery Deux Poissons, Tokyo (JP)
www.deuxpoissons.com

Fingers, Auckland (NZ)
www.fingers.co.nz

Gallery Funaki, Melbourne (AU)
www.galleryfunaki.com.au

Goldfingers, Copenhagen (DK)
www.goldfingers.dk

Galerie Noel Guyomarc'h Bijoux d'Art, Montréal,
Canada
www.galerienoelguomarch.com

Caroline van Hoek, Brussels (BE)
www.carolinevanhoek.be

Galerie Rosemarie Jäger, Hochheim (DE)
www.rosemarie-jaeger.de

Jewelers' Werk Galerie, Washington/DC (US)
www.jewelerswerk.com

Klimt02, Barcelona (ES)
www.klimt02.net/gallery

Galerie Rob Koudijs, Amsterdam (NL)
www.galerierobkoudijs.nl

Charon Kransen Arts, New York/NY (US)
www.charonkransenarts.com

Galerie Sofie Lachaert, Tielrode (BE)
www.sofielachaert.be

Galerie Sofie Lachaert, Ghent (BE)
www.sofielachaert.be

Kath Libbert Jewellery Gallery, Bradford (UK)
www.kathlibbertjewellery.co.uk

Gallery Loupe, Montclair/NJ (US)
www.galleryloupe.com

Heidi Lowe Gallery, Rehoboth, DE (US)
www.heidilowejewelry.com

Marijke Studio, Padua (IT)
www.marijkestudio.com

Galerie Marzee, Nijmegen (NL)
www.marzee.nl

Associazione Culturale Maurer Zilioli, Brescia (IT)
www.maurerzilioli.com

Mobilia Gallery, Cambridge/MA (US)
www.mobilia-gallery.com

Objectspace, Auckland (NZ)
www.objectspace.org.nz

OONA, Berlin (DE)
www.oona-galerie.de

Ornamentum, Hudson/NY (US)
www.ornamentumgallery.com

Galerie Pilartz, Cologne (DE)
www.pilartz.com

Platina, Stockholm (SE)
www.platina.se

Galerie Pont & Plas, Ghent (BE)
www.pontenplas.be

Galerie Hélène Porée, Paris (FR)
www.galerie-helene-poree.com

Galerie Ra, Amsterdam (NL)
www.galerie-ra.nl

Galeria Reverso, Lisbon (PT)
www.reversodasbernardas.com

Schmuckfrage, Berlin (DE)
www.schmuckfrage.de

Sienna Gallery, Lenox/MA (US)
www.siennagallery.com

Galerie Slavik, Vienna (AT)
www.galerie-slavik.com

Galerie Louise Smit, Amsterdam (NL)
www.louisesmit.nl

Gallery SO, London (UK)
www.galleryso.com

Gallery SO, Solothurn (CH)
www.galleryso.com

SODA, Istanbul (TR)
www.sodaistanbul.com

Galerie Spektrum, Munich (DE)
www.galerie-spektrum.de

Galerie Stühler, Berlin (DE)
www.galerie-stuehler.de

Galerie TACTILe, Geneva (CH)
www.tactile.ch

Galerie V & V, Vienna (AT)
www.kunstnet.at/v+v

Velvet da Vinci, San Francisco/CA (US)
www.velvetdavinci.com

Verzameld Werk, Ghent (BE)
www.verzameldwerk.be

Viceversa, Lausanne (CH)
www.viceversa.ch

Galerie Villa Bengel, Idar-Oberstein (DE)
www.jakob-bengel.de

Villa de Bondt, Ghent (BE)
www.villadebondt.be

Wittenbrink FUENFHOEFE, Munich (DE)
www.wittenbrinkfuenfhoefe.de

Galerie Annick Zufferey, Carouge (CH)
www.galerie-annickzufferey.com

Websites

www.klimt02.net
International art jewellery on line, Barcelona (ES)

www.artjewelryforum.org
A forum for contemporary art jewelry

www.metalcyberspace.com
Contemporary Jewelry Design + Modern Studio
Jewellery, Metalsmithing, Precious Metal Artists,
created by Susan Sarantos

www.francoisevandenbosch.nl
Françoise van den Bosch Foundation & Award,
Amsterdam (NL)

www.danner-stiftung.de
Danner Foundation, Munich (DE)

www.neuer-schmuck.com
Association to promote art in the field of contemporary jewellery, Munich (DE)

www.ethicalmetalsmiths.org
Jewellers for social and environmental responsibility

www.apparat.be
Showcasing international contemporary jewellery artists, created by Arnaud Sprimont (B)

www.artaurea.com
Platform for international contemporary jewel-
lery, crafts and design, created by Reinhold
Ludwig.

www.noovoeditions.com
Contemporary fashion, photography and jewel-
lery, created by Charo Gonzales y Santeiro and
Jorge Margolles, Barcelona (ES)

www.grayareasymposium.org/blog
Originally created as a forum for a group of Latin
American and European artists and jewellery
makers who, for a period of six months,
exchanged thoughts, experiences, ideas and
images on three main topics: jewellery, global
mobility and identity. Created by Valeria Vallarta
Siemelink (ME/NL)

www.pauadreams.wordpress.com
A website about contemporary jewellery in
Aotearoa (NZ)

www.snagmetalsmith.org
SNAG Society of North American Goldsmiths

Acknowledgements

This book would never have been written without the ongoing companionship of my fellow Think Tankers. Think Tank, a European Initiative for the Applied Arts, was founded in 2004 in the small Austrian city of Gmunden, situated within the beautiful scenery of Lake Traun, the Traun River and the upper Austrian Alps. While gathering there each year in September for our Think Tank symposium, taking part in wonderful discussions and sessions, the seed for my plan to write a book was sown. There, among good colleagues and friends, I found the trust to embark upon it. Special thanks go to Jorunn Veiteberg, Gabi Dewald and Mònica Gaspar for their good vibes, their positive response and their stimulating interest.

Further thanks go to Damian Skinner and Chloë Powell for reading along, their critical input and their enthusiasm. Thanks go to Chloë too for helping me to correct the book and realise the exhibition. Thanks to Maria Russo for translating chapters V and VI. Thanks to Hedwig Saam, director of the Museum for Modern Art Arnhem, for trusting me to make an extricable exhibition about international contemporary jewellery. Special thanks also to the museum's curator Eveline Holsappel who managed to keep up with my ideas and who invested too many personal hours in this project. Thanks to the Mondriaan Foundation, Ms Gitta Luiten and Mr Joost Vrieler for their generous financial support – without this the publication would have not been possible. Thanks to Arnoldsche Art Publishers in Stuttgart, including Dirk Allgaier for showing interest and making the book possible and Marion Boschka for her incredible and enthusiastic dedication. Working together with people such as Marion, Dirk, Eveline and Chloë was an inspiring and unforgettable experience. Thanks also go to all those jewellery artists for their wonderful work and cooperation. And last but not least, thanks to my dear Jim for always believing in me and never complaining, even when I worked during holidays, weekends and into the early hours.

Liesbeth den Besten, Amstelveen, 2011

About the author

Liesbeth den Besten is chairwoman of the Françoise van den Bosch Foundation for contemporary jewellery, member of the advisory board of the 'Chi ha paura...?' Foundation for serial jewellery and a founding member of Think Tank, a European Initiative for the Applied Arts.

Photo credits

Hans-Jørgen Abel 3
Aurelio Amendola 63, 64
Michael Anhalt, werkraum3149.com 152
Atelier Ted Noten 10, 75, 76 courtesy of Maria
    Cichy, 80–83
Ton Baadenhuysen 24, 42
Garth Badger 113
Peter Bauhuis 153
Rien Bazen 13, 25, 37, 122, 123
Anna Beeke 121
Richard Beer 101
Udo W. Beier 132, 133
Terence Bogue 114
Heidi Bollmann 159
Maurice Boyer 79
Paula Bray 89
Thomas Bruns 90
Claus Bury 158
Liesbet Bussche 156, 157
Bob Cramp 21
Kari Decock 33
Paul Duvochel 112
Dirk Eisel 140
Harry Ertl 97
Felix Flury 95, 96
Uri Gershuni 72
Michael Grenmarker 34

Eddo Hartmann 16, 119
Hogers/Versluys 98
Theresa Iten 99, 102
Rosemarie Jäger 39
Michael Jank 137
Georg Jensen 12
Eva Jünger 17, 143, 144
Mathilde Jurrissen 36
Stanley Lechtzin 155
Tanapol Kaewpring 7
Beate Klockmann 8, 9, 151
Dorte Krogh 6, 11
Tim Lehmacher 40, 84
Winnifred Limburg 49
Suska Mackert/Jens Niehus 85
Philipp Mansmann 154
Stefano Marchetti 147
Nanna Mclland 111
Marc Monzó 141
Bettina Neumann 77, 78
Iris Nieuwenburg, edited by Patrick Keeler 136
Gary Pollmiller 107
Ramón Puig Cuyàs 41
Patrick Reynolds 5
Audbjørn Rønning 18
Helga Schulze-Brinkop 145, 146
Robert Smit 32, 67, 68, 138, 160
Semuel Souhuwat 59, 60
Chris Springhall and Gavin Alexander 94
Kevin Sprague 69, 71 courtesy Sienna Gallery
Frans Strous 164
Michel Szulc-Krzyzanowski 23
Mirei Takeuchi 15
Lorenzo Trento 148
Pedro Mª de Ugarte 91
Tanel Veenre 161, 162
Rob Versluys 130
Leo Versteijlen 48, 50
Rainer Viertlböck 45
Lisa Walker 14
David Ward 26, 106
Becky Yee 88
Ron Zijlstra 53, 73, 74

Back cover:

left row (top down):
Pia Aleborg, necklace, series:
    Apartfrom, 2005 (fig. 34)
Bettina Speckner, brooch, 2003
    (fig. 39)
Paul Derrez, *Face*, 1994
    (fig. 59)

middle row (top down):
Helen Britton, *Big White*, 2009
    (fig. 125)
Hilde De Decker, *For the Farmer
    and the Market Gardener*,
    1999 (fig. 54)
Emiko Oye, *The Duchess 2*, 2008
    (fig. 124)

right row (top down):
Naomi Filmer, *Ball in the Small
    of My Back*, 2001 (fig. 94)
Hermann Jünger, brooch, 1993
    (fig. 143)
Mirjam Hiller, *Syspera*, 2011
    (fig. 20)
Hans Stofer, *Off My Trolley*,
    2009 (fig. 96)

ARNOLDSCHE project coordinator
Marion Boschka

Text editing
Wendy Brouwer, Stuttgart

Design
nalbach typographic, Silke Nalbach, Mannheim

Offset Reproductions
Repromayer, Reutlingen

Printing
Leibfarth & Schwarz, Dettingen/Erms

Printed on Profisilk 170 gsm and Galaxy Bulk 150 gsm

Bibliographic information published by Die Deutsche Bibliothek
Die Deutsche Bibliothek lists this publication in the Deutsche Nationalbibliografie;
detailed bibliographic data is available on the Internet at http://dnb.d-nb.de.

ISBN 978-3-89790-349-4
Made in Germany, 2011

Realised with the financial support of

The Mondriaan Foundation, Amsterdam

The Museum voor Moderne Kunst Arnhem

The Netherlands Foundation for Visual Arts, Design and Architecture, Amsterdam